T0158536

Real
Liverpool

To my mum and dad. Of course.

Real
Liverpool

Niall Griffiths

seren

Seren is the book imprint of
Poetry Wales Press Ltd
Nolton Street, Bridgend, Wales
www.seren-books.com

ISBN 978-1-85411-457-0

A CIP record for this title is available from
the British Library

The publisher works with the financial assistance
of the Welsh Books Council

Printed by Bell & Bain, Glasgow

Also in the Real Wales series
Editor: Peter Finch:

Coming Soon:

CONTENTS

EAST

THREADS

SOUTH

WEST

THREADS

CITY CENTRAL

CITY EYE

APPENDIX ONE

APPENDIX TWO

SERIES INTRODUCTION

Liverpool has a fair idea that it isn't quite England. Wales might imagine that this place is the capital of its mountainous north but that's not a Liverpool perception. Liverpool - the New York of Europe. The end of the line. A place where England reaches Wales and Ireland almost simultaneously. Where the population is a rich mix of immigrant, so rich that native no longer exists, if they ever did. Everyone got to Liverpool from somewhere else. The city itself is not mentioned in the Domesday Book. King John founded the port in 1207 because he needed an independent dispatch point from which to send troops to Ireland. Before that there was nothing. An ox-bow made by the bending Mersey. Liuerpul. Dank creek. Pool of mud. A dog and two fishermen.

The Earl of Derby built a four-towered castle here in 1232. This lasted until 1726 when it was replaced by a series of subsiding churches. The site today is occupied by the Victorian Monument[1]. The town grew because of the ships. Ships that went to America and the West Indies. Cloth, coal and salt from the Liverpool hinterland exchanged for the twin poisons of the Western world: tobacco and sugar. Ships that carried slaves. Liverpool's black community began when the first dock was built in 1715. It was the industrial revolution that turned Liverpool from burgeoning port to dynamic world city. Made it famous everywhere. The world knew of Britain and they also knew of Liverpool. Population rose from 6000 to 80,000 in the eighteenth century. That's quite a climb.

Trade expanded rapidly during the nineteenth century. Population continued to balloon. By 1851 around a quarter were Irish, fleeing the Great Famine, looking for work, safety, life, salvation. Their mark as indelible as the local Welsh walking in across the leaky and ill-defined border. Liverpool was the leading port of the British Empire. The weight and residual Victorian power of its major buildings are powerful reminders. They stood grand until the 1930s depression. The post-industrial slide from that time on, accelerating towards the millennium was as bad in Liverpool as it was anywhere. Local unemployment rates in the 1980s were the highest in the UK. Tear gas-subdued riots took place in Toxteth, the large working class walking suburb. A white immigrant place, a Welsh district and an Irish district but by the 1980s predominantly Asian and Afro-Caribbean.

Liverpool's twentieth century downs were many. Worst bombed city in the UK during World War Two. The stealing of Welsh water by the building of the damn at Tryweryn and the drowning of Capel Celyn near Bala in 1965. Far-left Derek Hatton Militant take-over of local services in the 1980s. Ninety six Liverpool football fans dead at Hillsborough. The James Bulger murder. The shooting of Rhys Jones. The demolition of large parts of the city's past in the late nineteen-nineties.

The rebuild in progress when I visit is in high gear. At the Albert Dock opposite the bus station, already looking like a part of Cloud City on the set of *Star Wars*, there are eighteen cranes in action redeveloping what looks like the entire of Liverpool 1. This is the Paradise Project – the redevelopment of 42 acres of prime city in time for 2008, the year Liverpool takes on the hard won mantle of European Capital of Culture.

It's a dull day. I don't remember ever having been here when it hasn't been. The visitor attractions of the sleek and repointed Albert Dock, the Maritime Museum, Tate Liverpool, the World War Two amphibious landing craft, American D-Day Dukws painted bright yellow which plunge with their waterproofed riders into the Salthouse Dock to shrieks and screams, they are all behind me. We go up the hill, along Duke Street, towards the Cathedral, one of them, the Art College, Chinatown and the Georgian once-Bohemia of Canning Street, Liverpool 8. Brian Patten lived here, tiny flat from which he ran his poetry mag, *Underdog*, No 18. Stuart Sutcliffe, almost Beatle, lived at 83. Adrian Henri, spirit of the age for the city that was the epicentre of the 60s, lived at no 64. This was where Allen Ginsberg stayed when he swept into this place to pick up the vibes in 1965. "Liverpool is at the present moment the centre of consciousness of the human universe." Just along Princes Road at Windermere Terrace lived Roger McGough. The Liverpool Scene identified by the critic Edward Lucie-Smith and launched on the world by Penguin in their classic Modern Poets No 10 *The Mersey Sound* changed the way we did things. "I have seen Père UBU walking across Lime Street / And Alfred Jarry cycling down Elliott Street", "And Marcel Proust in the Kardomah eating Madeleine butties dipped in tea."[2] They're still here too. In Chinatown, just below the Anglican Cathedral on St James Mount, is Cornwallis Street which has its nameplate in Roman script and below that in Pin Yin Chinese. In the Cathedral which looks as if it has stood for a thousand years but actually was only completed in 1978 after a century of build, I buy a postcard. 'Liverpool Historic Pub Crawl.' Thumbnails of The Grapes, Mount Street, Ye Cracke, Rice Street, Crocodile, Harrington Street, The Philharmonic, Hope Street, Carnarvon Castle, Tarleton Street. Fifty more. God and the grape close together once again.

Along Hope Street where Henri would have walked is the Art College. He taught here. On the corner of Mount Street is John King's public sculpture, *A Case History*. Boxes, bags, and cases made from concrete celebrating the famous who once lived nearby. Arthur Askey comedian, Josephine Butler pioneer in social welfare, Paul McCartney Sir and singer, Stuart Sutcliffe almost, Charles Dickens writer, R.J. Lloyd promoter of Esperanto, and a cast from a box of books addressed to the Liverpool Poets. Tourists have their photos snapped standing next to a case that might have held John Lennon's guitar.

At the opposite end of Hope Street the Catholic Cathedral is brutalist concrete made soft by its need to point like a crown at Heaven. It does not resemble the Anglican structure on St Stephen's Mount even though it was consecrated earlier. The Metropolitan Cathedral of Christ The King, architect Frederick Gibberd, took five years to realise and its two-thousand-three-hundred-seater cylindrical space sits on top of a Lutyens 1933 crypt. This is the only part of the first architect's pre-war grandiose design for the original cathedral to have been realised. The building's stark modernism is softened by bright coloured light coming through John Piper's contemporary stained glass. Inside the space is huge and open but somehow lacks awe, has little gravitas, lacks a sense of history. The crypt, the cathedral's one genuine connection with the past, hosts an annual CAMRA Beer festival. God and hop again. Couldn't happen deep in non-conformist Wales.

In Waterstone's on Bold Street someone in the history section is taking digital snaps of the index to a giant history of the city. Beats paying. The shop assistants take no notice. I find a loose pound coin on the settee installed to encourage browsers. I'll put it in the blind box. Can't find one. Back at the Tate is a wall map which shows Liverpool's position as the centre of most things. Echo and the Bunnymen at Erics. Brian Epstein and the Beatles. Jeff Nuttall, Maurice Cockrill, and Keith Arnatt at Liverpool College of Art. Yoko Ono and Mike McGear somewhere between Poetry and Music. The Boyle Family at the Docks. Le Corbusier at the Walker Art Gallery. A map of names and arrows and photos of places in squares. Beyond this I stumble on Henri's greatest painting, *The Entry of Christ into Liverpool*. Oil on Hessian. 68"x95". Père Ubu in his white suit with a black spiral on front. George Melly. Patten. McGough. The whole larger Liverpool cultural presence standing arrayed below a banner reading 'Long Live Socialism', next to an advert for Colmans Mustard, and then one for Guinness. The figures stand in line waiting to be recognised. If you were there then you'd be painted. Centre of the Creative Universe.

Amid the Welsh Streets in Toxteth where Ringo Starr was born in clapped out Gwydir there is no plaque. The Merseyside Bangladesh Association building stands in faded green paint, maroon coloured chipboard windows, deserted. All Items Of Value Have Been Removed From These Premises. A squatter hangs on, flowers in baskets hanging outside the only one of five hundred houses where anyone still lives. Flattening is days away. The council promise to rebuild Ringo's house as a tourist attraction, brick by brick, somewhere else. Would they be the same bricks? Same colour scheme on the restructured plaster inside? Will it cost £13 to visit as it does to the National Trust-run terrace at 20 Forthlyn Road where Paul McCartney once lived? Beatle music no longer leaks from the radios. There are none. All grey silence. Liverpool changing again.

Niall Griffiths' brilliant take on the real Liverpool gets into places that I only scratched. His book is the perfect guide. Listen to him talk, read his books, Liverpool is in his blood.

Peter Finch
September, 2008

notes

1. Monument to Queen Victoria, Derby Square, built 1902, intended to represent the spirit of patriotism of Liverpool's citizens, as well as the national self-confidence that Victoria's long reign had engendered.
2. From Adrian Henri's "Liverpool Poems", Tonight at Noon, Rapp & Whiting, 1968.

Some years later, in 1927, I obtained confirmation of my ideas about the centre and the self by way of a dream.... I found myself in a dirty, sooty city. It was night, and winter, and dark, and raining. I was in Liverpool.... I had the feeling that we were coming from the harbour, and that the real city was actually up above, on the cliffs. We climbed up there, [and] found a broad square dimly illuminated by street lights, into which many streets converged.... In the centre was a round pool, and in the middle of it a small island. While everything round about was obscured by rain, fog, smoke, and dimly lit darkness, the little island blazed with sunlight. On it stood a single tree, a magnolia, in a shower of reddish blossoms. It was as though the tree stood in the sunlight and was at the same time the source of light.... I had had a vision of unearthly beauty, and that was why I was able to live at all. Liverpool is the 'pool of life'. The 'liver', according to an old view, is the seat of life – that which 'makes to live'.

    C.G. Jung

A city named after an oik's pub game and offal.

    A.A. Gill

You could be worse
you could be scouse
eating rats
in a council house

    Popular terrace chant

PREFACE

'SCOTLAND TO THE NORTH, IRELAND TO THE WEST, WALES TO THE SOUTH, AND ENGLAND SOMEWHERE DOWN THERE'

What's your opinion of Liverpool? You'll have one – everybody does – and it usually tends towards the extreme, either involving such words as 'salty' and 'witty' and 'cocky' and 'charming' or 'feckless' and 'self-pitying' and 'filthy' and 'thieving' and 'sly' and 'junkie' and 'lazy'. It inspires wet-eyed wistfulness in the way that only certain countries (and hardly ever individual cities within them) can and flint-eyed frothy-lipped hatred and disgust which, of course, tells you more about the hater than the object: see Kelvin McKenzie on the Hillsborough catastrophe[1], or recall Thatcher's crusade to decimate the working class in Britain as a viable political force during which she propounded the desire to saw Liverpool away from the mainland and let it float out to sea, or listen to the vitriol that boils out of the away terraces whenever Liverpool or Everton play at home (or the home terraces when they play away, of course), particularly against London or north-west-based opposition. It arouses passions, like no other British, maybe even European, city can. The Loathers will claim that the city has brought such rank regard on itself, thereby evincing the denial and self-justification that is the root of all hatred; and interestingly, the Lovers say a similar thing.

On *The Idler*'s 'Crap Towns' website[2], the sardonically-named 'Ringo' lets fly:

> You could put your powers of taste and decency on hold for a while and visit [Liverpool] for a few bitterly unfulfilling hours but surely you've got more rewarding things to do, like cleaning the oven... [Take] that wonderful Scouse wit. That's the sort of repartee celebrated by the funniest man in the cosmos – Stan 'I could kill an Indian' Board-man – or that colossos (sic) of the comedy world Jimmy Tarbuck.

It's wonderful, the 'Crap Towns' website. It never fails to make me laugh. And I can't quibble with Ringo's comments on Boardman and Tarby, nor his attack on John Lennon's 'fat-arsed' hypocrisy. You can almost hear the blood beginning to bubble as he warms to his theme:

> Truth is the sense of humour's fine as long as it's directed at somebody else[,] but as soon as it's fired back at them, the thin-

skinned slimeballs launch into howls of self-pity.... If they're not cramming chips into their greasy maws, they're piling as many as they possibly can onto their round shoulders. They're misunderstood, they're misinterpreted, they're patronised, they're under-invested, they're unappreciated. They're Scousers.

Good Lord, Ringo's got twisted knickers. And how the apoplexy has been stoked further by the award of European City of Culture, which Liverpool celebrates in 2008, which has provoked, in turn, appreciative nods, widespread indifference, storms of derisive laughter, and something like profound indignation, which seems genuinely felt; Liverpool? City of Culture? Then get the Culture Commission on the next flight to Baghdad because if they can find evidence of culture in that God-forsaken shithole then they'll surely be able to find weapons of mass destruction in Iraq.

People can't leave Liverpool alone. They return to it – and not exclusively in figurative terms – again and again, like they might pick at a scab. It sits there, out on the edge, more sea than land, throwing black tendrils out over the country that lies behind it. It keeps its back turned, which further fuels the clamouring of the mob; seeking attention from a parent punitively stand-offish, the tantrums are intensified. The old pox-ridden crackwhore on the dip down the Albert Dock, once grand Maritime Dame, once Second City Lady, remains aloof and haughty. How *dare* she? Who does she think she is?

Yet this is part of the point of Liverpool, to remain isolationist, looking across the sea, resolutely resistant to the creeping embourgeoisement engulfing much of England (just one way in which the city resembles a Celtic country to the middle-England mindset[3]). It doesn't really care what's happening in the rest of the country and takes its cultural cues and points of reference from its maritime partners and now spiritual siblings, most notably Belfast, Dublin, and New York. In fact, the latter's position in America is helpful in a consideration of Liverpool's within England; in the country but not part of it; central to the historic momentum of the parent land yet adamantly apart from that same thing. Herman Melville remarked on such similarities during his stay in Liverpool in 1839[4]:

> Liverpool... was very much such a place as New York. There were the same sort of streets pretty much; the same rows of houses with stone steps; the same kind of sidewalks and curbs; and the same elbowing, heartless-looking crowd as ever.... I walked down Lord Street, peering

into the jeweller's shops; but I thought I was walking down a block in Broadway.

The two cities are officially twinned; New York stevedores were the first to down tools in solidarity with the striking Liverpool dockers of the 1980s, and the two unions have formed a strong and abiding friendship; Liverpool honours the destruction of the World Trade Centre with two vertical beams of blue light on the waterfront every September 11th; Brooklyn dockers in a bar in Red Hook took to calling me 'little brother' when they found out where I was born. Tony Wailey – writer, historian, film-maker – wrote[5]:

> Our shattered lives define our worth
> our children stampeding forth
> their bursts of joy defend the dark
> sweet Liverpool and New York

Kevin Sampson – music mogul (or ex, rather), novelist, fine fellow, whom you'll meet at greater length later – writes about being marooned in New York on September 15th, 2001[6]:

> I am not stateless. For years, many years, people have told me of the likeness between Liverpool, my city, and New York, theirs. I've been flattered by this - wanted to believe it. New York... home to a thousand nations and a hundred different soundtracks, the twenty-five hour city that never sleeps. Liverpool, Manhattan in miniature, the seaboard city that throbs to its own beat. Everyone tells you they're sister states, linked by their maritime past.

Note that word 'states'. And, to belabour the connection jus a wee bit longer, here's Paul Morley, himself not a Liverpudlian, with the most succinct and incisive summation of the city that I read in the course of my researches for this book[7]:

> Someone asked me about Liverpool. Liverpool is not part of England in the way that New York is not part of America. It is more Welsh, more Irish, a shifty, shifting outpost of defiance and determination reluctantly connected to the English mainland, more an island set in a sea of dreams and nightmares that's forever taking shape in the imagination, more a mysterious place jutting out into time between the practical, stabilising pull of history and the sweeping, shuffling force of myth.

Remember that Liverpool inspires hatred only amongst certain sections of the British populace; elsewhere – understandably excepting those parts of Italy connected to the Heysel catastrophe – I, personally, have encountered only intrigued and curious affection. Morley continues:

> Liverpool is always on guard. They know that the English look up and over with suspicion and doubt, stumped by the language, needled by the snappy, mongrel confidence, outmanoeuvred by the fast logic-shredding wit. The city is also always wary of what might appear over the horizon, from the endless heavy sea, at what unknown force, for good or evil, might wash up on their vulnerable, open shore. The city has had more money than some, and been poorer than most, it's seen better days, it's always on the up, it believes in itself, it's all on it's own. It's been associated with grotesque episodes in history, it's had ideas that have contributed to the immense civilised progress of the whole world. It's hands are dirty, but it's mind is open.

So the city I was born into was one of dirty back-alleys and goalposts painted on gable ends. Of vast and empty docklands and the Cast Iron Shore, of parks and bordering woods and fields and streams in which I'd search for sticklebacks and leeches and bird's nests in bushes. The city I left was one of dizzyingly-high unemployment and derelict shops and heroin epidemics and rusting cranes and echoing warehouses and a kind of pariah status and an all-too-easily-fathomable sense of desolation. And the city I've periodically returned to, especially in recent weeks, is one of litterless streets and vibrancy, investment and regeneration[8]. From the ferry terminal over the Mersey at Seacombe, the skyline is hugely impressive; the cluster of glass towers abutting the Three Graces, the new Pavilion building like a giant butterfly spread-winged, the brown bulks of the docks linking each horizon. It looks like Brisbane, or Baltimore, somewhere decidedly un-British. There is a forest of

cranes. Not all of this is down to the City of Culture award, and not all of it is down to Objective One funding, and very little of it is due to the venal machinations of a council tainted by accusations of corruption and incompetence. Booms have an echo, of course, even over the empty spaces between the sound-waves. It's not the city it was a century ago, but nor is it the city of two decades ago. It's a mad and fascinating place, possessed of a most peculiar life-force, part celebratory, part self-destructive, both insular and expansionist. My recent returns have revealed a more open and accessible city than I remember, one which now promotes The Beatles as a means of enticing the tourist quid rather than any pitiful clinging to past glories (that still exists, but it is subsiding). I doubt very much that this book will prompt you to alter or revise your opinion of Liverpool, whatever that might be, but I don't really care about that. I'm going to write it anyway. There'll be little of The Beatles within, or Gerry and the Pacemakers, and none of the mawkish twaddle that'll no doubt be foisted on and emanate from the city in 2008; if you want that, then take your pick from the tsunami of tat that'll be produced to 'celebrate' the City of Culture award. The city's not shy anymore about revealing its secrets. Or some of them, at least.

SOME STATISTICS/GENERAL INFO

POPULATION: The most recent census, of 2001, gave the population as 439,473, but five years later, Leo Benedictus in *The Guardian*[9] revised it up to 469,017. An increase of 30,000 in five years (although where the boundaries are drawn in such surveys, I've no idea); the exodus of the eighties is beginning to reverse. People are returning, and moving there for the first time. The crowd that greeted the Liverpool Champions League-winning team of 2005 was estimated at around 800,000, close to the peak 1931 population of just under a million, although of course many came from outside the city to celebrate. Of the permanent population, the Irish are by far the largest minority (so much so, in fact, as to make the term 'minority' questionable), followed by the Chinese, the Afro-Caribbeans, Indians, Somalis, Yemenis, and Nigerians, with smaller groups of Greeks, Russians, Poles and other eastern Europeans, Japanese, French, etc. To list all ethnic groupings would be to list almost every country in the world.

GEOLOGY[10]: This is important, here. The poet Paul Farley – whom you, and I, will meet later, and discover some incredible coincidences with between my upbringing and his – talks about how he loves the Liverpool sandstone[11], how 'the Lime Street cutting is like the eighth wonder of the world', with 'the hanging garden of the ferns' and the fallen hills that surround the city; 'big, gigantic forces', he says, and talks about the sandstone in the Anglican cathedral, and Picton library, 'this huge chunk of red rock we're sitting on'. Slate, too, which began as settling mud 500 million years ago in the seas and that would become the city's bedrock and which now dominates its roofs-capes; and coal, which began as vegetation 315 million years ago, a jungle-like forest cover blanketing the area, and which has been mined nearby in St. Helens, north Wales, and Wigan; and then 215 million years ago, the baking desert left after the waters receded gave us the sandstone formed in the temporary salt lakes caused by occasional rains or thawing snow from the close mountains, and, within the last million years or so, glacial murrains brought clay and sand and rock of all types and sizes which in turn offered varied soils and bricks and tiles and the glass industry of St. Helens.

'Gigantic forces' indeed. The city heaves and swells and falls away with the movements of the tides on which it is built, amasses and collapses, mirroring the pattern of stone.

HUMAN HISTORY[12]: I'll try, and no doubt fail, to be brief.

Around 3,000 BC, land clearance of the area by human agency began, as evidenced by the tools found in Toxteth and Wavertree and the chambered tomb in Allerton's Calderstones Park. This went on until 43 AD when Roman settlement began, primarily at Chester, but also in what is now known as Woolton. The Grassendale Pavement, a Roman road, linked Aigburth and Garston. Several centuries of Viking raids followed with Norsemen settling in Crosby and Kirkby, as well as on the Wirral. A hoard of coins found in Crosby dated in part from the reign of King Alfred, circa 883.

In 1086, the Domesday Book named Smithdown, Speke, Toxteth and West Derby, others. In 1190, the name 'Lifer pul' was first used, in a deed signed by Prince John; it is commonly accepted as meaning 'muddy pool', but Fritz Spiegl in his *Scouse International*[13] points out the various permutations of spelling, from Leverpool to Llyfrpwll, and proffers the theory that the name might come from the Welsh word for a type of edible seaweed, 'laver', a sprig of which is held in the Liverbird's beak, the iconic and famous emblem of the city (and pronounced to rhyme with 'fiver', not 'river').

Possible, and interesting. But anyway.

In 1207, on 28th August, King John granted the city a charter, recognising its potential as a safe port of embarkation to serve Ireland. He gave the citizens the right to hold an annual fair and a weekly market. Four years later he used the city as a base for military forays into Wales.

In 1229, Henry III issued a further charter, granting various civic privileges such as the right to levy tolls, before abandoning the nascent town by awarding it to the Earl of Chester. Population at this time was probably not above 1,200.

In 1235, William de Ferrers, Sheriff of Lancaster, oversaw the building of the now long-gone Liverpool castle, built, of course, out of sandstone. His son acquired control of his Liverpool possessions after some kind of typically medieval familial hullabaloo, which led to a group of burgesses being granted, in 1309, six acres at the head of what is now Brownlow Hill in the city centre. Edward II attacked the castle in 1315. The Mersey became a naval yard, holding vessels used to attack the French in 1328 and the Scots in 1335. By 1346, 196 burgesses existed in the town. Black Death then hit twice, bracketing the building of the first chapel, St. Nicholas's in Walton, patron saint of sailors. In 1357, Henry of Lancaster granted the lease of the whole town, excluding the castle, to leading burgesses for a decade, a grant renewed by John of Gaunt in 1374 and 1393 and probably involving a level of corruption that would make today's venal and underhanded power-propelled civic (un)dignitaries seem like choirboys in comparison.

1406, a fortified garrison was built at what is now Water Street at the behest of Sir John Stanley who, in 1424, came to blows with the castle constable, Sir Richard Molyneux. Belchem writes[14] that 'both families quickly accumulated high and influential offices... thus staking their claims to intervene in Liverpool's affairs for the next two centuries'. Told you so. In 1515, the first town hall was built, and a priest was installed to provide grammar school teaching. John Leland, author of *Piers Plowman*, visited in 1530, and described the city as a small fishing village with a number of vessels engaged in the linen trade with Ireland, and 'having well-kept, paved streets'[15]. Plague hit again in 1558, killing one third of the town's population, but Liverpool still managed to overtake Chester in 1586 as the north-west's leading port. Exports included coal, wool, knives, leather.

At the turn of the 1600s, a fleet of twenty vessels is recorded as using Liverpool's harbour, some weighing thirty-six tons, nearly all focussed on trade with Ireland. In 1664, the Molyneux family bought Toxteth Park. The Civil War reached the city in 1643, when Parliamentarian forces took the town, fortifying it against Royalist attack. Prince Rupert, in June of 1644, described the place as 'a mere crow's nest which a parcel of boys could take', but his initial assaults were repulsed until the Parliamentarians fled by sea, leaving the Royalist troops to sack the city and murder many, although they were to lose the city, and indeed the entire north, in the summer of 1644.

In 1648, the first recorded cargo from America landed in Liverpool. In 1670, London merchant Daniel Danvers set up business, bringing sugar refining to the town. A new town hall was built in 1673, roundabout the time the writer Celia Fiennes visited and wrote of it[16]:

> Liverpool... is mostly newly built, of brick and stone after the London fashion.... It is but one parish with one church though there be 2 streets in it, there is indeed a little chapel and there are a great many dissenters in the town.... The streets are well paved. There is an abundance of persons who are well dressed and fashionable.... It's London in miniature as much as I ever saw anything.

In 1699, Liverpool became an independent parish, gaining separate Customs authority from Chester. The first reference to slavery is made in 1700, with the sailing of the ship *The Blessing* (oh yes? For whom?), and construction of the first wet dock quickly followed, able to accommodate up to a hundred ships; contrast the motives behind that with those that led to the opening of the Bluecoat Hospital for poor children, in 1718. Strange city. The river Irwell was made navigable between 1720-1733, thereby connecting Liverpool with Manchester. The city was given a forestaste of sectarian strife in 1745 when the Roman Catholic chapel was razed. Wet dock number two was operative by 1754 – Salthouse Dock. Main industries, sugar refining and shipbuilding and rope-making and, by this time, slavery, in which Liverpool swiftly overtook Bristol and indeed everywhere else, achieving the status of Britain's leading slave-trading port by the 1760s, sending out between forty and a hundred voyages each year, peaking in 1799 when Liverpool ships alone carried over 45,000 slaves.

American War of Independence began in 1775. Recession in Liverpool. Wage cuts. Seamen attacked the town hall. France, Spain, and Holland declared war on Britain in 1778, which allowed Liverpool to profiteer and privateer, which it duly did. Also in 1778 a dispensary was opened in John Street where the poor could obtain free medicines.

Slaving fed on itself, growing exponentially, becoming an out-of-control monster despite rigorous campaigning against it by men such as William Rathbone, James Currie, William Roscoe and Edward Rushton, all of Liverpool. The population, too, metastasized, reaching 77,000 in 1801 and 118,000 by 1821, and 376,000 three decades after that. The slave trade was abolished in Britain in 1807, but the population and industrial/maritime boom continued with the rise of the cotton industry, which also indirectly helped to perpetuate the continuation of slavery in America. Slum housing began to dominate the docklands as cotton merchants branched out into property. Roscoe found the Liverpool Academy in 1810. Jesse Hartley, in 1824, dock surveyor, began to oversee the creation of the world's biggest fully enclosed wet-dock system, adding 140 acres of docks and ten miles of quay.

1825, Liverpool Merchants' Institute set up, the foundation of John Moores university. 1826, the Manchester-Liverpool railway was begun, to become the world's first passenger railway. Cholera killed 1,523 for the first time in 1832. But still the city grew. Became an Assize Town in 1835, with the Crown Court occupying St. George's Hall. First Grand National run at Aintree in 1837. Philharmonic Society founded in 1840, same year that Samuel Cunard established his transatlantic shipping line. Irish potato blight in 1844-1850 saw a huge increase in Irish migration to Liverpool, peaking in 1847 when

300,000 Irish landed, the same year that the city was declared to have the highest death rate in Britain, leading to the appointing of Dr. Duncan as the Medical Officer of Health.

1852 – 299,099 departures from Liverpool on 1,000 sailings; peak year of migration. 1857, Mersey Docks and Harbour Board was empowered to manage all shipping and commercial interests. Following year, Liverpool Society for Fine Arts was founded, and the Free Library and Museum in 1860. 1868, trams appeared. First Corporation housing in Britain, 1869 – St. Martin's Cottages. Tate's sugar factory began its operations at Love Lane in 1872.

Walker Art Gallery opened, 1877. Following year, Everton FC was founded out of the St. Domingo Methodist Youth Club. Things move even faster. City status granted, 1880. Underground links Liverpool with Birkenhead, 1886. Jewish migration to the city peaked in 1890. A rent dispute over the Anfield Road playing ground moved Everton FC to Goodison Park and Liverpool FC was founded. Overhead railway opened in 1893, first elevated electric railway in the world. The City of Liverpool swallowed Walton, West Derby, Wavertree and Toxteth.

Faster even faster. 704,000 citizens by 1901. Garston and Fazakerly eaten by the City. Work on the Anglican Cathedral begun in 1904 to a design by Sir Giles Gilbert Scott, twenty-three years old. Another colossus is born. The Three Graces built between 1907 and 1916 – the Dock Office, the Liver Building and the Cunard Building. 1909, Eleanor Rathbone became the first female councillor, same year as sectarian riots erupted in 'a perfect epidemic of terror'. Transport strike of 1911 saw gunboats poised in the Mersey. 13,000 Liverpudlians killed in World War One. 1919, race riots, in which one Charles Wootton is killed. Police strike = chaos. Unemployment rose, unleavened by the construction of the Queensway tunnel, which took nine years to complete. 1929, 30% of the citizenry living below the poverty line. Slums. Many slums. Limp men, 60,000 of whom appeared at the dockside each morning, seeking casual work. 1930, construction of Catholic cathedral begun, abandoned temporarily during World War Two. Peak population in 1932 of over 870,000. Work on the estates at Speke and Aintree and Kirkby started in 1936. 1939, 1,300 convoys used the docks carrying war supplies. Blitzkrieg between 8-15 May; 2,315 bombs, 119 landmines and countless incendiary devices dropped on the city. Deaths of 3,875 people, destruction of 10,000 houses. 70,000 homeless.

Slum clearance and re-building in the 1950s; 10,000 dwellings built on the Kirkby estate. Decline of sectarian politics is demonstrated by

Labour winning control of the city for the first time, but Jack Braddock dominates the administration and sectarianism of a different sort was begun. The overhead railway, or 'the Docker's umbrella', is closed. John Lennon formed the Quarrymen in 1957 and that's about all the Beatles-related stuff you're going to get, here. Industrial investment and expansion – Ford, Vauxhall, Standard-Triumph build three new car plants, creating 30,000 jobs, one of which was to be my paternal grandfather's. Hence the switch into present tense. 1967, Sir Frederick Gibberd's new design for the Catholic cathedral is completed. Further slum clearance between 1966 and 1972; 38,000 families rehoused in developments on the city's outskirts, such as Netherley, where I'll move to, aged three, in 1969.

1968, publication of *The Mersey Sound*. Sells nearly a million copies. 1971, second Mersey tunnel, the Kingsway, opened, linking Liverpool with Wallasey. Containerisation of shipping causes dock closure and mass loss of jobs. Severe recession follows; 40,000 made redundant. 450 factories close. Unemployment peaks at 25%, Tate and Lyle's closure highlights the city's economic desperation, two years after Thatcher came to power. Death knells are heard. A cataclysmic decade begins.

1980. People leave the city at a rate of 12,000 per year. 15% of Liverpool's land is vacant or derelict. Softer bombs fall, only slower and no less devastating in their effects on flesh and soul. Thatcher government creates the Merseyside Development Corporation to promote dockland regeneration, despite which, Toxteth riots for three days. Both black and white, poked into fury.

1983, after a decade of hung councils, Militant wins control. First

signs of revival begin to emerge with the Albert Dock development, the visit of the Tall Ships Race, and Britain's first International Garden Festival. Still, heroin and despair have much of the city in a grip, and on 29th May 1985, in Belgium's Heysel stadium, Liverpool fans charge Juventus fans and cause thirty nine deaths. The word 'pariah' is heard. Or heard more often.

Tate Liverpool opens in

1988, and an elite institution is forcibly introduced into an economically ravaged city. Still, it heralds a regeneration of sorts, and points towards a new kind of industry.

1989 – Hillsborough. 15th April. Liverpool FC go to Sheffield Wednesday's ground for an FA Cup semi-final against Nottingham Forest. West Yorkshire police make horrific mis-judgements concerning crowd-control and 96 Liverpool fans are crushed to death. Kelvin McKenzie gloats. Many others do too. West Yorkshire police attempt to deflect blame from themselves by pointing to the city's reputation as trouble. May they forever writhe in shame. Ninety-six dead.

Objective One status granted in 1993. Liverpool one of the poorest areas in the EU, with only 71% of the average EU GDP. A big boost for regenerative essays, but slightly shameful nonetheless. Much worse shame attended the abduction and murder of the three-year-old James Bulger on 12th February 1992 by two ten-year-old boys. National shock and disgust and outrage. Pariah city. Evil Liverpool. Even its children are beasts.

1999, first Liverpool Biennial of Contemporary Art is held. 2003, city secures the Capital of Culture award for 2008, meaning what? 2004, Liverpool Maritime and Mercantile City is designated a UNESCO World Heritage Site. 2004, work begins on the Paradise Project, one of the largest city-centre 'renewal' schemes ever undertaken in Europe. It will be vast.

2005, Liverpool FC win the Champions League, in spectacular and exhilarating fashion. One newspaper declares 'we are all scousers now', but then changes its mind after the vile and racially motivated murder of teenage student Antony Walker in Huyton in July of that year. And, in 2007, eleven-year-old Rhys Jones is shot and killed outside the Fir Tree pub in Croxteth, probably by someone not much older than himself. At the time of writing, a suspect has appeared in court and is in custody awaiting trial. 2007 is also the year that the city celebrates its 800th anniversary, not that that means much to the bereaved families. Or not that it helps them any.

2008 and beyond. Who knows?

★

The city that was, of course, is the city that is. Not much changes; everything changes. See what washes up on the tide.

notes

1.   Where, in his 'newspaper' *The Sun*, he accused Liverpool fans of pickpocketing and urinating on the dead. Some traces of urine were found on some of the bodies, undoubtedly, but they and others around them had been crushed to death. I'd relinquish bladder control, too. Wouldn't you? God rot the tabloid mentality.
2.   www.idler.co.uk/crap
3.   To be sure, recent developments, such as the Liverpool 1 'retail experience', might ostensibly be undermining this. But it still holds true, as I'll try to show.
4.   See *Redburn*.
5.   See *The Irish Sea*.
6.   See Mulhearn, ed., *Mersey Minis Three: Longing*.
7.   See the essay 'Liverpool Surreal' in Grunenberg and Knifton, eds., *Centre of the Creative Universe: Liverpool and the Avant-Garde*.
8.   Which has created its own victims, as we'll see.
9.   See 'Works Consulted'.
10. I'm indebted, here, to the catalogue accompanying the 'Blessings' exhibition held in the Catholic Metropolitan cathedral in 2007 to mark the city's 800th birthday. See Kiely, 'Works Consulted'.
11. In personal conversation.
12. Here, and indeed throughout, I'm indebted to the John Belchem-edited behemoth of a book *Liverpool 800: Culture, Character, and History*, a vast and absorbing encyclopaedic compendium and guide to all things Liverpool, which I found to be an utterly indispensable tool; and to an essay by Tim Lambert called 'A Brief History of Liverpool', which I discovered in my shoulder-high stack of printouts, and clippings, unfortunately unaccredited and undocumented. If it's been published before, I don't know when or where; nor do I know who emailed it to me. Nor, in fact, do I know who Tim Lambert is, but if he's reading this, thanks, and apologies.
13. See 'Works Consulted'. Spiegl, an inveterate writer of letters to newspapers, was very much a scouse polymath; collector of folk-song and sea-shanty, professional flautist, investigative linguist. The titles of his many books – for instance, *Learn Yerself Scouse* – shouldn't put you off; they're actually dryly-humourous, well-written, extensively-researched works. Honest.
14. In *800*.
15. Quoted in *800*.
16. Thanks to Lambert for this quote.

APPROACHING: BECOMING LIVERPOOL

TWO TUNNELS: KINGSWAY

The Kingsway – opened by the Queen in 1971 – was the second tunnel to link Liverpool with the Wirral, specifically Wallasey. No fanfare or flourish accompanied its opening as tunnel-enthusiasm had been exhausted four decades earlier by the Queensway tunnel, linking Liverpool to Birkenhead, opened by the then King. It just appeared, and people used it. Cars trundled down into it, sped under the Mersey bedrock and came back out on the other side of the water. Yes yes, very good. Seen it all before. I've been unable to find any information on it other than the year of its opening, so uninterested in it are the historians, so scanty its impact on the city's life. The Queensway was greeted with keen admiration for the remarkable feat of engineering that it undoubtedly was, but the Kingsway? Ho hum. More traffic. I don't know how the Queensway coloured Jung's visions of Liverpool, but I'd imagine that it made his mate Sigmund's slightly more fevered, if he dreamt of the place at all. But sometimes a tunnel is just a tunnel[1].

Still, here's a true story. Some years ago several toll-box attendants on the Kingsway were arrested on charges of embezzling thousands of pounds, found guilty, and incarcerated. They refused to reveal the whereabouts of the money, reasoning, I assume, that an extra bit of imprisonment was a fair price to pay when weighed against the moneyed fun and freedoms awaiting them on release. Round about this time, an old friend, who I haven't seen now for several years – let's call him Glen, because that's not his name – moved into a house in Birkenhead. Glen was, and maybe still is, one of those people to whom

luck sticks like a burr, like chewing-gum in their hair; extremely difficult to get rid of. The house had a long garden and Glen a lot of spare time so he decided to dig a vegetable patch. Stuck his shovel in the soil. Unearthed a sweet jar stuffed full of banknotes, almost a thousand pounds. Laughed and did a little dance. Dug again. Another jar. Then another, then another. Almost, as I recall, ten thousand pounds.

We assumed that it belonged to the ex-tunnel attendants, told Glen that when those fellers got out of jail they were going to come round looking for their money. If I was you, we said, I'd do a very fast runner. Did he take our advice? Yes, of course he did. Fled somewhere far away where the sun beats down on blue sea and white sand. I haven't seen him in years. I have no idea where he is.

FROM THE NORTH:
SOUTHPORT/MAGHULL/KIRKBY

Southport's not really a suburb of Liverpool, being separated from the city by miles of dunes and coastal arable land and small towns such as Ainsdale and Woodvale and Formby, but it's been utilised by the city as a place of seaside R-and-R for many years and, despite trains and cars cutting the journey time down to a mere hop, still is. The local accent sounds Liverpudlian, or almost; you get a strong sense of the big city boiling and a-throb nearby, its lights outshining the Southport stars (were they not smothered by the flashing and blaring bulbs of Southport's 'amusements' in the first place). Yet there is a feel to it of some removal from Liverpool, nevertheless; driving out to it along the A565 the city seems to end abruptly at Thornton and greenness spreads and rurality occurs. Signs in hedges point you to the Ince Blundell stately home, once the seat of medieval gentry landowners, or the airport at Woodvale, catering for training flights and private planes and gliders. Seagulls follow tractors and you are told that the Transpennine Way begins here, which surprised me somewhat, and the smells are of grass and soil and manure yet the brown bulk of Altcar prison is visible at the shoreline, outside the gates of which a young gang member was shot dead a few years ago, igniting the Croxteth/Norris Green turf/postcode war whose latest victim was the eleven-year-old Rhys Jones, himself uninvolved in the ridiculous and meaningless squabble in any way[2]. The 'Tourist Route' to Southport leads you through dunes spikey with marram, and alongside the pine woods of Freshfields were, as a boy, I'd feed red squirrels with peanuts (the nuts are still for sale, and the squirrels, amazingly, are still red). There's a Pontin's, razor-wired. Apart from that, it's pretty. I'm a passenger in my dad's car and he tells me of the Tiger Moth plane which would at one time use this beach as a runway, offering pleasure flights to paying passengers. Wouldn't be allowed, now. Marshgrass encroaches on the beach, threatens to

engulf as it has done further south at Parkgate, and across the estuary
I can see the tower and rollercoaster of Blackpool.

We enter Southport. The funfair closed a couple of years ago and
its rides lie empty, skeletally girdered, all stilled and silent. Saddens
me a little bit – I used to spend frantic days on those rides, on
Saturdays with friends and a bottle of Merrydown cider or on
weekdays with school truanted from and my tie bundled in my blazer
pocket. The town's shopping arcades remind me of Llandudno or
many another Victorian seaside resort and the grand hotels and
municipal offices pointlessly bellow of a wealth long gone.

Still, if Victorian grandeur is your thing, then the town's attractive-
ness isn't in doubt, but, like a lot of seaside towns, it's also become a
magnet for local junkies (the ocean as dark subconscious, the melan-
cholia of good-times-gone commensurate with skewed junkie
romance, the landfall of narcotics and the cheap drinking available in
the two-for-one tourist-trap bars), and the huge leisure/retail
complex under construction dominates the littoral side of the town,
uglifying the rows of townhouses that face the waves and the vast gas-
rig on the horizon like some giant alien invading machine. One
guidebook – *Liverpool: The Guide, 2005/06*[3] – states that Southport
'boasts more sunshine hours than anywhere else in the North West of
England', and maybe it does, but that's like praising Chester for
containing more wildebeest than any other border town in Britain
(the zoo there has three). The gas rig constantly brings to mind
empty promises; it's brought little or no wealth to the area, and only
made richer a few of the already-rich. Still, for all that, the town's not
completely unbeguiling; it's busy and lively, with many diverting
shops and pubs and with impressive statuary; the war memorial on
the corner of Lord Street and Nevill Street[4] never fails to grab the
eye. And there's the shelter on the promenade where, at age fifteen or
so, I got drunk on Concorde wine. And there's the bollard next to it
against which I was uncontrollably sick.

The town's young, really, dating from the late nineteenth century
as an offshoot of Churchtown, which itself is old enough to warrant
a mention in the Domesday Book. In 1792, a Churchtown landlord,
William Sutton, opened a hotel on the junction of Lord Street and
Duke Street, around which private dwellings were built to form a
hamlet called South Hawes. A stream ran up to Sutton's Hotel at that
time, offering anchorage to local fishermen, and so the 'port' was
appended to the 'south' in 1798. The visitsouthport.com website
refers to the 'little known fact' that Prince Louis Napoleon lived on

Lord Street before becoming Emperor of France in 1851 and suggests that the town's layout influenced the re-designing of Paris which he entrusted to 'the prefect of the Seine, Baron George Haussman', which is a tad fanciful but which I hope is true. In 1848, a railway linked the town to Liverpool and, from 1853, to Manchester and Wigan.

Most guides and websites use the word 'genteel', and it's not inappropriate, with the glass canopies and open parkland and tall granite townhouses and all. But there are, of course, darker sides, madder sides, legacies of that facet of the Victorian mindset which insisted on covering up piano legs lest they excite the humours of the loins whilst at the same time roping rebels across the mouths of cannons at the Lucknow uprising. Always the human animal rips through, always. The journalist and writer Nik Cohn visited Southport on the 12th July sometime in the late 1990s, the day of Loyalist marching, and found a 'stylish... Victorian resort, complete with pleasure gardens, arcades, and the world's oldest and longest iron pier', where, in the Edwardian public convenience, an old man enters, forces out a dribble, shakes off and exits with a cheery 'fuck the Pope'[5]. It's a great piece of writing, this, acutely observant, tonally urgent, disturbing and funny in equal measure. Cohn lists the brandished banners, 'a Loyalist roll of honour', reading 'Crown and Bible Defenders, Garscule Rising Sons of William' etc., but notes that this is really 'just a day's romp at the seaside.... They seem no more fanatical than a school outing, and far less threatening. Some of the bandsmen [,] unthinkably, are black. They even stop for red lights'. He follows the march to a small park where the marchers get even drunker than they already are and start to sing 'Oh Mammy dear, the Pope's a queer, he takes it up the arse' under a hoisted banner that reads 'For the Throne is Established by Righteousness'.

It's captured well, here, the miniscule distance from hideous violence that such sectarian gatherings stand. Which pretty much applies to Victorian seaside resorts in general, I've found; most of those memorials celebrate colonialist expansion, after all, the Maxim gun against the spear. No brave heroics. And the ordered grids of the streets and arcades suggest an utter intolerance of difference. Inevitable, then, that a town like Southport should act as a meeting place for such tribes, but its characteristic Merseyside maverickness has also drawn to it people such as J.G. Farrell, author of *Troubles* and *Singapore Grip*, and Booker Prize winner. Or, rather, it attracted his father; Farrell was only four when his family relocated to Southport

to escape the bombing of Liverpool in 1940, and so didn't have much
say in the matter. Farrell the younger never returned to Liverpool but
Ralph Crane, in his essay 'A Man from Elsewhere'[6], recognizes in his
work the influence of the city manifested in 'a sense of himself as a
man from elsewhere, a liminal position that is in line with being
Liverpool-Irish' (indeed, Farrell's first, and now largely forgotten,
novel was entitled *A Man from Elsewhere*). It's a paradox peculiar to
Liverpool, that a city with a powerful and profound sense of unique
identity should see its citizens leave the only place in which that
identity will be appreciated and unexamined. As if the strength of it
will remain resistant to dilution without but will contribute to the
weakening of it within the place in which it was forged.

And Jean Sprackland lives here, author of three collections of
poetry[7] and a handful of short stories[8]. She appeared out of the Dead
Good Poets Society, which we'll look at in more detail later, and was
listed as one of the twenty 'Next Generation' poets in 2004 (along
with Deryn Rees-Jones and Paul Farley, names you might recognise
by now). Her work is full of waves and sound, jetsam and undersea
cables, striking and lucid imagery. Take this, from 'The Currency of
Jellyfish' in *Hard Water*:

> What must it be like
> to have no bones, no guts, just that cloudy blue inside you?...
> Another tide had brought in hundreds more.
> They lay like saints,
> unharvested, luminous

Peter Barry, Liverpool-born critic and now senior lecturer at
Aberystwyth University, highlights Sprackland's[9] 'bizarre and surre-
alist... tone and control', as well as 'her strong political edge'. There's
also her sharp grasp of the melancholy inherent in a place like
Southport, which informs her published short stories; the town isn't
named in them, but a fading seaside resort is one of the connecting
leitmotifs, a place of collapse and demolition and drowning and
suicide with a gas-rig far out in the bay like 'an alien structure, a space
station'[10]. See? Told you.

We leave Southport and head towards Kirkby, cutting through a
tiny part of Lancashire on the way. These fields and woods and red-
brick farmhouses and stately homes are not what you associate with
Merseyside; where are the stoat-faced gangs in shellsuits and baseball
caps? Where are the cocaine dealers in Shogun jeeps? The pit-bulls,

the metal-sheeted shops and houses? Well, we'll get to them later. My dad points out a roadside ditch that I fell into when I was a small boy; it was a long drive home, apparently, and I cried and reeked all the way. The ditch is still there, still foul-looking. He also points to a farmhouse standing alone in a field:

"Your grandad worked on that house when I was a kid. He took me there one day to do some odd jobs and help him out. I think it was a way of making sure I behaved meself."

"And did yeh?"

"I painted some lad green."

We pass a gravel car-park which was once an old quarry-pit in which I'd fish with nets. Caught sticklebacks and newts and caddis-fly larva, little armoured creatures, tiny antenna'd tanks. A garish roadside sign reads: FARMER TED'S FARMAGEDDON! UNLEASH YOUR FEAR!, and lists a website: farmageddon.co.uk. Visions of fellers in wellies riding snorting skeletal horses, but the website reveals it to be a small music festival, and a pretty unexciting one at that. We drive through a village called Lydiate; anyone from there at school would be called the 'Idiot from Lydiate'. Next to it is a village called Lunt.

Maghull is city outskirts, really, but still there's a feel to it of rural market town. The knowledge of the city's contiguity, however, turns it into a typical suburb; redbrick houses, chain stores, busy roads serving the metropolis, all generic and commonplace. I had an uncle who lived here, a long time ago, an innately funny man who would cook me baked beans and gravy for tea. His own tea would often be Pollock'd up the wall above the gas fire; a sign of displeasure with his

sons, or to his wife that he'd finished arguing with her. The plate would be tossed with a kind of cheeriness, unangered and unaccompanied by shouting. Read the foodstains as functional, as punctuation; a full-stop, new paragraph, no more. He'd make me laugh, loud and long, when I was a boy.

We cross Switch Island and onto the busy new motorway that pierces Kirkby. My dad

tells me about the dump that used to be here for war machines awaiting dismantling; he'd search with his friends for bull-racers, circles of
steel enclosing ball-bearings (called, in this area, 'ollies', hence Olly
Dump). I remember those too; gleaming steel orbs of varying sizes
that could be used either as marbles or ammunition. What they were
used for, and in which machine, I don't know.

Shopping centre. Huge estate. A sports centre that is a giant
reinforced bunker. Such places as this on the outskirts of big cities
suggest temporal shallowness and immediacy, as if they have no
history that predates the 1960s, when they took on their physicality
which hasn't changed since. But Kirkby is old; recorded in Domesday
as Cherchebi, the 'town of the church' in Norse, and 'one of the six
manors held by that great Lancashire landowner, Uctred, the thane',
according to Derek Whale[11]. The first chapel here was built in 870, to
St. Chad, and not replaced until 1766, itself demolished in 1872 and
replaced by the present St. Chad's Church, containing a Norman
font, 1,000 years old, that had been used as a water butt for the old
school since he days of Puritan disapproval of 'unnecessary adornment'.

Excavation on one of the estates here unearthed a sandstone
obelisk, probably a Weeping Cross, where mourners/pallbearers
would lay down their coffins for a rest on their journey to the graveyard. It was restored in the 1880s by William Molyneux, Earl of
Sefton (which family you'll hear a lot about, in these pages), whose
mason re-designed the top into a pyramid shape. Why? Peat was cut
here, at Kirkby Moss. A dam built across the Simonswood Brook
drained the mossland. One of Britain's biggest munitions factories
operated here throughout World War Two, comprising over a
thousand buildings and eighteen miles of road, employing 23,000,
producing 10% of all ordnance used in the war. Two explosions, both
in 1944, killed sixteen workers, and buried over 4,000 bombs, which
took three months to recover. What work; digging in darkness, every
second promising a fireball. This factory's closure led directly to the
Kirkby-scape of today; the newly-unemployed munitions workers
were given the job of creating the huge estate that, effectively, Kirkby
is, of 10,000 houses and more than 80,000 residents.

The city now starts to give up its secrets. On the border between
Kirkby and Fazakerly (Anglo-Saxon, again, meaning 'meadowland with
a boundary field'), on the East Lancs Road, huge factories once stood;
in one of them, English Electric, my mother had her first job, directly
after leaving school. She worked as a clerk. The factory's gone, now.

FROM THE EAST: WARRINGTON/ST. HELENS

Nor can these places justifiably be called suburbs of Liverpool, really, but St. Helens is linked to the city by the Sankey Canal, and has been since 1755, and is classed as a District/Unitary Authority in the county of Merseyside, but the website visionsofbritain.org gives the population in 2001 as just over 176,000 – far too big for a suburb. See it, rather, as a town in itself with suburbs of its own; Newton-le-Willows, Ashton-in-Makerfield, Whiston, Rainhill, etc. The glass and copper industries spurred its growth; acidic fumes from the factories at one time turned horse-brasses green and blue, and destroyed most of the town's vegetation[12]. The town is probably most famous today for its rugby club and for being the birthplace of Johnny Vegas, stage-name of Michael Pennington, often called 'roly-poly comedian' by certain TV guides, whose drunken persona (if indeed it is an act) marks him out as something of a modern-day W.C. Fields. His act is funny, and compelling in its hysterical despair; he can be fascinating to watch. He apparently trained for the priesthood and, at the time of writing, has recently presented a Channel 4 series, *Johnny Vegas's Guide to Evangelical Christianity*, every episode of which I missed.

It's immediately south-west of St. Helens, however, that the isogloss lies, where the regional accent begins to take on its highly distinctive burr, and here's as good a place to discuss it as any. It's one of the most instantly recognisable accents in these islands, and as divisive as the city it comes frrom and the collective character of that city's denizens, inspiring on the one hand fondness and admiration and, on the other, contempt and recoil so abrupt and extreme as to appear to be genuine loathing. J.B. Priestley, in his hilariously snobby *English Journey*, wrote in the late 1930s: 'Liverpool is simply Liverpool. Its people – or at least the uneducated among them – have an accent of their own; a thick, adenoidy, cold-in-the-head accent, very unpleasant to hear'[13], whereas Nick Danziger saw in it that '*mix* [his italics] of accents which makes an egalitarian society all but impossible. Speech in Britain remains as much an emblem of social caste as when George Bernard Shaw wrote: 'it is impossible for an Englishman to open his mouth without making some other Englishman despise him'[14]. As far back as the early 1900s, its reputation had spread as far as Russia, where Isaac Babel wrote of a seafaring character who 'avoided speaking Russian; he expressed himself in the coarsish, abrupt language of Liverpool captains'. Fritz Spiegl, as always a reliable authority on these matters, writes[15] of the

varying accents *within* the wider vernacular, all characterised by the
'ur' or 'air' sound which is 'velarized, the tongue being shifted
upwards and backwards towards the velum, or soft palate, which
constricts the throat, in the way an oboist squeezes his reed'. Where's
it from? What are its origins? Liverpool didn't grow out of a collection of coterminous villages in the same way that, say Manchester or
Sheffield did; rather, it burgeoned exponentially and suddenly with a
rapid influx of immigrants, so the accent does not especially represent the locality. Spiegl sees the accent as adopting its familiar timbre
'only after Irish immigrants flooded in' after the potato famine of the
1840s and continuing with the influences from Northern Ireland, 'so
the truculent sounds of politicians and terrorists trying to justify
themselves in those whining upturned phrase-ending [sic] have
probably helped to give a bad name to the Scouse accent'. He sees a
strong Welsh influence, too, particularly north Walian; both accents
share dominant fricative and plosive ingredients, both sound insistent
even as they rise, both are possessed of a peculiar music. John
Kerrigan, in his introduction to *Liverpool Accents: Seven Poets and a
City*[16], writes that 'the staple argot... is by general consent a mixture
of Welsh, Irish, and catarrh', the last of which, along with 'adenoidal'
and 'nasal' and, indeed, 'whining', is one of the most common
epithets given to the accent by those who don't like it. Yet it's one of
its most intriguing qualities; Spiegl attributes it to the 'draught
coming up the Mersey tunnel'[17], whilst John Belchem in his essay 'An
Accent Exceedingly Rare: Scouse and the inflexion of class'[18] sees the
'pronounced adenoidal quality of scouse [as] a form of linguistic
bonding, an assertion of group identity, rather than a symptom of the
notorious problems of public health which made Victorian
Liverpudlians prone to adenoids and respiratory disease'. It even, in
the throat of the great poet and historian and effective abolitionist
William Roscoe, made him out to be something of a 'barbarian': the
novelist Maria Edgeworth, in 1813, after a visit to Allerton Hall,
wrote that she was impressed by Roscoe's learning but repelled by his
'strong provincial accent which at once destroys all idea of
elegance'[19]. Alan Bennett, in his *Writing Home*, had a good old snotty
grumble about it, as well, as have thousands more: 'There is a rising
inflection [in the accent],' he wrote, 'particularly at the end of a
sentence that gives even the most formal exchange a built-in air of
grievance.... They all have the chat, and it laces every casual
encounter... and it gets me down'.

   Well. Don't come back, then.

It's not an old accent, in truth; Gladys Mary Coles, poet and editor and publisher (the Wirral's Headland imprint is hers), sees it as taking root in the public consciousness not with The Beatles but with the Liverpool-Welsh playwright Alun Owen (who you'll meet in greater depth later) in the late Fifties[20], but, like other regional accents, it's more than the sounds that words make coming out of a speaker's mouth; it's a shibboleth, a verbal and linguistic badge, a

> micro-culture in historical formation.... [Liverpudlians'] identity is constructed, indeed is immediately established, by how they speak rather than what they say. Instantly recognisable, the accent is the essential medium for the projection and representation of the local micro-culture, the 'scouse' blend of truculent and defiance, collective solidarity, scally-waggery, and fatalist humour which sets Liverpool and its inhabitants apart[21].

And a sense of 'apartness', for both good and ill, has always been an essential component of the Liverpool soul; it's why so many people leave the city; it's why so many stay there; it's why so many are starting to return. The accent defines the city; a little bit Irish, a little bit Welsh, it nevertheless sounds like no other argot anywhere. I've lost a lot of my own accent, but still I was bemused – and strangely pleased – to be asked to repeat my question in English when I asked a passerby for directions in Ottawa. The accent displeases certain people because it deepens the impression that 'Liverpool [is] an island with arcane customs and rituals, loosely attached to the north-west coast'[22], and exclusion tends to offend, even if it is to do with something the offendee doesn't want to be a part of anyway (or thinks s/he doesn't). The dark and gathering sameness that threatens to engulf this small archipelago of many once-diverse cultures and is exemplified in the epidemic of accentual blandness that is Estuary English encounters an insurmountable obstacle at St. Helens, as it does at Gateshead, Coventry, the Severn. Applaud that.

Oh, and Warrington; I haven't mentioned Warrington. Novelist Helen Walsh is from there; her second novel, *Once Upon a Time in England*, is set there. You'll meet her later. Warrington isn't Liverpool, in fact is half-Manchester, so we won't go there. But here's a couple of stanzas from Kevin Fegan's fine poem 'Bridgebuilding'[23]:

> At Junction 7
> on the M62, Warrington
> is waiting with divided loyalties

like a newspaper salesman,
Manchester Evening News in one hand
Liverpool Echo in the other...

On the stone bridge
over St. Helen's canal, Warrington
is waiting like rival gangs
warring over words like private
and rented, money and pride, east
and west, borough and new town.

FROM THE SOUTH: RUNCORN/WIDNES

Runcorn is grim hinterland, frontier Merseyside, beyond which, to
the east, the accent becomes more Lancastrian than Liverpudlian. It,
too, is less a suburb than an autonomous town in the Borough of
Halton, with, in the late 1990s, a population of around 65,000, but as
a physical conurbation it is linked to the city through Hale and Speke.
It lies on the opposite side of the Mersey, facing Widnes, and there's
not a great deal about it that needs to be said, in a Liverpool context;
it has a huge shopping precinct which, as a child, I'd visit often; the
sitcom *Two Pints of Lager and a Packet of Crisps* was filmed there;
there was a car sunk in the mud beneath the transporter bridge over
the Mersey that would intrigue the younger me (don't know if it's still
there). It was granted New Town status in 1964, which saw the
appearance of some really quite astonishingly brutalist architecture,
including stacked cabins not unlike shipping containers masquerad-
ing as housing, but, despite that appellation, the place is old, with a
Saxon name, and a trove of various archaeological treasures, including a Bronze Age stone axe-hammer and a bronze palstave. The
Romans passed it by, seemingly, but Queen Aethelflaed built a
fortress on what is now called Castle Rock, in 915 AD. This was
shortly followed by a church, and a Priory, dedicated to St. Berthelin,
and another one at Norton (opened to the public in 1975), a ferry
service over the Mersey and sea-links to north Wales and, in the late
1700s, a canal and docks, fairly successful; between 1873 and 1884
the Bridgewater Navigation Co. handled, on average, 490,000 tons of
goods each year, including china and blue clays, pig iron, slate, stone,
coal, and salt[24]. The Port of Liverpool collected dues on all such
goods handled at Runcorn until 1861 when an Act of Parliament

transferred the duties to the Upper Mersey Navigation Commission. Quarries appeared, supplying the sandstone for Peel church on the Isle of Man, the New York Docks and, of course, Liverpool's Anglican cathedral. Then came heavy industry, and chemicalisation of the town and environs; soap works, acid and alkali works, slate works, brewery, steam mills. Pollution. Three firms producing Leblanc alkali. The Aluminium Co. of Oldbury. Chemical stink, effluent, burgeoning population. Ill health, stupefaction. Tanneries. Chloro-ethylene solvents. Local employment dominated by ICI, and, in more recent times, the YKK zip factory at Whitehouse. New town status increased the population exponentially, as it did in others (Milton Keynes, for example), for reasons which I've never really understood. Shopping City, my remembered precinct, was opened in 1972, when I was six years old. It covers an area of thirteen acres and can accommodate 2,500 cars.

And that's it, really. Of the lives and loves and longings of Runcorn's no doubt fine populace, I know next to nothing, so I won't hang about. Before we go, though, look out over the river, towards the Widnes side; see that range of small hills? They're grassed-over mounds of chemical waste, known as the 'Widnes Alps', homes to two-headed moles and earthworms that glow. So, yes, let's not hang about.

Stay on the southern banks of the Mersey for a while, keeping the city at a safe distance, over the river's gravy waves. Circle those towers and stone mountains for a while. Scoot quickly through Cheshire, skim the Welsh border and enter the Wirral peninsula, where you'll find Birkenhead, which you'll smell before you see.

FROM THE EAST: THE WIRRAL/BIRKENHEAD

'The wilderness of Wirral', an anonymous yet perspicacious poet once wrote many centuries ago; 'There few people lived/Whom either God or good-hearted men could love'[25]. Once the haunt of pirates and cut-throats and smugglers and brigands, parts of it have been gentrified to a great degree and are perceived as the 'posh' parts of Merseyside, the mansions at Caldy and Meols, especially, providing homes for soap actors and football players and drug dealers (the notorious and astonishingly successful Curtis 'Cocky' Warren had a house here). The novelist Malcolm Lowry – more on whom later – was brought up in Caldy, in a house called Inglewood, 'an eight-roomed mock-Tudor mansion set in two acres of land', part of 'an estate for affluent gentry and the nouveau riche'[26]. It's a wet and windy peninsula, as rural as Merseyside gets, with, from the southern flank, great views over the Dee estuary and north Wales. The largest conurbation, Birkenhead (say it with a catarrhal blockage in the throat and a mucal clearing of the nose: *Birrrkkh-n-edd*), is big enough to have its own satellite towns, and, despite so many commonalities between it and the city across the river as to make the two almost indistinguishable to an outsider, likes to define itself as being most definitely not Liverpool; as the Tranmere Rovers (the Wirral's football team) followers sing in Kevin Sampson's first novel, *Awaydays*:

> Don't be mistaken and don't be misled
> We are not Scousers, we're from Birkenhead
> You can fuck your cathedrals and your pierhead
> We are not Scousers, we're from Birkenhead[27]

It has a unique smell to it, Birkenhead; amphetamine and exhaust and brine and chips and fags. Glenda Jackson has a theatre named after her on Borough Road, the main thoroughfare, next to a block of flats that was once a college of further education where I did my A-levels; Lily Savage's alter ego, Paul O'Grady, was born here; the writer Nathaniel Hawthorne was American consul here in the 1860s, in the Washington Buildings, and he begins his reminiscences by complaining how, 'in a stifled and dusky chamber [I] spent wearily four good years of my existence'[28]. Perhaps the town's[29] most famous musical export is Half Man Half Biscuit, 'four lads who shook the

Wirral', tirelessly championed by the late John Peel, and favourably sketched by Paul du Noyer in his historical overview of the Merseyside music scene *Liverpool Wondrous Place: From the Cavern to the Coral*[30]. He writes:

From their Wirral bastion they issue occasional dispatches of wry hilarity and downbeat, satirical bite. The songs... suggest a very real world of people too educated to be on the dole but too luckless or lazy to be anywhere else. They take a witty revenge on the drive of popular culture, without denying their fascination with it. They seem flintily incorruptible, and scan the London music media with a mocking eye for cant.

They're well worth a listen. The basic post-punk jangle of their music is supported by often brilliant, surreal and beguiling wordplay. You'll find them either repellent or addictive. They've been around a long time, and are still fuelled by the petrol of satire, which, of course, will forever geyser from the wells as long as the world and many people in it remain ridiculous. Asked, in a recent interview, how he chooses his targets, lead songwriter and singer Nigel Blackwell replied: 'I don't seek targets so much as they themselves sort of come knocking at my door, whereby some form of lambast duly manifests itself'[31]. Can't argue with that.

And remember Orchestral Manoeuvres in the Dark? Big-haired, rolled-up sleeved, slightly pretentious early 80s synth-band? Their 'Enola Gay' reached number one. A Wirral band, too. In detention at school, I'd sneak surreptitious peeks at the ledger when the teacher was out of the room, note down which members of OMD had been held back and for what misdemeanour, but I can't divulge any details here. I've said too much already.

We'll visit a few specific towns on the Wirral later, and intermittently touch Birkenhead, but this is a good place to look at the term 'scouse', widely thought to have originated in the Birkenhead docks, coined by either Norwegian sailors or Welsh dock-men, depending on who you'd prefer to believe. The word refers to a food-stuff, a basic stew, consisting of sheep-meat, carrots, onions, and potatoes, served with pickled beetroot or red cabbage and bread ('Blind Scouse' omits the meat), although the details and nuances have been widely and pointlessly argued over; seal the meat first? Add herbs? Include swedes? Daft matters, really. What's interesting is how a localised dish has supplied the name for an accent, an origin, indeed an entire demotic culture; to my knowledge, this has occurred nowhere else in these islands. Fritz Spiegl, in his *Scouse International*[13], points out that the food-stuff 'predates... the person', and how it was 'born of hard times', consisting basically of anything the housewife or ship's cook was able to find. A recent discussion in *The Guardian* newspaper included a letter from a Peter Williams of Old Llandegfan, pointing out that the distribution of the dish throughout various sea-ports

(Holyhead, Hamburg, Oslo etc.) 'tells us something further about the history of the 'Pool: it is one home of that great brotherhood of itinerant and iron-stomached sea cooks.... So lob scouse, in its various versions and spellings, [means] "throw the cheapest meat in the pot"'[32]. It began, probably, as the German *labskaws*, and became *lobscows* in Wales in 1706, according to Spiegl; 'lobscouser', meaning sailor (not peculiar to Liverpool, necessarily), first appeared in 1888. When it began to refer to anything specifically Liverpudlian is anyone's guess – not until after World War Two, probably. But it's stuck.

Spiegl lists some interesting variations; Bombay Scouse – add some curry paste to the broth; Spanish Scouse – use diced chorizo sausage; Hungarian Scouse – a pinch of paprika and tomato puree, and so on, as befits a multi-cultural maritime city, although the notion that the Welsh song *Sospan Fach* is actually a corruption of 'Scouse-pan Fach' is fanciful. John Belchem, in *Merseypride*, talks about the Saturday night 'scouseboat', a vat of the stew doled out at the junction of Wellington Street and Scotland Road, or the Scouse alley which ran underneath Paddy's Market in St. Martin's Hall, offering scouse for 1d. a bowl and wet nellies for a halfpenny (another local delicacy, a kind of curranty sponge). Somehow, and at some point, 'a sense of pride and identity with the dish seems to have developed', says Belchem, most strongly in the Scotland Road area, even though the most popular pauper food in that area was, at one time, Portuguese saltfish, or bacalhao. Who knows how or why these things occur. They just do. They're mysterious, and intriguing, but I don't think there's any deeper meaning to be quarried out. They just happen. And sooner 'scouse' than 'wet nelly'.

TWO TUNNELS: QUEENSWAY

In the 1920s, as sea-trade continued to decline, so certain municipal bodies within Liverpool began to look east, to the industrial hinterlands, for some suggestion as to best boost ailing fortunes. Civic Weeks were held, promotions of the city's past glories and present potential, during one of which the construction of a tunnel beneath the Mersey was proposed, primarily to 'remove Liverpool from its geographical corner'[33]. Trade continued to decline at a greater rate than production. Of course, Liverpool had been linked to Birkenhead by ferry for centuries, and Brunel had first planned a road tunnel in 1825, but the growth of docks and population on the Wirral, and the decline of such in Liverpool, obviated the need for an efficient transport link. So the railway tunnel was opened on 20 January 1886, the first passenger trains going through on 1 February, carrying 36,000 people on a single day. Thirty-eight million bricks were used to line the tunnel, much of it initially dug out with pickaxes and explosives until the Beaumont Cutter was brought in; a huge machine for a huge undertaking. Ventilation fans failed to clear the smoke but electrification occurred in 1903; the first under-water electrified railway on the planet.

Which still left the problem of road traffic, and the transportation of goods. Long queues still formed at the luggage-boat-quays or on the roads to Runcorn to use the Transporter Bridge there. Bridges were considered over the river from Liverpool, but were reckoned to be more expensive than a tunnel, so an Act of Parliament was passed in 1925, authorising the construction of such; engineer-in-chief would be Sir Basil Mott. Construction began in December of that year, with the sinking of 200ft vertical shafts at the dry (and, by now, disused) George's Dock on each side of the river. Two pilot tunnels were cut; on the Liverpool side, the main portal ran under Old Haymarket with an additional smaller one to serve The Strand docks by Bootle's Chapel Street. When the two tunnels met, they were no more than an inch out of alignment, and on the 3rd April 1928, the Lords Mayor of Liverpool and Birkenhead shook hands through the hole in the rock divide[34].

Work went on. Walls lined with bolted cast-iron plates, backfilled with rubble and grouted. All joints sealed with lead and a gunite rendering of cement, plus a bituminous emulsion and then plaster and paint. The work must've been filthy and strenuous and claustrophobic and dangerous. Ventilation was effected by six massive shafts, each containing twenty-eight fans which could remove 2,500,000 cubic feet of air per minute. Herbert J. Rowse designed these shafts, made out of Portland brick and stone, as he did the tunnel entrances and toll booths. The tunnel was opened on 18th July 1934, an amazing feat of engineering. King George V's opening speech contained the words 'it is a deep pleasure to us to come here today to open for the use of men a thoroughfare so great and strange as this Mersey tunnel, now made ready by your labour'[35]. Love that 'strange'. The opening ceremony was marked by Royal Tunnel Week with various festivities 'representing all the life and interests of Liverpool as a great seaport, a great centre of industry and a place of culture'[36]. Each day of the Week was marked with street processions led by women on horseback dressed in medieval garb, representing the Spirit of Liverpool (impersonated by Miss Joy Miller, daughter of the commander of the *HMS Indefatigable*) and the seven lamps of charity, faith, remembrance, youth, progress, vision, and commerce. Following them were decorated vehicles, 'triumphal cars carrying representatives of the civic enterprises and industries of Liverpool', writes Belchem[37]; he includes a photograph of the Mersey Docks and Harbour Board float that carries the legend 'THEY THAT GO DOWN TO THE SEA IN SHIPS AND DO BUSINESS IN GREAT WATERS·THESE SEE THE WORKS OF THE LORD AND HIS WONDERS IN THE DEEP'. During the royal visit, the opening ceremony was marred by the high droning of an aeroplane circling overhead, trailing a banner for Crawford's biscuits.

The moment seems an innocent one. By 1967 the tunnel was struggling to convey eighteen million vehicles a year through it. So then came the Kingsway.

A memory; driving in a friend's van through the Queensway tunnel, over to the clubs and pubs in the city. On an excited high. The van started to chug and cough and labour. Fuel gauge pointed to a red 'E'. Aware that a breakdown recovery within the tunnel would, at that time, incur a charge of £40 whereas one without would be free, we got out of the van – very much forbidden, that – and pushed it out of the tunnel proper, to be met panting and sweating by two laughing policemen who'd watched it all on CCTV. They took my friend with them to get a can of petrol, while I sat in the van just outside the vast cathedral-like tunnel vestibule. That was the only time I've been in the tunnel outside of a vehicle, and I remember the traffic roar bouncing off the insides of the hangar, the whoosh of hot air, the cold

wind blowing through, the sense of space and exposure and my soft and breakable body rocked by the passage of fast glass and speeding steel. It was inexplicably peaceful.

And another memory; how, as a child, the movement of car headlights across the smooth tunnel walls would look very much like the rippling of water. Wherever you go in this city that element insists on being recognised.

notes

1. Except for those whose culture was buried beneath the despoil, driven into the river's bedrock with the pilings; the Kingsway tunnel effectively wrecked what was left of the Scotland Road way of life. But more on this later.
2. Apropos of the Altcar victim, graffiti in Croxteth reads 'RIP brave soldier'. Jesus Christ.
3. Edited by Cottrell, David.
4. See Cavanagh, Terry, 'Works Consulted'.
5. See *Yes We Have No*, 'Works Consulted'.
6. In Rees-Jones and Murphy, eds., *Writing Liverpool*.
7. Of which I have two: *Tilt* and *Hard Water*. See 'Works Consulted'.
8. Collected in *Ellipsis 1*. Ditto.
9. See his essay in Rees-Jones and Murphy.
10. From 'Three Villages' in *Ellipsis 1*.
11. See *The Lost Villages of Liverpool Volume Three*. See also *Domesday Book*, 'Works Consulted'.
12. See the website sthelenschat.co.uk.
13. See 'Works Consulted'.
14. See *Danziger's Britain*, ditto.
15. In his *Scouse International*.
16. In Robinson, ed.
17. Op.cit.
18. In his *Merseypride*, 'Works Consulted'. The essay's title is taken from the refrain of the song 'In My Liverpool Home': 'We speak with an accent exceedingly rare/Meet under a statue exceedingly bare/If you want a cathedral we've got one to spare/In my Liverpool home'. Opposing football fans have changed the lyrics to: 'You look in the dustbin for something to eat/You find a dead rat and you think it's a treat/ In your Liverpool slum'.
19 Quoted in Belchem, ibid.
20 There's an excerpt from his *No Trams to Lime Street* in the brilliant anthology *Both Sides of the River,* a wondrous compendium of writing often referred to as 'The Liverpool Bible'.
21 Belchem, op.cit.
22 Adam Sweeting, *Guardian* journalist, quoted in Belchem, ibid.
23. Collected in Coles, op.cit.
24. See www.runcornhistsoc.org.uk
25. See Winny, trans., *Sir Gawain and the Green Knight*.
26. See Bowker, *Pursued by Furies: A Life of Malcolm Lowry*.
27. At the time of writing, filming on *Awaydays* has recently been finished. You'll meet Kev, later.
28. From Our Old Home: A Series of English Sketches, quoted in Murphy and Rees-Jones, *Writing Liverpool*.
29. Despite continuous optimistic lobbying, Birkenhead still hasn't been granted city status.
30. Yet another bad title, but the text within it is superb. We can see, in such titles and the content underneath them, some encapsulation of the Liverpool psyche; a tendency to mawkish self-aggrandisement trowelled over some incisive, interesting, and stirring analysis. The titles of many books in the 'Works Consulted' might put you off. Don't let them.
31. See Tarpey, Paul, 'Bards, Barbs, and Biscuits', Works Consulted.
32. See Williams, Peter, 'Works Consulted'.
33. See Belchem, *800*.
34. Much of the information here is to be found in the Maritime Mercantile City book, no listed authorship. See 'Works Consulted'.
35. Quoted in Coles, *Both Sides of the River*.
36 See Belchem, op.cit.
37. Ibid.

THREADS

WATER: MERSEY/ ESTUARY/OPEN SEA AND DOCKS

Water features even in the city's name. The sea and shipping inform its life. You won't arrange to meet a friend at, say, six o'clock; the nautical term 'six bells' will be used. Sea-smells imbue the soft sandstone of the buildings and bedrock, the upholstery in pubs and taxis. Behind the traffic noise will be the cries of gulls. 'That terrible city whose main street is the ocean', wrote Malcolm Lowry[1], who surrendered to the promise of escape offered by that main street, like so many others before and after him. Jack Kerouac referred to the city's 'liquid belly'[2,] but it has liquid limbs, also, in the Mersey and the Dee rivers, and a liquid spine in the ship canal. Its pavements aren't solid. Look up, and the tall buildings seem to roll and reel around you as if with the motion of waves. The main city is built on a dingle; the pull of the sea seems gravitational, a fact felt in the diaphragm.

In August 1848, the *Ocean Monarch* sailed out into Liverpool Bay, carrying 322 steerage passengers, mostly poor Irish heading for America. A fire broke out, forcing the ship to return to dock; other ships arrived to help, but many passengers tried to escape the flames by leaping into the sea. A roll call back in dock revealed 178 missing[3]. So the sea gains its salt. Tony Wailey, in his poem 'Dingle Beach'[4], writes:

> The Liverpool river, the Irish Sea
> land of shithouses and bad poetry.
> Hurtled from our jiggered homes
> millions of us went to roam
> on ships that rode and stalked these waters...
>
> Go on home Bill find your way now
> find your way when every sinew
> strives to make the hours continue

with every fucken port you've been to.
And the sea still crashes deep within you.

He also writes, in the intro to his *Edgy Cities*, that:

> Movement continues to define [Liverpool] as much as the irregular
> tides define the river and the city's place on the Atlantic Ocean and
> the west coast of Europe. A city where the Gulf Stream meets the
> Irish Sea and melts into its own illusions like any city of the hurricane
> ports. Liverpool may be based within a temperate zone but it is not a
> temperate city.... This suits us fine because any port city is related to
> its physical landscape.... A shifting shoreline produces edgy cities and
> 'edgy' people.

Yes, and eyes are forever focussed on the waves, beyond the dark
geometry of the docks; port cities always feature strongly in the
narrative of diaspora, both as destinations and origins of exodus.
Such 'currents and flows gave port cities separate dimensions of time,
space, and movement; rhythmic qualities which like the shape of the
earth [are] circular.... The tides carry the rhythm', writes Wailey.[5] The
insights of his *Edgy Cities* into the psyche of a port people – the
almost proprioceptive evolution of their collective character – are
arresting; Wailey moves from a consideration of the unique topography of port cities, the interconnecting lanes and alleyways ensuring
the fast transit of goods, to this: 'Everything had to be quick. So the
inhabitants took on those same qualities; quick minded, witted,
making quick money, and with a pace of speech which slows notice-
ably the further inland you go'.

I like that. And I like, too,
and very much, the fact that
Mr. G.W. Lennon in 1963 had
to explain to the Royal
Meteorological Society that it
was impossible to place
Liverpool on a weather map
due to 'the unique natures of
its tidal storms and swells'; he
referred to, as Wailey quotes[6],
'the transient [and] complex
nature, the irregular and
unpredictable, the turbulence

which is impossible to stabilise because it comes and goes in the opposite direction to the normal'. Says it all.

Astutely, Wailey chose for the cover of *Edgy Cities* a photograph of one of the figures from Antony Gormley's great sculpture 'Another Place', which consists of a company of cast-iron figures, reputedly modelled on Gormley himself, standing scattered across the beach at Crosby, facing out to sea. For this, Gormley has been awarded a Fellowship from Liverpool John Moores University, and although the piece was originally intended to be a peripatetic one, he has given his permission for it to remain permanently on the Crosby sands. I go to see it with my youngest sister on Boxing Day. A large sign at the boundary of Crosby reads: 'NORTHWEST IN BLOOM/MOST IMPROVED TOWN 2005'. It's freezing. The beach is strewn with a thousand empty razor shells. People are walking off their Christmas feeding frenzies, weaving bigly in between the iron figures which stand lonely and aloof across the beach, many of them, each weathered almost black. One, inevitably, is wearing a cheap Steven Gerrard replica shirt; another sports bladderwrack dreadlocks. They have pronounced peni. They have the air of sentinels or guardians but also a quality of terrible longing, as if they're dreaming of elsewhere, of another place from whence they've either come and wish to return to or to where they yearn to initially escape. Some of them are way out in the waves, only their backs visible; the tide will cover them and they'll re-emerge, slowly, as it ebbs. The furthest ones no doubt bear barnacles and limpets. Their resilience stirs. They regard the sea, endlessly, and will be, in achingly slow increments, shaped and changed and altered by it, but never – or at least in no time-scale

graspable by the individual human mind – defeated; they'll continue to re-appear.

It's a magnificent piece of work, moving and inspiring. Unimprovably conceived, too; I can't imagine a more precise and incisive concretisation of this city, the windmills and cranes and towerblocks of which can be seen in mist across the small waves like beige crépe-paper. I ask my sister for her verdict and she replies: 'They've got nice tight little bums'.

Leaving the beach, we pass a substation covered in graffiti: LFC CHAMPIONS LEAGE (sic) WINNERS 2005, a woodpecker-thing apparently called SQUIGGLES, and U COULD PUT THE CHEESE IN UR BUM BUM. What cheese? And why would anyone want to put it there? Who knows what this means. If anything.

'Another Place' is a haunting, emotive sculpture. Crosby, and the adjoining Waterloo, were once somewhat wealthy places; they're certainly not rundown now – there's a holistic health shop, the huge Merchant Taylors' private school, an Oxfam which has numerous designer outfits on its racks (charity shops are a reliable index to an area's prosperity) – but I remember a recent shooting in Jalon's restaurant and, in the *Echo* the following day, I read about a young man beaten up so badly in Crosby that his lower jaw became detached from his skull. 'Most improved town'? Hmm.

All this rage. Ebb and flow. Jetsam.

A DIVIDED CITY: FOOTBALL

St. Domingo, or Dominic, is a Catholic saint, founder of the Dominicans or Black Friars, patron of astronomers[7]. He gives his name to the Latin American Republic of Dominica and to an area of north east Liverpool between Kirkdale, Anfield, Everton and the Sefton docks; St. Domingo Road, Vale, Grove etc. The first football team in the city was also named after him, in 1878, set up jointly by the Reverend Chambers and John Houlding, Tory MP and city mayor, a 'strictly amateur affair', according to one Liverpool FC website[8], 'created amid the belief that young lads could better be kept on the path of religious well-being through a healthy passion for competitive team games'. Their first home games were played in Stanley Park, and after a year or so they re-named themselves Everton Football Club, after the district location of their founding church (also

called St. Domingo's, and now long demolished). They met at the
Queen's Head Hotel, which served Houlding's products (he was a
brewer), and set up a stadium on a field between Anfield Road and
Walton Breck Road. Houlding has a short street named after him in
the area, on a corner of which stands the Sandon pub, which he once
owned, and whose bowls pavilion soon became the changing-room
and meeting place of the new team. Houlding had a friend, another
brewer called Orrell, who owned some land which he rented out to
the team, around which a dispute developed, as it did over the fact
that only Houlding's ales were to be sold at the ground; so venality,
self-interest, and heavy drinking marked Merseyside football from the
outset. Rent on Anfield was increased further in 1890, to £250 p.a.,
up from £100 in 1885; Houlding offered to sell the land to the local
club, who refused. Houlding affected outrage; this disrespect of the
team's founder and original investor, harrumph, shoddy treatment,
splutter, etc. The official split between himself and the team took
place on 12th March 1892, and Liverpool Football Club was formed
three days later, at Houlding's house on Anfield Road, with input
from William Barclay, first secretary at Everton. First, Houlding
attempted, unsuccessfully, to legally steal the Everton FC name, then
a group of Everton fans bought land, so he was left with an empty
stadium, which meant he was losing money, so he shortly had a team
playing there, wearing red and with the Liverbird emblem as a crest.
This team had to be built from scratch, as most staff had left for
Goodison, as Everton's new ground was now known; luckily, John
McKenna stayed loyal to Houlding, a dynamic and committed
Irishman, who became director at Anfield for thirty years, and who,
with a loan of £500 from Houlding (which was never repaid),
recruited an entire team from Scotland; hence LFC's first nickname,
'the Macs'. Their first game, against Rotherham, was won 7-1, with
McVean scoring the first ever goal for Liverpool. Only a handful of
people turned up, however; more than 10,000 went to Goodison.

And so Everton became 'the People's Club'; its genesis in rebellion.
And Liverpool became the representative team of the Celtic Fringe;
founded by an Irishman, comprised of Scotsmen, which later, and
short-lived, appellations as 'the Protestant's Club' did little to dispel.
Puzzlingly, Houlding has become a largely forgotten figure in the
city, a bronze plaque outside the Director's Lounge at Anfield, the
name of a short thoroughfare, and an oil portrait within the club
museum his only mementoes (apart from the club itself, of course);
maybe such a proudly left-leaning city prefers relative oblivion for its

unreconstructed capitalists (contrast this with how it once honoured its slave-traders). An Everton FC website[9] states that 'a fierce rivalry has existed between EFC and LFC, albeit one that is generally perceived as being more respectful than many other "derbies" in English football', which raised my eyebrows so high and suddenly that I tore the skin on my face. It might've been true in the 1980s, when fortuitous FA Cup draws saw both sets of fans mingling on public transport and two-tone seas of mixed red and blue in the stadia, but recently... well, I was in the city for a derby in 2007 at Goodison which Liverpool won, contentiously, 2-1. The referee seemed so biased that I could sympathise with Everton fury at the unfairness, but they could only blame their defender (an ex-Manchester United player, to boot) for blatantly and shamelessly punching a goal-bound shot off the line and giving away a penalty in the last minute; nobody else was to blame. And I saw the abuse spray-painted on the memorial to the Hillsborough dead, saw the Everton fans, children included, pressing their spread fingers to their faces (a reference to the 96 people crushed to death against a chainlink fence at Hillsborough), heard the vile and spat chanting. In a Red pub in the city centre that evening, I joined in with the songs, until they turned to bellows of hate. Everton fans appeared outside and began to stone the pub, which emptied in seconds of almost all men, mass brawling outside, inside the barman screaming 'gerraway from the winduz! AWAY from the winduz!', riot vans, ambulances, helicopters, chaos, pools of blood on the pavements, crying women, 'they've stabbed him!'. The rivalry never used to be like that. It's black, now, and bitter, intra-fraternal, friend against friend. Civil war. Senseless.

More on the two clubs later, and separately. They need to be kept apart.

A DIVIDED CITY: RELIGION

I was making my way back to the flat I was staying in after a party. Mid-morning, this was. I was tired and could hear the hangover hurtling towards me like a runaway juggernaut. I needed sleep and food and a bath, in no particular order. Along Hope Street I was stopped by an ageing lady, as well-dressed as she could be, in obvious distress. She'd missed Mass, she told me, in a brogue thick as mud. She'd got to the church and it was empty but she was in plenty of time so why was it empty? Did I know why that was? She was close to tears. I reminded her that it was Daylight Saving Time; the clocks had gone forward at 2 a.m. Relief began to creep across her face.

"Ah, so... then I didn't really miss it, did I? I tried to get to it, didn't I?"

"You did, love, yes."

"He'll not be seeing it as a sin, then, will He?"

I told her that I doubted it very much and she gave me a big and sudden smile.

"Ah, well, then. Pubs'll be opening now. Might as well go for a drop."

She doddered off in the direction of Peter Kavanagh's pub and I went bath and bedwards.

★

It suits some to see the city as creedless, even God-forsaken, or as hypocritical in its fawning over the trappings of institutionalised religion and its keen pursuit of theft and inebriation and fornication. Let them wallow in their myths, and see the city as, rather, a place in which mild piety has no anchor; as a place which recognises that atheistic despair has more in common with the passion of the divine than with self-satisfied sanctimoniousness. The despairing, too, have fallen to their knees in anguished awe at a terrible and immense power. See the two cathedrals and the hundreds of churches of varying nationalities and denominations and the streets and squares and parks named after saints and then see much of the traffic that occurs amongst them in its steady hysteria as representative of Swedenborgian yearning, prayers articulated in deed not word and the need for recognition from a God that is profoundly loved yet always unacknowledged. Just worship of a different kind.

Well, maybe. At the time of writing, Liverpool staged a Nativity play a few days ago, broadcast live on BBC3, with a cast of 300, music by the Royal Philharmonic, and a technical crew of 150. It took place in various venues throughout the city, in pubs, bus-shelters, even on the Mersey ferry. Mary cleans tables in a cafe in Seaforth; Joseph is an asylum seeker sent to Liverpool to renew his visa. Herod is a woman and the shepherds are rough sleepers, sheepless. The writer, Mark Davies Markham, was quoted as saying: 'I wanted [the story] still to be familiar but to help people look at it in a different way. If they see it in terms of hope for humanity, that would be good!'[10]. So the angel Gabriel addresses Mary through a TV screen and informs her of the conception. Joseph is enraged by the news and sings 'There She Goes' by The La's, a song about heroin addiction, but let's let that slide. Joseph and Mary then head across the river to the passport office in Birkenhead, singing 'Comedy' by Shack (a beautiful song which describes the human story as a 'long-lost comedy' and 'foregone tragedy'). Jesus is born in the Roscoe Arms. Jennifer Ellison and Cathy Tyson and Nerys Hughes and others appear in various guises. It was, by all accounts, very successful.

But, of course, this being Liverpool, there are voices of dissent, one of which, here, belonged to Andy Capper, who saw Liverpool's terrible bad fortune (in, for instance, being swamped with subversion-quelling heroin by Margaret Thatcher and in being associated with people like Stan Boardman and Carla Lane) as worsening with the performed Nativity[11], which has been 'put together by the same people who made last year's Manchester Passion fiasco, an event similar... in that it was embarrassing and reflected nothing of the culture of the city itself, rather the crazed dream of some pantomime dame who works in the BBC Classical department'. He's got a point, there. And here, too: 'Sorry, Liverpool, but... I'm down on this whole idea. To follow something up that Mancs did first is pretty bad, but to have millions of choreographed stage school kids following *Brookside* characters down to the Albert Dock holding candles and singing Zutons songs is even worse'.

There were many who felt that way, I'm sure. The Nativity was performed anyway, to both applause and disgruntled rumblings. It wouldn't be Liverpool, if all voices were in accordance. Religion, and the diverse expressions of same, divide the city as much as football does, or musical allegiances. Let's not even get started on the Catholic/Protestant thing. Yet.

GHOSTS/GUILT/SLAVERY

Go back. Go back to June 5th, 1919, when Charles Wootton, a twenty-four year old Trinidadian, was chased and drowned in the Queen's Dock by a white crowd who had ripped him from the hands of protecting policemen and hurled him in the water. Just one horrific event in the race riots of the years immediately following World War One, which raged through Glasgow and Hull and Cardiff and Barry too but which, in Liverpool, were 'particularly intense, reflecting tensions that extended far beyond the local waterfront' and which turned London Road into 'the Ypres of Liverpool'[12]. The cause of the trouble was, according to the Head Constable then quoted in the press, 'the arrogant and overbearing conduct of the negro population': the propensity of 'blacks' to 'swank about in smart clothes'; and the provocative stance of the 'white women who live or cohabit with the black man boasting to the other women of the superior qualities of the negroes as compared with those of white men'[13]. Apparently, Scandinavian seamen, seeking to obscure their foreign-ness, attacked a West Indian man, which produced violent reprisals; soon, those from the 'volcanic' area of Scotland Road – hooligans, rough-looking women, the dockland mob[14] – joined in and the city centre was ransacked and looted. Xenophobia, fear, quick and eager leaps to violence were everywhere in 1919. All Europe was a smoking ruin.

Now go back further, to the beginning of the nineteenth century, when Liverpool had control of 90 per cent of Britain's share of the trade in slaves. Ninety percent. In one city. The slave-trade began in Liverpool in September of 1700, when the *Liverpool Merchant* carried 220 slaves from Africa to Barbados, where they were sold for £4,239[15], and was followed in October of that year by the *Blessing* (horrible name, in this context), which made a second voyage in 1701, from which date the city began to boom and burgeon, buildings appearing mortared in blood and vast warehouses sheltering tea and cotton and tobacco and the wails of those who had been bartered for such goods. Many men grew bloated as others, of darker skins, began to vanish from view, and the city honoured such vampires with streetname and statuary; the famous Penny Lane, indeed, is named after James Penny, slave-trader who made eleven voyages to Africa[16] (there is a movement to re-name Penny Lane, along with other streets of similar nomenclature which, I feel, would be a mistake; history is the past we have, not what we would like it to be. If certain of its echoes and signposts prompt shame, then so be it; shame is what some of us should feel. Besides, what better way to ascertain that the city ignores its shameful past than by eradicating the reverberations?). They're all around; Atherton Street, Bamber Street, Dorans Lane, Hardman Street, Rodney Street, Tarleton Street (Cameron and Crooke list scores); slavers all. There's also Roscoe Street, of course, named after the powerful abolitionist William Roscoe, who wrote in his long poem *Mount Pleasant* 'yet whence these horrors? This inhuman rage,/That brands with blackest infamy the age?'[17]. And indeed Liverpool, to an extent, was instrumental in ending the slave-trade, as well as galvanising its growth in Britain; but blood and tears dry and crumble, and a city built on such must, at some point, and to some degree, collapse. Karmic consequence and all that.

Now jump forwards, to 30th November 1988, when the Gifford Inquiry into race relations in Liverpool issued a statement expressing 'shock at the prevalence... of racial attitudes, abuse and violence' of a 'uniquely horrific nature'[18]. Jump again to the turn of the century when the city welcomed thousands of Somalian refugees fleeing the civil war in their country. And again to July 2005 when the eighteen year old Anthony Walker was murdered in Huyton in a racially-motivated attack; the estranged brother of the thuggish footballer Joey Barton, with an accomplice, left an ice-pick buried in Anthony's head. Sick and stupid and utterly senseless.

Such historical moments as slavery never really end; there is no closure. They spread tentacles through distant days, their poison has a long life. We'll return to it, as the city itself does and must, again and yet again. I visited the Slavery Museum in the Albert Dock recently, during Black History Month[19], where you're greeted by words from the former slave William Prescott: 'They will remember that we were sold, but not that we were strong. They will remember that we were bought, but not that we were brave'. There is a chalkboard covered in messages. Children of all skintones run whooping in and out of the Anthony Walker Exhibition Centre; some kind of schools event going on in there. I discover that the Bluecoat Chambers were built as a school by Bryan Blundell, who traded in enslaved Africans and tobacco. Posh kids go to the Bluecoat. They always did. Liverpool's black area used to be focussed on the south docks, but World War Two's bombing moved it to Granby/Toxteth, during which time 'black' became a political term referring not just to Afro-Caribbean people but also Asians, Chinese, and Arabs. Liverpool in general supported the South during the American Civil War; ships were secretly built on the Mersey for the Confederacy. The *Alabama* was constructed as a raider at Lairds in Birkenhead. The *Shenandoah*, the last ship to surrender in the conflict, hauled down its flag on the Mersey on November 6th 1865. I guess the cotton-masters just couldn't relinquish their need and greed.

This, apparently, is the first museum in the world to deal solely with transatlantic slavery. It's absorbing, fascinating, and confers an intense emotional kick; at the end, as you're about to leave, you stand and watch a recording of Martin Luther King delivering his 'I have a dream' speech, projected onto a wall. As you watch, you gradually become aware of a presence looming behind you. You turn, and there, in a glass case, is a full KKK Grand Wizard outfit, the pointed hood, the soulless eyeslits, the yawning sleeves. Regarding it, you see King reflected in the glass of the case. If this part of the museum's layout is deliberate, then its inspired; if it's not, then there was some kind of innate and subconscious genius for space-management at work. Either way, it leaves you shaken.

REGENERATION/CITY OF CULTURE?

On the 11th January 2008, Liverpool kicked off its year-long European City of Culture awards with a display of dance and music and acrobatics on the cobbled apron outside the monolithic St. George's Hall, and on the roof of that huge building. Faces in the audience smirked with the pleasure of confirmed prejudice as the letters in the lit-up 'LIVERPOOL' winked out, leaving only the 'POO'. Hard-hatted workers ascended the scaffold to remedy the lighting; immediately after doing so they fell off. Gasps. Then they emerged from the hidden safety net, removed their hard hats, and took a bow. Some laughter and applause. The Wombats played a set, as did Pete Wylie, flanked by amazingly graceful aerialists. Then Ringo Starr appeared and what could any right-thinking person with a strong sense of dignity do but cringe hard enough to dislocate their spines at his words: 'Destiny was calling/I just couldn't stick around/Liverpool I left you/But I never let you down'. It hurts me even to write those words, and I sincerely apologise for exposing you to their evil effects. Many of the criticisms levelled at the city's

character by those who begrudge the Culture award – mawkish sentimentality, contrived salt-of-the-earthness etc. – were encapsulated in Starkey's shameless bleatings. I know that you can't really have such a celebration *without* the surviving ex-members of The Beatles, but Jeez.... The city's collective shudder of embarrassment was measurable on the Richter Scale. Or maybe that was just me.

Still, Liverpool – along with Stavanger in Norway – remains the European City of Culture for 2008. The award, of course, was not without its protests, usually of a tiresomely predictable sort; culture? In Liverpool? You sure? And, again of course, the award remains meaningless in many ways due to the diffuse refusal to engage with the notion of what culture actually is for some people, particularly as  applied to narratives on the societal margins, and instead present and promote one committee's notion of cultural endeavour, often referred to as 'high culture', and exemplified by the orchestra and the ballet and the theatre. So are more opportunities missed, but only by some; others, of course, have used the chance to debate and air grievance with sharp aplomb. The film-maker Alex Cox, for instance[20], took the opportunity to train his guns on the Council and asked:

> In a city blessed with great museums and galleries and a biennial art show, how much space has ever been dedicated to the work of local artists? How many local writers, painters, actors, composers and film-makers have seen their own offerings shunned by the city's cultural establishment in favour of art imported from Iceland or a lecture by Yoko Ono?

It's a valid question; Liverpool City Council have ever seemed ashamed of their perceived provincialism and are thus overly-concerned with stressing the cosmopolitanism of the city by bringing in work from abroad, rather than promoting the million stories and experiences within[21]. This can be seen in the differing programmes of events scheduled for 2008, the more exciting and intriguing of which have been arranged not by the official C of C people but by those involved in the Writing on the Wall festival and other clandestine organisations (more on whom later). Little wonder, then, that many Liverpudlians themselves are casting a cynical eye on the award which they're referring to as the 'Culture of Capital', the irony being, to quote Cox again, that 'when the advisory committee for the

European Capital of Culture gave its reasons for recommending Liverpool, it emphasised that it had been influenced by the culture of the city's people.... It picked Liverpool... on the basis of the scousers themselves', rather than the proposed new buildings and tram systems, which now look like never materialising anyway. But shopping, well, that's another matter; the Liverpool 1 project is vast and expensive, yet the Welsh streets will probably be demolished, and Arthur Black[22] points out that 'by the time Liverpool [celebrates] its much-vaunted Capital of Culture status, it will have lost swathes of its Victorian infrastructure... By 2008 the only traditional pubs surviving in the [city] could well be the Philharmonic on Hope Street and the Vines on Lime Street. These undisputed architectural gems will undoubtedly feature in Council publications as outstanding examples of Liverpool's rich pub heritage', yet it's the same council who are demolishing many others of their kind.

And, indeed, infighting, rancour, and venality have marked and marred the build-up to 2008, and a measure of redemption only really came with the appointing to the panel of Phil Redmond in 2007. An example; it's customary, and polite, to invite representatives from the previous year's City of Culture to the opening of the new one, yet, as far as I'm aware, no-one from Sibiu was ever invited to Liverpool (by contrast, I was taken to Sibiu in 2007, treated like a king, and enjoyed myself immensely). Inter-council squabbles and careering costs threatened to call down chaos from the outset, when a general 'inability to separate the cultural programme from local politics'[23] led to a feud between then-council leader Mike Storey and chief executive Sir David Henshaw, and the resignations of both men. Plus, the appointment to Festival Director of Australian cabaret singer Robyn Archer was greeted with bafflement; can no-one in Liverpool do the job? In Britain, even? Archer worked in the city for four months, and then left with a £125,000 pay-off. For not being very good at the job she was enlisted to do. Then the Matthew Street festival was cancelled. Then Storey and Warren Bradley (the current chief) came under investigation by the Standards Board for England, accused of holding secret meetings at which they conspired to remove the then-acting LCC chief executive[24]. Early in 2008, the city council 'identified a budget gap of about £20m for the next year: a result of hosting the capital of culture'[25], which may well have to be raised through borrowing, selling off land, or asset re-financing (some council tax increases have been capped at 5 per cent, one of the highest levels in the UK, for one of the poorest cities). Those payoffs have to be met somehow. And so it goes on.

And yet, a big point is being missed if the focus remains on puerile political machinations, rather than that part of the city which purportedly garnered the award in the first place – its people. There's a felt air of excited anticipation, even of re-invention. Cranes are everywhere, and for once they're not swinging wrecking-balls (well, not all the time, at least). The dockside Three Graces and the Walker Art Gallery and World Museum have been around for a long time but the modern skyscrapers now visible from their grand steps and entrances now re-situate them in a momentous history, in an upward spring, in a step away from generalised decline and gone-grandeur. The bars and bistros and boutiques buzz[26]. The Culture Company's 'noisy troubles are an essential part of Liverpool life'[27], are certainly demoralising and disillusioning, in part, but the black moods of the 80s and early 90s have largely faded away. The maverick spirit has taken a different turn; the empty warehouse spaces are being turned by art collectives, like the Red Wine, Curve and Wolstenholme Projects, into studios and galleries. The counterculture that has nourished and energised the city for decades – yes, even through Thatcher's reign – remains resiliently strong, which isn't due to the C of C award, but can certainly benefit from it. In 1997, Nick Danziger visited the city, rocked by drugs and related crime as it was then, and by the time he left had 'come to understand part of the scouse mentality.... No amount of decay can extinguish their absolute energy and irrepressible spirit.... [They] won't put up with emotional camouflage'[28]; and that particular eye for the scam, that 'displaced creativity' that may or may not be a legacy of piracy, will now be able to apply itself in ways that will draw praise, not a prison sentence, when discovered. This is no panacea, of course, but 'where Liverpool will triumph, in 2008 and beyond, is by virtue of what is already here, was always here; heart, soul, wit, wisdom, music, fun, footy', as Kevin Sampson rightly says[29].

I'm still a wee bit cynical about the whole thing, to be honest, and we'll look at some dissenting voices throughout, but having renewed my relationship with the city on something approaching a more-than-muscle-deep level, I'm getting pissed off with those whose tendency is to sneer; it's a pinched opinion, an ungenerous one, all pursed and puckered and smug, proffered by the kind of people whose neighbour's fence is encroaching half an inch into their garden and they're losing sleep over it. What about Stockholm, they say, Barcelona, Rome, Prague; well, yes, but the C of C award only lasts a year – some other city will bear the monicker in 2009. Liverpool's not taking it away from anyone. And would they sooner the city sink deeper? Would they wish further crime, poverty, ill-health? To deny whatever benefits and comforts the award might bring (and there will be some), would that make them happy?

Well, the positive is that such people, I suppose, won't be visiting Liverpool, in this or any other year. Culture, indeed.

Anyway. Here's the city.

notes

1. In *Hear Us O Lord from Heaven Thy Dwelling Place*.
2. See Mulhearn, *Mersey Minis Four: Loving*.
3. See Bagshaw, *Bloody Britain*.
4. See *The Irish Sea*.
5. In *Edgy Cities*.
6. Ibid.
7. See Farmer, *A Dictionary of Saints*, and:
    http://encyclopedia.thefreedictionary.com/Saint+Dominic.
8. Liverpoolfc.tv/lfc_story
9. Liverpoolcityportal.co.uk/sports/everton_fc.html
10. See Ward, 'Miracle on Merseyside', 'Works Consulted'.
11. See 'Music' column for the *Guardian* guide of 15/12/07.
12. See Belchem, 800.
13. Ibid.
14. These terms basically pseudonymous for the North End Liverpool Irish.
15. See Cameron and Crooke, *Liverpool: Capital of the Slave Trade*.
16. See Thomas, *The Slave Trade*. For more on the origin of Liverpool streetnames, see Westgaph, Laurence, *Read the Signs*; or log on to english-heritage.org.uk and follow the links. It's good work, despite those who decry it as focussing on the negatives; Andrew Pearce, editor and chair of Liverpool Heritage Forum, asked in the *Echo*: 'What other city focuses mainly on the downside of its history?', prompting a spirited and angry reply from Westgaph. See 'Why we can't ignore our city's shameful past', *Liverpool Echo* May 27 2008.
17. Quoted in Coles, *Both Sides*.... Coles also quotes John Wesley: 'Many large ships are now laid up in the [Liverpool] docks, which had been employed for many years in buying or stealing poor Africans, and selling them in America for slaves. The men-butchers have now nothing to do at this laughable occupation.... So the men of Africa, as well as Europe, may enjoy their native liberty'. This was written in 1777. There was also John Newton, slaver, who had a spiritual awakening during which he wrote 'Amazing Grace' and thereafter became an active abolitionist.
18. Belchem, op.cit.
19. See liverpoolblackhistory.com.
20. See 'Scousers are the Culture', 'Works Consulted'.
21. And, to those of you who'd sooner go and see Sigur Ros than Stan Boardman, I'd have to agree. But the argument goes beyond that.
22. In his 'The Save Our City Campaign', published in *Mercy*. See 'Works Consulted'.
23. See Topping, 'Party Cross the Mersey', 'Works Consulted'.
24. For more on such dumb skullduggery, see liverpool.subculture.blogspot.com.
25. Topping, op.cit

26. For an excellent guide to such things, see the Angie Sammons-edited website LiverpoolConfidential.com.
27. See Ward, 'Liverpool moves out of the shadows with a little help from its friends', 'Works Consulted'.
28. See his *Danziger's Britain: A Journey to the Edge*.
29. From a personal email.

CITY
NORTH

AINTREE

You'll know Aintree by its races, no doubt; it's the home of the Grand National, due, in part, to the area's flatness and open-ness (indeed, its name comes from the Anglo-Saxon 'an treow', meaning 'one tree'); horse-racing here entertained Elizabeth I[1], and the very first Grand National, then known as the Liverpool Grand Steeple Chase, was held here on February 26th, 1839. The grandstand's foundation stone was laid by Lord Molyneux (from the family which, for generations, had a finger or two in many a scouse pie). The first race run on the course – the quarter-mile Croxteth Stakes – was won by Mufti, owned by a Mr. Francis.

And, for a time, people rode steeds of a different sort. The flatness of the area allowed for its use as a basic kind of aerodrome and in the early 1900s Sir William 'Pickles' Hartley, the jam-man (who was to open a huge preserves factory at Aintree), offered a £1,000 prize for the first person to fly from Liverpool to Manchester. Colonel Samuel Cody, in his bi-plane, got as far as Eccleston Park, ten miles from the city, and was forced to return by thick fog, but on 7th July 1911 the prize was claimed by Henry Melly and his wife, Ellen, probably the first woman to take to the air in Britain (if Henry was any relation to the late jazz troubadour, raconteur, and flamboyant suit-wearer George Melly, who was born by Sefton Park, I don't know). In a logical progression, the National Aircraft Factory was built here, abutting the race-course, and which, of course and pardon the pun, boomed during World War One. In 1924, the first Belfast-Liverpool airmail service took off from here, making the return journey, including a landing on Southport sands to pick up newspapers, in two hours. Four passengers paid the £3 fare.

In 1925, the Aircraft Factory was taken over by the British Enka Artificial Silk Company, later known as Courtauld's[2], although the district remained overshadowed by Hartley's jam factory, in Long Lane. Hartley – like Leverhulme over the river in Port Sunlight – was one of those socially pioneering capitalists who introduced 'profit-sharing, pensions, health service and recreational facilities for his employees, not to mention giving huge sums of money to charity'[3]. He sold out to Schweppes in 1959 in a £2m deal. In 1977, when the site was being dismantled, a desperate bid was made by conservationists to save its four-face tower clock from being sent to America. The bid was successful; the clock was destroyed. If I can't have it, no-one else can. How ridiculous.

And then there was the mortuary, by all accounts a filthy charnel-house of a place, a foul midden: 'When [it] is washed out', said Dr. Glover, police surgeon, in 1932, 'some of the blood and filth goes on to the grass. It is an insult to the human body – one of God's master-pieces – to put it in such a place'[4]. Coroner Brighouse joined in: 'If my good wife had been found dead in this district and she had been placed in this dirty, disreputable outhouse... with a dirty sheet over her, and I had come to see her, I would have walked out and I would have cursed everyone. This place must be closed'[5]. Which, shortly, it was. Bodies were then taken to Ormskirk.

Aintree is now a dull suburb (and how many suburbs can escape that epithet?), quintessentially modern British, with regimented housing and chainstores and retail parks. The race-course dominates everything. The Blue Anchor pub still stands (as far as I know), from the back of which the race-course can be seen, and whose bowling green nudges the Leeds and Liverpool canal. It's all exhaust and quick steel and sunlight bouncing back and dazzling from the windscreens of the incessant traffic entering or exiting the city on the A59. If you're not here for the races, then *why* are you here? Not much to detain you. In nearby Melling, however, once scene of many a highwayman hanging, is the church of St. Thomas, built on a mound used, for millenia, as a tumulus. In 1319, the church's cemetery was said to have been 'polluted with blood'[6], after some terrible crime, its details long-forgotten, so attempts were made to move the bodies, during which it was discovered that the church had never been consecrated. Cue tales of hauntings and restless souls and en-purgatory'd disembodied shriekers. Naturally.

LITHERLAND/SEAFORTH

The Molyneux family – yes, them again – once owned Litherland, as it was given to them by King John in the early 1200s in exchange for their hunting park in what is now known as Toxteth, one of the most infamous ingredients, in David Lewis's wonderful phrase, in Liverpool's 'awkward mythology'[7]. It's a Viking name, meaning 'sloping land', as so much of Liverpool's north-western districts are, being built on a long dingle, land that rushes to meet the sea. Neighbouring Seaforth was once host to a huge hall in which Dickens and Sheridan stayed, and to a colossal hotel which failed in that venture due to its distance from the docks and so became a convent for a while until the Dock Board bought it out, whence it remained empty until 1912 when it was taken over by the Lancashire Asylums Board and, in 1913, set on fire by the Suffragettes. After repairs it was used as a home for 'mentally-retarded chuldren', to quote Derek Whale[8], then as a naval hospital, then as north-west headquarters of the Inland Revenue. It was demolished in 1967.

Barracks were here, too, scene of riots in 1914, when the families of the soldiers stationed inside tried to force their way in to say their – probably final – goodbyes to their sons or husbands or fathers or brothers. Lord Baden-Powell had been stationed here too, in the 1880s. This was where his scouting days really began, he declared[9], and where he trained with machine-guns in the nearby dunes, exhibiting, apparently, a great enthusiasm for the weapon, which resulted in his posting to Africa, and the defence of Mafeking. Dib dib dib.

A dog-track was here. Closed in 1966. The overhead railway had its terminus here, the first elevated electric railway in the world, knocked down in '56. But the Darwin Cottage still stands in Litherland, on Sefton Road, home of a farming family not quite powerful enough to rival the Molyneuxs. Still standing too is Sefton Church, bearing a stone in its outer wall dated 1111. Litherland Town Hall, where the Beatles gave some of their earliest performances, commanding fees of £8 a show between them. And so on. History accrues, in Litherland as elsewhere. But you wouldn't know you were in Litherland and not Aintree or Bootle if there wasn't a roadsign telling you so.

BOOTLE

Bootle. Boot, *ill*. Boot, *I'll*. An ugly name. It comes, simply, from the Anglo-Saxon 'Botelai', meaning a 'building or settlement of some importance'[10], and is mentioned in Domesday, but you'll be familiar with it, probably, as the site of the Strand shopping centre, from where, on February 12th, 1993, at 42 minutes and 32 seconds (as the data on that notorious and awful CCTV image has it), the ten-year-olds Robert Thompson and Jon Venables abducted the two-year-old James Bulger, walked him to a nearby railway embankment, and slowly murdered him, leaving his body to be run over by a train. It's a heartbreaking story, profoundly disturbing and upsetting, and truly, deeply alarming in its ramifications. I won't discuss it here, as any necessary abbreviation of the matter would be a trivialisation, and it requires an ever-expanding library of material to even begin to approach some sort of, if not understanding, then meagre accommodation. Instead, I'll steer you in the direction of work which will not only offer you more information about the horrific events but also assist you in coping with that knowledge (be warned, though; these writings will steal your well-being). They are Blake Morrison's *As If*; David James Smith's *The Sleep of Reason*; and Gitta Sereny's *The Case of Mary Bell*, the 1995 edition[11]. Not dry, scholarly tracts, these; they're emotive, angry, sad, impassioned. Some threads that have led us to the pit we're in. Recently, Venables and Thompson were released from prison, under assumed and secret identities, of course, which event prompted a new round of foam-lipped rage and calls for the re-instatement of capital punishment from the tabloids (as if killing the kids that killed the kid would solve anything at all. But that's the country and age we live in), and more sober, and productive, reflections from the broadsheets[12]. Such material will shatter and shred you, but sadness is the price we pay for wisdom. I won't say anything more on the issue, except this; that the two boys – and remember that they were children – who were so attenuated and brutalised to the state that they were able to murder another child have been deemed rehabilitated enough to be released from prison is a cause for commendation, not condemnation or disgust. The story begins, and is immersed in, darkness; maybe we ought to welcome some measure of light. That's all.

And Bootle is decline in miniature, in many ways, or it was; social moribundity in microcosm. It's one of the links in the chain of docks that surround the city on three sides, and Collingswood Dock, which leads us into the district, is a standing testament to the area's gone wealth; the walls that guard it display mason-work of exquisite finery, containing a powerful sense of highly skilled artisanry, each stone chipped and honed and bevelled to fit its neighbours, stretching for miles. My dad, who's been a bricklayer for 45 years, is awestruck by these walls, as am I; the labour, the craftsmanship, is astonishing. Nearby Canada Dock, still in operation, contains an Alps of scrap-iron bound for China; lifting machinery, hidden behind the high walls, screams. The old Dock Road itself still sports a few dingy cafes and bars, and is still busy, in a sense, but it's cold and empty compared to what it was, even in my own lifetime; two decades or so ago it was a place that, let's say, had an extremely liberal interpretation of the licensing laws, and no end of clientele with a shindig in their souls. It was the place to go when everywhere else had closed. It was a sea-fogged thoroughfare of music and drizzle-veiled light. Further back, Brunel's steamship the *Great Britain* sailed out of these docks, and William Ewart Gladstone had a residence here; the dock's prosperity built Bootle's Town Hall, art gallery, law courts. Inevitably, it was targeted by the Luftwaffe, and 'Bootle suffered the heaviest and most destructive bombing of anywhere in Britain', according to Lewis[13] (although I imagine Coventry might argue with this claim), who quotes an Andrew Richardson: 'the 1939 population figure of 80,000 was reduced by 1941 to a daytime figure of 30,000, with only 10,000 remaining in the area at night'. Only forty houses out of 17,000 escaped some form of damage, and in sixty eight raids, 3,966 people were killed. Victorian Bootle was largely obliterated, and re-building was, as usual, ugly, although the present juxtaposition of dark and baroque churches at the feet of high-rises carries a quirky visual appeal. A windfarm at the docks now generates electricity for the district, and the docks themselves still process much freight, although machinisation has, of course, reduced the workforce.

In the Welsh history of Liverpool, Bootle is significant. Derek Whale[14] tells the story of Klondyke Jones, a builder from Llanerchymedd, responsible for Gower Street, Holywell Street, Denbigh Street, Bala Street, and Anglesey Street, some of which still stand. He built his own estate, named after himself, along Hawthorne Road, for which he made his own bricks and generated his own electricity. By all accounts a personable fellow, Klondyke served Bootle Town Council for forty years as a Liberal, but his fierce teeto-tallism meant that he refused to let any land for taverns, and even today, if you're looking for a drink along Hawthorne Road, you'll stay thirsty (and sober). He became Mayor of Bootle in 1886, the first Welsh-speaker to do so (indeed, he insisted on delivering some of his public speeches in his first language). He died in 1918. He's emblem-atic of how 'the pattern of Welsh settlement [on Merseyside] tended to follow the path of residential development', to quote Belchem[15], which stands to reason given that the growing city, geographically contiguous with north Wales, attracted Welsh builders. An Eisteddfod was held in Bootle, in the early 1900s – a smaller, localised event complementing the larger one – for 'children of Welsh descent'.

WALTON

Walton is full of pubs. The Prince of Wales was once called The Sodhouse due to the landlord's practice of a), stacking grass sods around his beer-barrels to keep them cool, and b), of responding to complaints about his notoriously bad beer with the words 'if you don't like it, sod off'. The prison here has housed many a ne'er-do-well, roustabout, and jackanapes, including the infamous Billy Grimwood and Charlie Seiga in the Sixties, powerful gangsters who, reputedly, opened up a cocktail bar in a basement cell, 'like a little nightclub'[16]. The prison's address is officially 4, Hornby Road, so widely used on bureaucratic documents as to become something of a euphemism for the place; the address would, instead of 'Walton prison', be written as place of birth on the certificates of any child born in the institution. It's like any other prison anywhere else in the country – big and beige and brutalist and bulwarked. What surprises me, however, are the pretty tree-lined avenues that surround it, ablaze with autumn when I pass down them.

The place's full name is Walton-on-the-Hill. The 'wal' part comes probably from the Anglo-Saxon word 'walas', or 'foreigners', from which, of course, the word 'Wales' is derived. St. Mary's Parish Church appears in Domesday and was originally made out of timber, being replaced by stone in 1326, although Walton itself, as a settlement, predates Domesday by several centuries. It's old. The churchyard contains the grave of actor John Palmer who died on stage in 1798 with the words 'oh God! There is another and better world'[17], and in 1810 the church spire collapsed onto a school party of little girls, crushing twenty five of them to death. Mysterious ways? You're not kidding. The fine Welsh-language poet Goronwy Owen was curate here, and the Welsh building dynasty sired by Owen Elias and taken up by his son William were so keen to be remembered that they made an acronym of the streetnames built by them off County Road: Oxton, Winslow, Eton, Neston, etc. Check it out on an A-Z. Robert Tressell, or Noonan, author of *The Ragged-Trousered Philanthropists*, is buried at Walton Park cemetery, as is John William Carling, pavement artist at five years old and, later, illustrator of Poe's *The Raven*. Died in Brownlow Hill workhouse, aged twenty-nine. Pauper's grave, although it's now topped with a memorial stone. Brendan Behan was incarcerated in Walton prison; have a look at his *Borstal Boy*, the early chapters. Walton borders Anfield, but it's predominantly an Everton supporting area, being the heart of the north end of the city; a red shirt here is as rare as a bear in Sefton Park.

And that's Walton; interesting place, even if the *Liverpool Echo's* 'Celebrate Walton' feature of October 25th 2007 makes it seem like the most boring place on the planet: 'There's a choice of solicitors in Walton too,' it reads, 'so if you need advice on moving home, making a will or any other legal matters it makes sense to pop in and see them.' Good Lord. The real draw about Walton, however, the quality that magnetises it, is its status as the main settlement on Scotland Road, or rather the miles-long thoroughfare that becomes Kirkdale Road and County Road etc. but begins smack in the heart of the city by Lime Street and heads north out of it and is probably the city's most famous street (after Lime and Mathew), synonymous with scouseness, the quintessence of the metropolis. If Liverpool is cocaine, then Scotland – Scottie – Road is its crack:

> [It] was not merely the major route out of town northwards, but an entire district comprising the numerous streets and courts leading off it.... It is among this mass of streets, alleyways and tightly packed courts, slums and cellars that much of the Irish population lived.... The inhabitants... were all desperately poor and that the district bred many hardened youths should come as no surprise[18].

Its proximity to the landing-stages of the docks meant that it 'came to serve as the hub of Irish Liverpool, the main artery through the North End with a pub on every corner and a riotous reputation'[19]. In the 90s David James Smith visited the area and found that a 'potential for ruination still persists along Scotland – Scottie – Road.... There is a press of pubs along the last stretch [of it]. Within a couple of hundred yards, on one side of the road, stand the Foot, the Widows, Dolly Hickey's Pub and Wine Bar, the Parrot, the Corner House and the Clifford Arms; and, on the other side of the road, the Eagle Vaults, One Flew Over the Throstle's Nest, the Newsham House, McGinty's Bar and the Europa'[20]. Some of these hostelries have gone now, but enough still stand on Scotland Road for that unbreakable link between penury and alcohol to remain as strong in this part of Liverpool as it does elsewhere, and as it always has: 'In 1888... in the district lying between Scotland Road and Vauxhall Road... police registers show that no fewer than 158 fully-licensed houses, eight beerhouses and one off-license were necessary to supply the drinking capabilities of the residents'[21]. J.B. Priestley got all sniffy about the place when he paid a visit to Paddy's Market in the

30s – 'surrounded by slum streets, dirty little pubs, and the Irish'[22] – one sneer amongst the many that contributed to 'the demonisation of the Scotland Road district [that] can be traced back to the 1880s when its inhabitants were described as the 'lowest type of squalid life'[23]. Not surprising, then, that the characteristic maverickness of the city has fastened on to a connection with Scotland Road as something to be fiercely proud of; this occasionally results in a daft kind of inverted snobbery – I was once told that the only 'true' scousers are those born on Scotland Road, which, if correct, would make the city a village – but more often than not succeeds in creating a sense of heartland, a wellspring of identity for this 'coastal statelet divided by accent and attitude from the English heartland [that] seems to crackle with a special charge'[24]. John Belchem, in, of course, *800*, talks about how 'Scotland Road has established itself as the 'hallowed path' of Liverpool's heritage and identity... [It] epitomised Liverpool and that special Liverpool spirit that could survive any disaster and then recount the event with typical Scouse humour'.

Well, yes, but this unwittingly offers ammunition to those who'd like to camouflage the real misery that must accompany decline and decimation. Bernard Fallon, in the introduction to his collection of photographs *Bernard Fallon's Liverpool*, writes about the impact on the Scotland Road area of the construction of the Kingsway tunnel:

> It must have given work to hundreds, but changed the lives of thousands. As one man said, "all this, just to get to Birkenhead?"... I photographed a partially roofless block of flats being dismantled that still housed an elderly couple waiting to be evacuated. It could have been a recreation of the Blitz, if the building hadn't been so new. The couple didn't want to leave and go to Kirkby. They'll have to make new friends and he'll have to find a new pub. "You get moved into a new flat with a bath and things. You haven't got no friends. Yer in a box watchin' another box. You'll just fret and die".

It needs to be remembered, this kind of thing. Interesting, though, how one of the main roads *out* of the city has become synonymous with rootedness, identity, the value of belonging. Scotland Road's endless stream of high-speed traffic, moving perpetually with an escape velocity, hurtles through a place that sums up unmoving solidity. That's good, isn't it?

NORRIS GREEN AND CROXTETH

The city's north end has always been notorious for its wildness and danger and gangsterism. It was here that the High Rips first appeared[25], where emigrant Irish formed secretive criminal societies, and where, currently, the Crocky and Nogzy Crews have been fighting an ongoing turf/postcode war, whose lethality is in no way undermined or alleviated by the puerile ridiculousness of its motives. The area was given newsworthy status on the 23rd August 2007 when eleven year old Rhys Jones, himself not a gang member in any way and by all accounts a shy and polite and studious boy, was shot dead through either mistaken identity, a twisted initiation ceremony, or mere bullying bravado – take your pick. He bled to death in his mother's arms. Senseless and awful, an immeasurable waste. At the time of writing, police have arrested a suspect, who awaits trial, but they were long hindered in their investigations by the code of *omerta* in operation here, as well as the fear of recrimination.

This is an age of easy self-publicity, and of legitimation through representation, and the Youtube postings of the two rival gangs – the Crocky Eds and Nogzy Eds – reflect that hollow hunger for fame and notoriety and the commodity of 'respect', now twisted so much as to have become completely detached from its meaning. There's a soundtrack of gangsta rap; boys in hoods showing off their pitbull pets and their abilities with trailbikes and stolen cars and their weaponry – revolvers, shotguns, even machine pistols. They're at first laughable images, pathetic, but then you think of Rhys Jones and they become profoundly disturbing, images of a society in a meltdown that might well turn out to be irreversible. A kind of respect was once awarded to those who could fight fearlessly, fist-to-fist; now it's measured by the nonchalance with which one young man can shoot another and run away. It's cowardice, of course, and the very worst kind of selfishness, but one that is born from hopelessness, 'the most lethal weapon', as Mary Riddell wrote in the *Observer* at the time[26]; 'in the midst of outrage at the loss of another young boy's life, there is some recognition that society's monsters are often also frightened kids, allowed to fail and fall from infancy until they discover the awesome power of destroying the lives of others while also throwing away their own'. Understand, too, that the Fir Tree Pub in Croxteth Park, outside of which Rhys was killed, is not an inner-city booze-bunker with sheet metal for windows, and nor is the area of which it is a part a smack-rotten sink estate; in the same

Observer, the journalist Euan Ferguson – who appears to possess an empathy with and respect for and deep appreciation of the city rare in his profession – wrote:

> The media swooped, again, on Liverpool, having half-heard the word Croxteth, and the circumstances of a pub car-park, expecting to find another grim tale of run-down Liverpool, dirty, mean streets and unhappy kids, and revenge shootings. They arrived to find something more akin to Basingstoke: happy streets, and school ties, and articulate, dignified, aching parents. How to explain? How to even begin to explain? To begin, you have to start walking, the long half-mile[,]to the heart not of Croxteth Park but of Croxteth proper[27].

Croxteth *Park* is part of the estate of Croxteth Hall, where the Molyneux family (again), earls of Sefton, lived from the sixteenth century until the last earl's death in 1972; but Croxteth *proper* is the second-biggest housing estate in Europe, ill-supplied with shops and pubs, and abutting Norris Green is home to the Boot estate, built in the 20s, 495 houses made of brick and 1,511 built of concrete and steel which 'started crumbling almost as soon as the first paint was dry on their front doors'[28], and have been crumbling since[29]. None of this is any kind of excuse, or even reason; its status as mere mitigating factor is debatable, even, given the frequent attempts at prettification in evidence as I drive around the two estates – window-boxes, well-kept gardens, a kind of pride. The sickness, I feel, is deeper, and wider, and to do with a culture that reveres renown at absolutely any cost and instils in developing minds the notion not only that they can have anything without working for it but that it is deservedly theirs, and offers no way of coping with the frustration and self-loathing that results from the non-acquisition of what was so shoddily promised. There is culpability, oh yes; it's not diffuse or amorphous, although it's so widespread and pervasive as to seem that way. We're at a point where none of us wanted to be. So how did we get here? And it's not just Liverpool; London and Manchester and Nottingham too have seen their children murdered. But as Ferguson wrote: 'it seemed that it was to be Liverpool, again, which had to outdo them all in horror; Liverpool which would become synonymous once more with a broken country'[30]. No amount of gesture-politics[31] will ever help, here, will ever in any way alleviate the Jones family's grief. Only one word works here, and that is 'lost'. In all its meanings.

My family has roots in this area. My parents lived in a house on Unicorn Road, and my grandfather and auntie lived on Carr Lane and Lewisham Road. I'd visit often. People from Croxteth and Norris Green at that time had a rivalry, but not a vicious, or even particularly serious, one; they'd often join forces in fights with Breck Road gangs (Anfield) or Shiel Road (Kensington). Norris Green was largely Catholic, and Croxteth Protestant (which doesn't lie behind today's idiopathic hatred). The Sants ice-cream-van driver, when serving Norris Green, would shout from his window 'ice-cream and rubber goods!'. The Western Approaches pub still stands, named after a World War Two shipping lane. Pitch-and-toss games would be played against its walls on summer afternoons. There's the Lobster pub, opposite a row of shops, one of which has a banner which reads 'Just Perfect' and sells cushions. There are a few weaselly faces beneath the bills of baseball caps outside the off-license. Speedbumps make the houses unsteady, as if on a choppy sea. Some years ago, the tower-blocks here – those in Croxteth christened Smack Heights, due to the prevalence of heroin dealers, although the need for that particular drug has largely disappeared now, overtaken by cocaine and ecstasy and weed, always weed – were demolished and replaced by pebble-dashed semi-detacheds. There is a respectable air, yet the Dog and Gun pub remains empty and boarded up, closed some years ago on police orders as guns were being sold on its premises. Today it bears graffiti: 'JOCK' and 'BOMB'. They might be nicknames. Taken together, they might constitute some kind of imperative. I don't know. But what appears increasingly self-evident to me is the fact that we, as a race, have entered an age in which the utter annihilation of behavioural and inter-personal norms and restraints has been welcomed, gleefully and without any stay of shame. What should one do with this knowledge?

APTLY NAMED: STANLEY PARK: EVERTON AND ANFIELD

Visitors or newcomers to the city often express surprise at the proximity of the two football grounds, separated from each other only by the green space of Stanley Park, traversable in a ten-minute amble. It's named after the Stanley family, who had their main residence at Knowsley; Sir Thomas Stanley was given the title of Earl of Derby by King Henry VII in return for his support at the Battle of Bosworth in 1485. They controlled the royal forest in what is now Toxteth and were influential for many decades in the internal politics of Liverpool, especially during the immediate post-Restoration years when William Stanley became mayor of the town between 1662-3, which Liverpudlians seemed to welcome and willingly 'to subordinate [their] interests to the Stanleys in return for their protection'[32], which sounds pretty much like extortion, but given the choice of the rock of the Stanleys and the hard place of the self-serving Molyneuxs, the former seemed the safer option. The park as it is today was laid out in the 1860s to a design by Edward Robson and built by the firm of T.D. Barry. It had a boating lake, aviaries and a glasshouse, and, from its elevated position, views all the way to the Yorkshire hills and north Wales. Such open space was welcomed in the cramped and close north end of the city, and its green lungs quickly became congested. In the 1970s and 1980s, however, at the height of football-linked tribal violence (not only in Liverpool of course but in every town and city across the country), many an away supporter was bushwhacked as they crossed the park to one of the stadia or down into the city centre; fights would often feature the weapon of choice, the Stanley knife, ironising the park's name. At that time, this was a culture which baulked at death but thought little of horrible facial scarring. Boots to blades to bullets; it's just evolution.

Yet I like this area; I like the sardined red terraces and the cosy corner pubs, these buildings like minnows shoaling around the enormous twin whales of the football grounds.

Anfield – from 'hangfield', or sloping agricultural land – is the flat land behind Everton brow, with roads that have stayed unchanged for over two centuries, and which seem to expand to accommodate the huge crowds on matchdays. The aorta of Anfield is Breck Road, both shopping area and route into the city, shops on the ground floor, living quarters above, all built in red-brick and terracotta and amongst the most impressive examples and echoes of the city's Victorian heritage. There's the Richmond pub, which David Lewis calls a 'Gothic fantasy'[33]; there's the Holy Trinity church with its octagonal spire. There's the huge cemetery on Priory Road, once described as Liverpool's Père Lachaise[34], an expansive necropolis with tree-lined drives that allow, in summer, the spangling of the many tombstones, and with a set of catacombs which accommodate only a handful of coffins, one containing the remains of the wife of a Russian nobleman who died on a visit to Liverpool and was deposited there 'temporarily' until he could build a church on the spot, but he returned to Russia, re-married, and forgot about it[35]. There's a memorial here, too, to the nearly 4,000 victims of World War Two air-raids, which covers a mass grave of 554 people, 373 of whom remain unidentified. Another shrine, erected in 1950, commemorates all Chinese ex-pats who have died on these islands. The great artist William Hardman is buried here, although he lived in Everton, Jem Mace the boxer, Jacob Stone, and Fred Parry the footballer. Famed bones a-mouldering. Canon Thomas Major Lester too, the Protestant half of the first Catholic-Anglican partnership in the city (the other half was Father Nugent, 'Father of the poor') set up to help destitute children, most of which were, at the time, to be found here, in this immigrant-Irish dominated end of the city. And there's a birth-claim, too; actor and comedian and writer Alexei Sayle was born in Anfield. And, in 2006, a well-known gangster was shot in the groin and leg outside the Salisbury pub; at a loss as to how to keep tabs on him, the police served him with an ASBO banning him from the city centre; in the three months following the order, 'thuggery in the city centre... decreased by 21 percent'[36]. Tony Soprano this isn't.

What else? Oh yes; on 18th October 2005 a woman telephoned police to report the discovery of a foetus in an alleyway off Oakfield Road. Paramedics and police doctors couldn't identify the body. Rumours spread; aborted baby, discarded. *Dismembered* baby, some said. Within five days the alleyway had become a shrine filled with flowers and teddy bears and cards, one of which read 'RIP little baby. Safe in the arms of Jesus. From someone who is a loving mother xxxx'. On the 24th October police announced that the investigation was over; the 'body' had been identified as a raw chicken carcass[37].

Funny story. Yet it fed those eager to believe about the city what people like Boris Johnson tell them to believe; he approved the *Spectator* article in which an anonymous writer berated Liverpudlians for typifying the 'mawkish sentimentality of a society hooked on grief'[38]. But the flowers weren't laid for a chicken; they were laid for the dead and discarded body of an infant – *that's* what people genuinely believed it was. The situation turned out to be humourous, yes; but, for a real while, it was horrific. Honestly horrific.

Anfield's going to change; the famous stadium will be demolished and a larger one built in Stanley Park. Some of the terraces will fall which, in part, is to be welcomed; the impermanence which has attached itself to them since the announcement of the new stadium go-ahead has contributed to a ghettoisation of some areas. Those still residing in the non-boarded-up houses will be bought out. LFC needs a bigger stadium; more seats = more money = more, and better, players. Football both trashes and builds cities. It's godzilla with architectural blueprints in one claw.

Cross the park to Everton, the 'highest point on the long stone spine that runs through Liverpool parallel to the river'[39]. The vista of the city from up here can stun. When part of the barony of Roger de Poitiers – cousin of William the Conqueror – it appeared in Domesday as Hereton, although Whale[40] traces the name to the Saxon Efer, meaning wild boar. It's old. The writer Thomas de Quincey lived here, in 1801 at age sixteen, with his mother in what is now called Everton Terrace, and witnessed the cotton fire in Goree Piazza in 1802. The artist William Gavin Herdman lived here too, at St. Domingo Vale, for several years before his death in 1882; a much neglected figure, his watercolours and architectural drafts are a fascinating window into Liverpool's growth. He has been quoted as saying 'I have done more for art in England than any man living'[41], which is an exaggeration, but he undoubtedly warrants wider recognition[42]. It was once healthy and fashionable, at some remove from the city below, and attractive to those who had made large sums of money from maritime traffic. In 1812, 70,000 people came here to watch an ascent by the well-known balloonist James Sadler; he came down in West Derby village, a couple of miles away. Fewer people saw him land.

Everton was built up from a rural village to a city suburb by Welsh builders, who dominated the city's construction trade (remember Klondyke Jones?). Welsh-language newspapers were printed here;

Welsh-language churches operated, too, and in fact churchery still dominates the roofscape; there's St. Polycarp (once fiercely Orange, now a workshop), St. Anthony's. And the spikes of St. Francis Xavier's, where the poet Gerard Manley Hopkins would deliver Mass, and which Spring-heeled Jack clawed his way up, cackling and spitting blue sparks (I'll introduce you to him in a later chapter, but you won't thank me; he's a scary feller). The late twentieth century turned the place into an urban gargoyle; Lewis writes that 'it is one of the poorest districts of modern Liverpool and has been shamefully treated by successive generations of city planners, which in many cases demolished what was good and built badly.... The fine Victorian houses... were demolished and eventually replaced by the soulless Everton Park, a strangely useless and vainglorious piece of urban landscaping'[43]. I doubt if this surprises you. Yet there's the iron St. George's church; Brougham Terrace, on which was built the country's first mosque; the grandly ornate Locarno ballroom and theatre on West Derby Road; the huge water tower, dating from the 1850s; the Round House, built in 1787 as a lock-up; and there's yet another necropolis, the city's first, which, until 1997, bore the skull of Yagan, an aboriginal warrior, shot dead in 1833 outside Perth in western Australia as he led resistance to European settlers. His head, taken as a trophy, was kept in Liverpool museum but interred in Everton cemetery in 1964; four years later, twenty stillborn children were buried above it which meant, under the terms of the Burial Act of 1857 which protected remains from being disturbed, that aboriginal demands for the return of Yagan's skull were rejected. In 1997, however, aboriginal leader Ken Colbung flew to Liverpool and said he would remain there until what was left of Yagan was surrendered to him, and it was, without any disturbance of the infants' remains[44]. So a happy ending, of sorts. Deeply miserable beginning, though.

It doesn't always feel a part of the wider city, Everton – not exclusively because of the separating wedge of the separately-named football club, but because of its physical distance from the city proper, made tangible by the vista of the centre and the docks some miles below. But there's a shared history, of course; umbilici that hold the two entities close.

The day is quiet and rainy. The giant letters that spell out 'THE PEOPLE'S CLUB' on Goodison Park are just about discernible through the grey drizzle. Dixie Dean's statue kicks a raindrop. There's no graffiti on him today, and nor is there any on the monument to the Hillsborough dead outside Anfield's gates. The flame below the list of names flickers, never to go out. I meet an Australian feller there; it's his first visit, he says. A pilgrimage. He'll be going to the game tomorrow, against Derby County. Where are you from? Melbourne. I've just come back from there, I tell him. Few days ago. Welcome to Liverpool. He asks me to take his photograph in front of the monument and I do, the never-ending flame dancing on his shoulder. Should we bump into each other tomorrow in a crowd of about 50,000 people, say hello.

For some reason, none of the photographs I take of Anfield can be developed, but there's no problems with those of Goodison. I hope the Aussie's had better luck.

OLD SWAN

A wonderful name – evocative, poetic. Old swan. Some grizzled grey in his white feathers. Pretty prosaic origins, however; the area is named after a pub that stood on the corner of Broadgreen Road and Prescot Road, where the Red House boozer stands today. See, the Walton family's (local landowners) coat-of-arms featured three swans, and they were responsible for the building of three pubs – Old Swan, Middle Swan, and Lower Swan. These have all gone, now, but the Cygnet, on Derby Lane, maintains something of the tradition. The area contains more red-brick terraces, more sandstone temples huddled around a busy junction; there's St. Oswald's church, designed during the Victorian Gothic Revival by Augustus Welby Northmore Pugin in 1842, the spire of which is said to be the first Catholic spire built in England after the Reformation; there's a very impressive Barclays Bank built out of the red masonry that was once quarried in the area, occupying the site of the lock-up which was used primarily to chain violently-disposed individuals to its walls. And there are ghosts; lots and lots of ghosts, because, when the foundations for St. Oswald's primary school were being dug one day in 1973, a mass grave was uncovered. Building work was delayed for eighteen months while the remains, some piled sixteen deep, were exhumed and examined, cremated and/or re-interred in Anfield cemetery; 3,561 of them in all. A plague pit? Possibly, because Old Swan lay on heathland some miles removed from the town during the plague age, but, according to Tom Slemen – the foremost authority on Liverpool hauntings and horrors, author of many books and compiler of several compendia on scouse spookery – the Home

Office investigations revealed that the plague claimed no more than a few hundred Liverpudlians, and the Old Swan bodies had been 'grouped according to their age'[45]. An unsolved, abiding mystery.

The railway line here saw the death, too, of William Huskisson, who has a street and a dock named after him in the city centre. Stephenson's engines chugged and farted and bugled through the area, and Huskisson, I imagine, would've huzzah'd at the sight, maybe even tossing his topper into the air, had he lived long enough to witness the spectacle. What happened was this; Huskisson, born in Newton-le-Willows in 1870, became M.P. for Liverpool and a powerful supporter of rail development, so much so that he was invited to the opening of the Liverpool-Manchester Railway on 15th September, 1830. He and other guests rode on the Northumbrian, and, overjoyed out of his senses at the experience, Huskisson attempted to climb from his own carriage into the Duke of Wellington's as the train was in motion. Stephenson's famous Rocket, coming the other way and driven by a Mr Joseph Locke, hit Huskisson, mangling his leg. Stephenson rushed him to hospital in the Northumbrian but he died on the way of his injuries, becoming the first British railway fatality. It must've been traumatic, really; all that blood and screaming. And this stretch of track also claimed another civic dignitary, in 1873, when Joas Caffareas, Brazilian Vice-Consul in the city, was hit by a train at Broadgreen Station. Apparently killed instantly.

Now? Well, there's a Tesco superstore, built on the site of a tenement block which at one time dominated the city-scape here as much as the red terraces do today, and of which there are hardly any left[46]. There's a Melbourne Hotel (another Oz connection; today's thrown up several. I wonder why). A sandwich shop called 'Big Baps'.

DIDDYLAND: KNOTTY ASH AND DOVECOT

If you're over, say, thirty five or so, you'll probably remember, or have been told about, the Knotty Ash Diddymen. Dickie Mint and Nigel Ponsonby Smallpiece. Funny little puppets, creations of Ken Dodd's, the shock-headed and terrifyingly-toothed comedian and singer who had a hit in the early 70s with 'Happiness' ('the greatest gift that we possess', apparently). Doddy's an institution, seemingly as old as the city itself, and still performing five-hour-long stand-up routines with his tickling stick. Don't lump him in with the likes of Stan 'The

Jeermans' Boardman or Chirpy Jimmy Tarbuck; he's more of an absurdist bent, more in the tradition of Edward Lear (who lived, for a time, in Knowsley; see next section), representing 'a Liverpool character less often celebrated: the droll suburban sceptic, the Dale Street cotton clerk or low Tory stockbroker in the lunchtime pubs of Hackins Hey', says Paul Du Noyer, in his *Liverpool: Wondrous Place*[47]. Knotty Ash became Dodd's imaginary fiefdom, a place of jam butty mines and broken biscuit repair works and black-pudding plantations, peopled by Mick the Marmaliser and Wee Hamish, little fellers in barrel-like costumes and hig hats, probably based on Dodd's diminutive Great Uncle Jack, who, according to Derek Whale[48], is still remembered, by Knotty Ash's older residents, as bumbling about in a long coat and bowler hat. When he drove his two-wheel, pony-drawn float, he could hardly be seen holding the reins; only his voice could be heard, trilling out old music-hall songs.

The place gets its name, unsurprisingly, from an old ash tree, which stood on the site of the Knotty Ash Hotel at the top of Thomas Lane. Lewis, in his *Illustrated History...*, refers to the Yates and Perry map of 1768 which, for the first time, mentions Knotty Ash as an independent area. A crossroads here led to an increase in traffic (as it did in Old Swan) – mail coaches etc. – which led to an increase in accommodation and service structures, and so the area was built. Some of old Knotty Ash remains; there is a row of cottages that borders the main Prescot Road, known as Little Bongs. They're small and snug, incongruous in this area (not that it's an especially ugly one, in an way); I imagine hedgehogs and badgers living in them, drinking tea and wearing waistcoats. A ticking clock. 'Bongs' might refer to 'bungs', as in 'barrel bungs' – a huge brewery once operated nearby. Many of these older dwellings were occupied by American troops on their way to France during the 1914-18 war; Knotty Ash railway station was a significant transit point for men and supplies.

It's a pleasant enough place, really. Suburban, not quite swallowed by the city, although it presses at the backside of Alder Hey hospital. The Knotty Ash pub has a banner which reads 'The Best Local Ever!'; how do they know? Adjacent Dovecot, however, huge housing estate, is only just beginning to lose its reputation for roughness. Where the Eagle and Child pub once stood (or, in local parlance, the Bird and Bastard), there is now just a patch of struggling grass; attempts to obliterate the black-market economy of which the pub was a hub. It was an ordering station; you'd go in with a request for a TV, or a DVD player, or a pair of jeans, or a type of car or whatever, and then you'd return some hours later to pick up and pay for the item. See it as piracy. Continuing a tradition.

The name 'Dovecot' comes, possibly, from the name of a manor house called Dovecot House, owned by Margaret Molyneux and featuring in its grounds a shelter for white domesticated birds of the pigeon family. The district was a rural one until as late as the 1930s, when rapid and extensive 'redevelopment', with staggering speed, urbanised it. Now, it's a low-rise sprawl contained by the howling arteries of Roby Road and Prescot Road. The Apostolic church bears a sign: 'Hope for the Hurting', it says.

A Doddy anecdote, before we leave the area: Parkinson once had him on his chatshow as a guest. Aware of Doddy's scientific approach to the analysis of comedy, Parkinson asked him for an insight. Well, said Dodd, you can tell a joke which will bring the house down in Glasgow, but they won't laugh in Manchester. Yes, an eager Parky said, why is that? Doddy replied: Because they won't be able to hear you.

notes

1. See Whale, *Lost Villages of Liverpool: Volume 2*.
2. My paternal grandfather worked here, for over three decades, shortly after he was demobbed. An anvil fell on his thumb, and for as long as I knew him the nail remained black.
3. Whale, op.cit.
4. Quoted ibid.
5. Ditto.
6. Ditto.
7. From his *The Illustrated History of Liverpool's Suburbs*.
8. Op.cit.
9. See Whale, ibid.
10. Lewis, op.cit.
11. For bibliographical information on these books, see, of course, 'Works Consulted'.
12. A selection of which can be found in 'Works Consulted'; see Ferguson, Riddell, Morrison (B) and Preston.
13. Op.cit.
14. In Volume One.
15. In 800.
16. See Johnson, *Powder Wars*.
17. See Whale, *Volume Three*.
18. See Macilwee, *The Gangs of Liverpool*. This is a book that tries to do for Liverpool what Herbert Asbury's books do for various American cities. It doesn't quite succeed, but it's still well worth a look.
19. Belchem, op.cit.
20. See *The Sleep of Reason*.
21. See Miller, *Poverty Deserved?* A gripping book, this, extensively-researched and stirringly-written. The reek of desperation wafts from its pages.

22. See *English Journey*.
23. Belchem, op.cit.
24. See Barnes, Elias, et al, *Cocky*.
25. See Macilwee, op.cit., and Barnes, *Mean Streets*.
26. In the article 'Don't seek revenge in violent gangs: Take responsibility', 26.8.07.
27. See 'The grief of Liverpool', 'Works Consulted'.
28. See Ward, 'From bad to verse', 'Works Consulted'.
29. In 2005 the estate's resident poet, Jane Canning, released a DVD containing verses and apothegms, including this one by the Reverend Mark Coleman: 'Salvation is not just a spiritual thing; it's about having homes to live in and food on our table'. See Ward, ibid.
30. Op.cit.
31. More laws, they say, we must have more laws. What, such as making it a crime to shoot an eleven year old boy in the head? Don't we have that one already?
32. Belchem, op.cit.
33. See his *Illustrated History...*
34. Lewis, ibid.
35. See Whale, *Volume Two*.
36. See Jenkins, 'ASBO bans gangster from city centre', 'Works Consulted'.
37. Unacknowledged article, *Fortean Times*, issue 206.
38. Quoted ibid.
39. Lewis, op.cit.
40. Op.cit.
41. See Elson, 'Liverpool's Greatest Artist', 'Works Consulted'.
42. Photographs of his works have been collected in Parrott, *Pictorial Liverpool* (see 'Works Consulted'), and are well worth checking out.
43. OP.cit.
44. See Jones, Catherine, (A), 'Works Consulted'.
45. See Slemen, *Haunted Liverpool 1*.
46. There's just one remaining block, I think, down by Bootle, below Kirkdale and Everton Brow.
47. Dale Street is one of the main streets in the central business district, Hackins Hey a narrow pub-lined cobbled ginnel in the same area.
48. See his *Volume Three*.

EAST

DANGEROUS ANIMALS RUNNING WILD: KNOWSLEY AND THE SAFARI PARK

There's an oddness to Knowsley; it's had a safari park since Edward Smith, the thirteenth earl, kept a menagerie in the grounds of the hall in the early 1800s and so the area's unpretty conurbanity is broken by hoardings bearing the giant forms of roaring lions and tigers and the fearsomely-tusked mouths of hippos (not that different from Knotty Ash and Ken Dodd, then). The presence of these animals colours the place; they're just there, over that wall. Beyond those gates. Big teeth and claws and muscles. On those rare occasions when the nights are quiet you can hear roaring.

In 2007, Knowsley was listed as one of the tenth worst places to live in the UK on Channel 4's *Location, Location, Location: Best and Worst* live programme. Knowsley's mayor at the time, Cllr Eddie Baker, was mildly miffed, and told the *Echo*: 'I don't take a lot of notice of this, really. As mayor, I see a lot of positives every day in Knowsley and I like living here'. What kind of positives? Well, the same article listed ten[1]; crime in Knowsley dropped 13.4 per cent in 2007; GCSE results went up by 15.2 per cent in four years compared to 5.6 per cent in other parts of the country; two thirds of the borough is greenbelt, and it has won eighteen national environmental awards in the past decade; a project in north Huyton helped reduce the teenage pregnancy rate in the area by 32 per cent; and Knowsley is the only authority in the country to completely rebuild all its secondary schools. Not negligible statistics, these, to be fair, but of course they beg the question; how bad must the place have been before all this redevelopment?

Its reputation for wildness is reflected in its origins and nomenclature; the Anglo-Saxon warrior-king Kenulf – the 'Bald Wolf' – gave it its name, a corruption of Kenulf's Ley, 'ley' meaning 'meadow', and meadowland it was for centuries until post-war redevelopment dumped huge estates on it to house those uprooted by bombing and inner-city slum clearance. Before that, it was held by the Lathom family since the twelfth century, a daughter of which married into the Stanley family, and was said to have been the largest single estate south of Scotland, at about 30,000 acres, much of which was sold off in the 1920s and 30s; 1,700 acres in 1932 for £185,000. Land becomes money and that money changes hands. The land stays as it is. The huge Hall which still stands bombastically on the estate and was occupied, in the 80s, by Merseyside Police, was given to the Stanleys after the Battle of Bosworth in 1485. Shakespeare is said to have played there[2] with Lord Essex's troupe in 1589 and, in keeping with the peculiarity of the place, the nonsense poet Edward Lear was employed there in the 1830s, sketching the menagerie's bird specimens, which, as R.L. Mégroz points out, 'explains the superiority of Lear in so many nonsense drawings [in which] the non-human forms constantly reveal a highly sophisticated technique subdued to the nonsensical *élan*[3]. Derek Whale[4] has it that Lear wrote his 'Nonsense Songs and Stories' for the children of Knowsley Hall, and Deborah Mulhearn, with the literary archaeological intrepidity that characterises her *Mersey Minis* series, unearths a letter from Lear dated 1842, which reads, in part: 'I should much like to know – when anyone writes from Knowsley... to learn if the green plot before the Stillroom window & up to the trees by the Chapel, is yet turned into a Flower Garden:- and if my unprincipled friend the Chough is still alive and proceeding in his old habits'[5]. Isn't that sweet? Parts of the Hall were opened to the public in 1949; for the first time the plebs were allowed to see the little oak chair on which the seventh earl, the notorious Royalist James, knelt to be beheaded in 1651, and the engravings of the family motto 'Sans Changer' everywhere, which, when you look at the fairly recent photographs of Knowsley as a village complete with parish church and central green and war memorial and compare those with the unlovely views of the outlying estate through the windows of the Hall's upstairs rooms, seems entirely inaccurate.

Still, Knowsley's no worse, really,than many of the functionally featureless and visually bland flat splats of post-war housing estates that rim most British cities. And, here, at least you can be amused as a primate drops a turd on your car bonnet and feel the thrill of danger as you leave your car window down and risk being dismembered by untameable feral beasts. Plus you can pay a visit to the safari park (sorry, I know, that's cheap. But I couldn't resist).

PRESCOT

Prescot's a surprise; between St. Helens and Liverpool proper, abutting the green of Knowsley Park and a huge reservoir system, its telephone numbers still have the 0151 prefix and its post offices a Liverpool postcode, but it feel distinctly separate, villagey, a self-contained little town. Big factories surround it (Pirelli cables, etc.) and retail stores and supermarkets, but, encircled by them, Prescot seems to tick along as itself, not really anywhere's or anyone's suburb. Its name comes from 'small home of the priest', and was designated by archaeologists in 1978 as the oldest settlement in England's north, retaining much of its medieval structure. It's thought that the place had a religious sanctuary of some sort (on, of course, the site of the present Church of St. Mary the Virgin) even before Christianity; Celtic mendicants built a timber and clay chapel here long before the Conquest.

The present church was built in 1729 and designed by Nicholas Hawksworth, pupil of Christopher Wren. John Wesley attended a service here in 1757, delivered by the Welshman Augustine Gwyn, 'a tolerable sermon', Wesley called it[6]. It's been through many generations of royal fists; John De Nevill, John of Gaunt, Henry IV.... In 1930, three charters granted to the town – by Henry VI, Henry VIII, and Charles I – were found in a solicitor's office, bestowing such privileges as freedom 'from toll, pannage, pantages, wharfage, and murages', whatever they are. Liverpool market-folk didn't like this, understandably, so Prescot people set up their own weekly market in 1587, which is still held, on alternate Tuesdays in Lent and up to May (hence its name of the 'May Fair'). The original charter also bestowed immunity from arrest on any felon who escaped to Prescot after committing a crime, even murder, outside the town limits. Hence the reputation the town once had as a harbour for miscreants, gamblers and drunkards; four centuries ago it boasted twenty pubs, twice the then national average. There's a few today, but no more than anywhere else of the same size, although I'll wager that they witness the same level of desperate drinking at weekends.

Prescot's a place in which to while away afternoons, drifting between the pubs, ambling the sloping sandstone streets, sitting on benches and feeding birds with bread. Intriguingly, in 1759, Liverpool and Prescot almost went to war, the latter's folk reacting against the former's turnpike tolls, three in seven miles with others at every branch road. Liverpool council bought arms from a Mr. Adams, gunmaker, 'a parcel of musketts and bayonets... when the town was in danger of being plundered by a mob of country people and colliers in and about Prescot', weapons to 'defend the town from the insults of the Prescot mob'[7]. Letters to Liverpool were once addressed to 'Liverpool, near Prescot'. After you've done with the pubs and the benches and the birds here you can catch a bus into the little satellite metropolis, somewhere in that ocean of lights to the west.

HUYTON

Another monument to misery. Another site of unfathomable pain. The facts are these; on 29th July 2005 the eighteen year old Anthony Walker, a popular young man, was killed in a racially motivated attack by Paul Taylor and the seventeen year old Michael Barton, estranged brother of premiership footballer Joey[8]. The murder weapon was an ice-axe, which penetrated Anthony's brain to a depth of seven inches. This was in McGoldrick Park, on St. John's Road, in Huyton. Before the murder, Taylor had carved a swastika sign and the word 'nigger' into a bollard outside a pub. He and Barton have been jailed for life. Anthony's family continue to function through what is unimaginable anguish; the interview that his mother, Gee, gave to camera outside the court on the day of sentencing revealed a woman of extraordinary forbearance and dignity, so much so that she re-instilled in the watcher a measure of hope for the human race that Barton and Taylor and their monstrous act had done so much to dispel. Remember the names; Anthony's to honour him, Barton and Taylor's to shun and deplore and as reminders of how irredeemably vile your fellows can be.

The early twentieth century saw brutal race riots in Liverpool (as in many other cities), but, in truth, racially-motivated violence of this kind is thankfully rare. In December of 2005, *Observer* journalist Mark Townsend visited Huyton, however, and discovered, as the tagline to his article had it, 'a lingering subculture of venom and violence'[9]; I don't doubt this, but the word 'subculture' is important, implying as it does a loose group of socially excluded nurturers of their own bitterness such as Barton and Taylor who 'would attack anyone they felt was an outsider'. The murder, Townsend wrote, was the 'single, horrific moment [that] grotesquely articulated [a] complex meld of causes and entrenched bigotry', and was the culmination of lesser hate crimes that occurred across the country following the suicide bombings on the London transport system on July 7th; between that date and August 8th, Merseyside police alone recorded a quadruple increase in the number of racially and religiously motivated attacks on the person. Lay the blame for some of this at Fleet Street's doors. *Some* of it. So the council's slogan for City of Culture 2008, 'The World in One City', began to appear as mere spin and to clang discordant as a risible untruth, particularly in the 'white ghetto' of Huyton, where, out of the 150,600 residents listed, only 2,100 are from an ethnic minority, and which is the third most deprived area of the UK with more than one in four young men unemployed, and where theft is, as Townsend wrote, 'the principal vocation'[10]. Disenfranchisement gets into the marrow, and victims become victimisers, which fact doesn't, of course, excuse or condone anything; yet travel less than two miles from Huyton, to Woolton, and there is a multicultural mix in which racial tensions have not gained a toe-hold. Liverpool's long been a rainbow of pigmentation; in most areas, the days when stolen African children as young as eight were sold for pennies along with '10 pipes of raisin wine and a parcel of bottled cyder' in Canning Place coffee-shops[11] remain resolutely at several centuries' remove, but in others, shrivelled souls and wizened hearts harbour darkly a belief that the only way to relieve their own suffering is to give it out to others. Skin colour, really, has little or nothing to do with this; at root, it's about solipsism, and a lack of empathy staggering in its inhuman breadth. Others will discuss this, and at greater length than I can here. One anonymous mourner who left flowers at the spot where Anthony died recognised the uniting potential of shared ordeal when s/he wrote: 'It's not black, it's not white. A young boy lost his life here. For God's sake will they understand?'

★

After that, it seems unfeeling and of a piece with trivialisation to write anything else about Huyton. The place, as do so many others in this extremely peculiar city, drips with sadness, is shocked with loss, and grinds with rage. The prow of a Viking ship has been found here. Flint arrowheads. During World War Two, Huyton was an internment centre for 'enemy aliens', 4,000 of them to 340 beds. Other stuff. See Whale's *Volume Three*. I've had enough of it. He was eighteen years old.

GATEACRE/NETHERLEY

Gateacre's pretty. It's surrounded by huge and ugly estates, but honestly, it's pretty; there's a village green and old Tudor buildings and several rickety pubs. Rows of cottages called things like 'Grange Mews' and 'Paradise Row', dating from the 1500s. The green sports a fountain, built in 1883 as a memorial to Cllr John Hays Wilson, a brass founder, chairman of the Liverpool Water Committee and so instrumental in 'impounding' the waters of the Welsh Lake Vyrnwy (Liverpool has long had a – to say the least – problematic relationship with Welsh water, which we'll later discuss). The Hall on Halewood Road has The Slave Gate – a wrought iron gate, through which slaves were reputedly passed into the Tower building to await shipment, although both Lewis and Whale dispute this. The names of the pubs – Black Bull, Brown Cow, Bear and Staff – reflect the area's farming traditions. It's a pretty place.

But Netherley *isn't* Gateacre. Part of the urban renewal strategy begun in 1964 and initiated by William Sefton[12], which cleared vast tracts of 'slum' housing and constructed 95,000 new dwellings in a little over a decade, Netherley, and nearby Cantril Farm, were the two areas in which newbuild housing was prioritised. This is the very edge of the city; the estate abuts open greenery, and beyond the little brown trickle of Mill Brook, you're not in Liverpool anymore. The place *feels* urban, but in actuality it's fairly rural; you can smell grass and fertiliser, see the green fields, hear cows lowing and the chirrup of birds. In the 80s, the place became synonymous with poverty, crime, squalor; Beryl Bainbridge visited in 1984, when retracing the route of Priestley's *English Journey*, and noted that if the Russians could see Netherley, they'd send us food parcels. See, the estate, and others like it, were jerrybuilt; the speed of construction meant that there was a ten-year-gap between the first wave of residents and the completion of the main shopping and leisure facilities, and the cheapness of construction resulted in dampness, vermin, and an imposing and repetitive aesthetic with the linking decks between blocks saving money on lifts and staircases. The blocks were declared a mistake even before they were completed, and quickly christened Alcatraz; plans which seemed open and airy on paper in offices for walkways and underpasses etc. proved dehumanising in practice, a mistake made several times before and since, but of course financial exigencies forever get the nod over human comfort[13]. The blocks themselves were demolished in the 1980s, but the terraces and rows are still there, including those of Appleby Walk where, between the ages of about three and nine, I lived. It's called the Woodlands Estate (and, indeed, it does contain a wood, still; a small one, true, but it was huge to me, as a child). My family moved there from Toxteth when we were all, including my parents, very young. When, in the 90s, I would tell people where I'd been brought up they'd express shock and horror; Christ, *Netherley*? Smack city, bandit country? But I don't remember it being like that; I remember abundant birdlife and frogs and sticklebacks in Mill Brook and herons at the pond on the fields; of course there was domestic violence on the estate and much cruelty to animals and various other forms of bullying but the place wasn't a hell-hole, or at least it wasn't then, and we'd left before Thatcherite economics dropped its bombs on the area. I'm slightly restrained here as to what I can write concerning my personal reminiscences of Netherley as I've written about them for the summer 2008 edition of *Granta* and I must avoid stepping on copyrighting toes but, physically, the place hasn't changed much; my old house still looks exactly the same, as does the White Bridge (under which I was convinced gila monsters lived) and the woods around it and the meadows beyond. There are no goalposts painted on the gable ends of Kirkbride Close and the chippy's completely gone and the underpass is filled in and most of the shops in the row have been closed down but the free-standing wall by them is still there, still with the same three-decades-old graffiti and the small greens that separate the ranks of houses haven't been built on. Whether they're still dotted with dogshit, I don't get close enough to find out (I fell in a pile once, face-first; the taste and the stink still linger, at thirty year's distance. Vomited like a fire-hose).

And there's a marvellous coincidence; as research for this book, I get in touch with the poet Paul Farley, winner of the Somerset Maugham Award and Whitbread Poetry Award, and we arrange to meet at the Philharmonic pub on Hope Street in the city centre. I ask him where he's from. An estate on the outskirts, he says, you wouldn't know it. Try me, I said. And so it turned out that he'd been close friends with my brother (he's a couple of years older than me), would come round to my house for fish-finger butties etc. We share a past, and didn't know it, had read each other's work but never made the connection. For some reason I find this heart-lifting. *Granta* commissions us to return to Netherley and co-write a piece for them, which we do, and on our stroll around the estate on a day sharp with frost I interview him; our talk is constantly interrupted with visually-stimulated reminiscences and stories but I get to know a bit about him nonetheless.

He left Netherley, and indeed Liverpool, at age nineteen. He traces his Irish roots back to the 1850s. He teaches at Lancaster University which suggests to me that the city is in some ways drawing him back; 'it's exerting a pull', he agrees, 'definitely'. He went to Belle Vale School, as I did. Remember Mrs. Jump and her woolly boots? Pupils would be made to wear them if they were caught kicking anyone: 'It made me cry, putting them on. It was a real emasculation'. He recalls the 'siege mentality' of the off-license, which had anti-ramraiding bollards set into the cement in front of it long before that particular form of robbery was even given a name. Paul did an evening paper round, so got to know the estate intimately; the different letterboxes, the smells of different teas. We agree that it wasn't a bad place in which to grow up, although we can't fathom where our literary obsessions and needs to write come from. Paul would spend his Saturdays in Picton library, a voracious and uncontrolled reader, although his first forays into artistic endeavour weren't literary; rather, he'd draw babies for money, his 'own cottage industry, really'. Writing supplanted drawing in his early twenties when, on a whim, he walked into a class given by the poet Michael Donaghy in London and thought 'so *this* is where they've been hiding it'. This was his Damascene moment, and Donaghy would later give Paul's work his imprimatur. Paul 'couldn't believe that Liverpool would have poetry, especially Netherley', but reading the Liverpool Poets (McGough, Henri, Patten etc) taught him otherwise; 'raw materials are just raw materials. That sounds trite, I know, but it wasn't at the time of discovery'. In Netherley, writing poetry 'had no currency. Drawing did – it could be sold. But poetry didn't'.

We stop on the White Bridge, a short concrete and steel structure that spans Mill Brook. Gila monsters (why did those colourful Mexican lizards fascinate me so as a child?) lived under here only in my head, but in the real world it was a place of water rats, which would often be hunted down by local lads and stoned or beaten to death. We talk about the violence that surrounded us; not of a particularly physical sort, and certainly never in our own households, but there was a pervasive and general coarseness and brutality, 'and the way to not get battered was to align yourself with the brutes'. Paul points to the isolated barn in the field over the brook. It always reminded him of a Dutch master, he says. There was no-one he could share that observation with.

The simple fact that he writes poetry is 'radical enough', given his background; the poetic impulse is all the experimentation he needs. 'A poem is a meeting space. It's a dynamic space'. He tells me that he sees peculiarity of rhythm in the scouse dialect, but could never presume to impose poetic syllabics upon it (would that other dialect poets felt this way). A kid from Netherley writing poetry? 'It's squatting'. So why poetry, then, particularly? Why not prose? He doesn't believe in the prose he writes, he says (and does himself a disfavour; Paul's sections in our shared *Granta* piece are superb); 'I know where I am with organised poetry, and lyric verse. I like shape and symmetry, all those things that Netherley didn't have'. Hence his mistrust of modernism; the same principles were applied to those parts of Netherley that were demolished in the 80s and 'didn't work'. Yet Paul did, once, compile a non-literary guide to William Burroughs, collating everything that Burroughs wrote that wasn't in book form. I tell him I find that strange and he agrees, 'but it's left no footprint on my work at all'. He's also written a monograph on the films of Terence Davies[14], although whether Davies's work is overly modernist in tone or structure is moot.

We walk through the woods and up onto the playground; swings, shelter, a five-a-side pitch behind wire mesh. 'Writing feels so right. I don't think too long or too hard about where it issues from. Liverpool people are good bullshitters, which is a skill, it's a talent'. So maybe that's the wellspring, I say; maybe it's of a piece with talking one's way out of a beating, and is linked to the blag, or as a way of gaining approval. It's a survival mechanism. There's an instinctive element to writing which it *needs* to have, 'otherwise', Paul says, 'what's the fucking point?'

I get specific; so, Paul, your poem 'Liverpool Disappears for a Billionth of a Second' that everyone's going on about. Tell me about it (the fact that I loathe this question when it's asked of my own work doesn't prevent me from dumping it on other writers).

Well, he says, it's about quizzing yourself where home lies... is it in the future, waiting to be regained? It's about trying to make the extraordinary ordinary, not the other way round. Not that much happens in it... and I *do* wish Liverpool would vanish, but only for the tiniest fraction of time. It was the perfect place to grow up as a poet, a 'city of the mind, so far away from the stupid clichés... it's an infinitely more mysterious city than people give it credit for. The clichés totalise and flatten it, do it a disservice'. What clichés, in particular? 'The chirpy sense of humour, the mouth and solidarity... they're not even amplified half-truths'.

He continues: Liverpool 'went through the mirror' in the 1960s, and became self-conscious. Even in the accent – it became harder. 'The city's now become used to seeing itself on screen, and the accent's now a noisy, mediated racket'. All the nuances have been burnt off and gone. The refusenik nature, the awkwardness, is to be highly valued. 'It's the most un-English of English cities... it's on the edge of something. It's a great place to come from as a writer, because it's indefinable', and in poetry, 'if you're not saying one thing and meaning another, then you're wasting your fucking time'.

We stand at the bus-stop. A passing teenage boy recognises Paul;

his teacher, who also taught Paul, has given him a copy of Paul's first collection to read. He's thrilled to meet a living breathing poet and I'm touched. He asks us if we'd like to go and see his school's Capital of Culture exhibition but our bus arrives.

Capital of Culture, Paul? 'All I can think is 'please don't let them fuck it up'.... These things are very artificial. It was a city of culture anyway, it already had the raw materials. The Capital of Culture thing, how deep will it dig? How Liverpudlian will it be?'

We talk about the lost years of the 80s. 'The world has caught up with Liverpool, and the city has become more corporatist'. The vast decline of river commerce – 'blunt economics' – has made the city what it is now.

Back in the city centre, I see Paul onto the Lancaster train at Lime Street and take two collections of his poetry into a pub and order a Guinness. I've read them before, but I read them again. And, no doubt, will do so again; within its formality it's brilliant and inventive and thrilling, and it and the day and the Guinness exhilarate me – the coincidental weight of our meeting is in itself an excitement, and our shared explorations into our writing impulses have made my scalp tingle. Why Netherley, at that time, should have moulded us both into writers – superficially very different ones – I don't know; but the common irreducibility of our obsessions must have something to do with the place, and the time. It's not something I feel the need to look into too deeply; I don't want dissection, or explanation. I simply want it to never go away, as Netherley won't, ever, and nor will it for Paul, as his poetry testifies. 'The Newsagent' and 'Paperboy and Air Rifle' and 'Brutalist' and, especially, 'I Ran All the Way Home' (all from *Tramp in Flames*) stun me with the shock of recognition. The lines 'a newsagent will draw/The line at buttered steps' jolts me into remembering how the newsagent lived in a flat above his shop and how thieves would first smear the steps leading down from it with margarine before breaking in. I go to the bar for more black beer.

WOOLTON

Woolton's *not* Walton. It's another one of those places which, if you were shown a decontextualised photograph of it and asked to guess where it was, you'd miss by a mile. There are trees and, again, Tudor houses. The Coffee House pub, dating from 1641. The Woolton Cheese Company, whose 'Cheese of the Month' is Cornish yarg.

WAG territory, this. There's a quarry nearby, hence the name of John Lennon's first band, The Quarrymen. He was a middle-class son of Woolton, Lennon was. The proximity of the Netherley and Cantril Farm estates meant that Woolton once had a reputation for roughness, but that's changed now; to be sure, weekend nights here see a large proportion of cocaine-gurned faces between Burberry, but much random violence is yesterday's, including that meted out by the Teutonic chief Wulf who settled on nearby Camp Hill, with its views across the river and Wirral peninsula and Welsh mountains, and who gave the place its name.

It has Hospitaller associations, as reflected in the Woolton Cross and the water mill, built by the Knights, below Naylor's Bridge; if you don't know, they were an order of Knights who, supposedly, cared for sick pilgrims. Their land here was seized by the Crown in the 1540s, after the dissolution of the monasteries, although, according to Lewis[15], 'for many years after it was compulsory for Woolton residents to have a cross set upon their houses'. Queen Elizabeth I then took ownership, and after her, Robert of Upholland, then James I, then the Sixth Earl of Derby, then Isaac Green (a local lawyer who invested heavily in land), and then the Marquess of Salisbury. The Hall dates from 1704 but is possibly built around a much older structure; it was erected for, again, the Molyneux family, but is now a pub/restaurant. The population of the area boomed in the nineteenth century, after the Waste Lands Enclosure Act of 1805 demanded labour to build walls and fences, and with the influx of Irish people during the Great Hunger; in 1851, 24 per cent of Woolton's population were Eire-born. Pigs and pubs appeared. Rowdiness and poverty, grindingly hard and poorly-rewarded work on the new docks and railway system at nearby Garston. Liverpool city swallowed the place in 1913.

Close by is Strawberry Fields[16]. When I was a boy, it housed a pre-Borstal correctional facility which was locally referred to as the Naughty Boy's Home. Useful for a parental threat. When Lennon was a boy, though, it housed a Salvation Army home on Beaconsfield Road and would host open-air summertime concerts which he'd attend; the original building has long gone, but the ornate red gates, of course, remain a shrine to Beatles obsessives. Lennon's childhood home on nearby Menlove Avenue, which leads onto Penny Lane, is now owned by the National Trust. This is not, and never has been, a working-class area. Something to be, indeed.

And that's enough of Lennon and anything else Beatles-related, now, here, but we'll stay in Woolton and have a blether and a pint with

Mike Morris, who's not from here (he was born in Ormskirk and brought up in West Derby) but now lives here, and is a founder and organiser of the annual Writing on the Wall festival, along with Janette Stowell and Madeline Heneghan. WOW's fast becoming a Liverpool institution, if it's not already, and should supply everything you need if you're looking for cultural festivities alternative to those promoted and made by the mainstream. I meet him for a spree on a rainy night in early winter. He's a man for whom cultural and political activity is propulsion; so much so that he joined Militant at the age of fourteen, and quickly became a full-time organiser for thirteen years. You might remember Militant; with rent-a-gob Derek Hatton as its mouthpiece, it reinvigorated the Liverpool Labour Party in the late 1970s, seeking to, in Belchem's words[17], 'revitalise a moribund Labour Party [and] fill... the leadership vacuum that had existed since the discrediting of the party machine in 1972'. It magnetised trade unions at a time of futile isolated struggles over factory closures and redundancies and offered them a broader political outlook. It came to encapsulate scouse awkwardness and bloody-mindedness and, eventually, what many saw as hypocrisy and counter-productive intransigence 'when the local authority was formerly disowned by the then Labour party leader Neil (now Lord) Kinnock, and redundancy notices were infamously delivered to staff in a fleet of taxis'[18]. An inevitable reaction to the crush of Thatcherism, Militant is now often regarded with suspicion and mistrust and is even sometimes saddled with some of the blame for the city's 80s decline. Mike was at the epicentre when the movement splintered and turned factional, at the time of the docker's dispute; he tells me that the much-prophesied crash wasn't supported by what he saw in the city – the cranes, the amelioration of poverty in some areas. At a National Committee meeting for the Labour Party Militant was threatened with suspension, so they voluntarily left. But some members didn't want to. Hence the rift. And the isolation.

Mike was politicised in the early 80s; the miner's strike, the South African and Chilean refugees arriving in Liverpool. Militant had the potential, he says, to be more than it was, but it hasn't left much of a positive legacy. Labour movements in, say, Spain or Latin America often encouraged, and were in turn encouraged by, cultural activity but this didn't happen under Liverpool Militant and, like a lot of sectarian organisations, 'it lost a toehold in reality'. Are there *any* positives, I ask? Well, Militant was responsible for the construction of 5,000 houses. Rents and rates were frozen, jobs created on the council, the education system was re-organised, four new sports centres were built... it grew out of 90% youth unemployment, heroin epidemics, slum housing etc. Of *course* there was anger. But isn't a lot of regeneration privately funded? Of course, says Mike, but Militant was never hostile to private investment. And it recognised the importance of stabilising business rates.

We're on Hardman Street now, in the city centre, smoking in the beer garden of a bar, our fags wilting in the drizzle. A heart-stoppingly pretty French waitress keeps bringing us drinks. Mike returned to university in his mid-twenties. Became a Leaving Mentor at a comprehensive in Anfield and was made redundant when the school became an academy. He started WOW in 2000, and since then it's been an annual feature on the city's cultural calendar. In 2006 he made a film with Dave Cottrell called *Cunard Yanks*, which premiered to an audience of 1,500 in the Philharmonic Hall[19]. WOW, Mike says, will make the kind of literary festival that the C of C year will need; not a Cheltenham kind of thing, middle-class and apolitical with no direct emotional involvement, uninterested in developing new audiences and new work.' There's a place for that', Mike says, 'but it's not our bag'. WOW is concerned with issues of social justice; it's not just about *who'll* be performing, but also *where*. Tickets for a Linton Kwesi Johnson performance in the Blackie were sold in shops along Granby Street, for instance. This city's, this country's, cultural pursuits have become exclusive and cliquey, ignoring many for whom the creative urge is immensely powerful. 'WOW reaches out to such people'.

And Capital of Culture? 'Well, the opportunity was lost when they failed to think. You can't *not* have Paul McCartney, really, but... I doubt this will leave a cultural legacy for the city'. Regeneration, he says, began years ago, with Objective 1 funding and privatised enterprise. The C of C award capitalises on this. It's *not* the other way round.

We're now outside the Prohibition Bar on Bold Street. The human traffic here.... It's always been like this – fevered, frantic – but there's a difference, now; there appear to be more smiles, more laughter and relaxation, less beggars, junkies, sirens. But still the same heart beats.

notes

1. See O'Keeffe, 'You've got Knowsley all wrong, Kirstie', 'Works Consulted'.
2. See Whale, *Volume Three*.
3. See the introduction to the *Edward Lear Omnibus*.
4. Op.cit.
5. See *Mersey Minis Volume Four: Loving*.

6. Whale, *Volume Three*.
7. See ibid.
8. Who is a thug, but was uninvolved in the murder.
9. See 'Works Consulted'.
10. For the 'phenomenal' growth of estates like those at Huyton, when, in a few post-war years 'the rural idyll of hedges, broccoli and carrots disappeared underneath. . . bricks and concrete', see the essay 'City of Change and Challenge: Liverpool since 1945' in Belchem, 800.
11 See Fryer, *Staying Power*.
12. See Belchem op.cit.
13. As Jenny Roche wrote in her poem 'Netherley – 1985' (see Coles, *Both Sides of the River*): 'They solved housing problems,/We lived them'.
14. See 'Works Consulted'.
15. Op.cit.
16. You'll know the song, I'll wager, and might even be as bored by hearing it as I am.
17. See *800*.
18. Says Hetherington in his article 'Clash of the Titans', 'Works Consulted'. He also sees this same tendency reflected in the political infighting that preceded the Capital of Culture year.
19. Google this – it's fascinating.

THREADS

WATER: MERSEY/ESTUARY/OPEN SEA AND DOCKS

The city's collective brain is hydrocephalic. Water moves through its vital organs as alcohol does through a dipsomaniac's. The Mersey was once as blackened and corrupt as an alcoholic's blood but industry's affluent appears to have been washed away now and salmon have returned to the river, even porpoises. Thank the Mersey Basin Campaign, set up in 1985, which took on the task of cleaning all of the river's 110km and its many tributaries. It used to stink, and now it doesn't. Or only of the sea.

For a 2007 collection of essays and photographs about the Mersey[1], the journalist David Ward took a ramble along a section of its banks[2], an inland section, where the rivers Goyt and Tame meet behind the Sainsbury's in Stockport. He also stood on New Brighton pier and spoke to anglers who were preparing to fish for cod. In the Mersey – cod. And its attendant predators; small cetaceans, grey seals, even octopi. Birds, too; according to the RSPB, the Mersey Estuary supports more than 100,000 ducks and waders. Within a ten minute walk from the city centre you can see dunlin, wigeon, teal, shelduck, bar-tailed godwit, redshank, curlew, heron. Not bad for a river described only two decades ago by then environmental secretary Michael Heseltine as 'a disgrace to civilised society'[3].

There are people on it, too, as there have been for many centuries. The ferry that crosses the river is one of the world's iconic short boat-crossings, up there with the Staten Island trip and the one across the Bosphorous that links Europe with Asia[4]. The photographer Ken Grant is fixated on the Mersey and the human life on its banks. Liverpool born, Ken now lectures on photography at Newport (he's one of my oldest friends), but is drawn constantly back to the city of his birth and the riparian traffic of it; his collection, *The Close Season*, bears as a cover image children playing on the beach at New Brighton, with footballs, on bikes, with bucket and spade, an upturned supermarket trolley and all elongated shadows pointing at the city skyline over the flat water. It's brilliant stuff, moving and intimate and angry and wistful[5]. There's the image of a man and a boy at a sea-wall, the river grey before them, cranes blurred and barely visible through the haze. Caught in mid-flight a metre or so away from the man's face is a pigeon. It is all longing. It is lovely.

'The city and its river are forever linked', wrote Ron Freethy in 1985[6], but the river changes. Tony Barnes, in his *Mean Streets*, has a story about how the contours of the Mersey's bed have been altered by the amount of mobile phones thrown in the water, used once for a drug deal or related transaction and then tossed untraceably away. 'There's a giant mobile phone sand bank built up in there', a detective is quoted as saying. I know they'll be destroyed by the water, but I imagine them going off; all those different ringtones blurred with gurgling. The octopus using them to text his friends, eight at a time.

A DIVIDED CITY: FOOTBALL

Football; greed, money in obscene amounts, spoilt and pampered boy-men accountable to no-one behaving in whatever hideous ways they wish, both on and off the pitch. And the worst kind of tribal hatred, of corrosive and poisonous base emotion. Three days previous to the time of writing, Liverpool were comprehensively beaten by Manchester United, their bitterest rivals. One of United's fans, evidently a playful scamp, had painted on a motorway bridge over the M62 so that all visiting Liverpool fans would have to pass underneath them, the words '96 DEAD NOT ENOUGH', a reference to those Liverpool supporters crushed to death at Hillsborough in 1989. On the pitch, a United player harangued the referee, albeit unsuccessfully, into sending off a Liverpool player, a fellow professional, with Liverpool already reduced to ten men. In the last seconds of the game, with United three goals up, one of their players took his usual dive in the penalty box, attempting to con the referee. The game was won; why cheat? This kind of thing goes on constantly, and, although United are amongst the worst practitioners of bullying and cheating, they're by no means the only guilty team. Liverpool can do it, too. But not as often. Or as cynically. There is a side to football today that is vile and vulgar and vicious.

But, God, it can be glorious. How it can make the heart soar, make your blood rejoice, if football's already in it. Take what happened on 25th May, 2005, in Istanbul; Champions League Final, probably the most prestigious club cup competition on the globe. Liverpool versus AC Milan. Liverpool three nil down at half time, but in the space of six second half minutes they score three times to take the game into extra time and then a penalty shoot-out which they win. I was supposed to be there, in Turkey, but the organiser of the trip was suddenly bereaved so it all fell through. So I watched the game in Downie's Vaults in Aberystwyth, and when the goalie, Jerzy Dudek, saved that final penalty I collapsed in rapture in a puddle of beer beneath the fruit machine. It was glorious. The story of the game, and the build-up to it, is traced in Guillem Baleque's book *A Season on the Brink*, which stands out from others of its type due to the quality of its prose. It's quite gripping. He also looks at Liverpool's Basque and Spanish connections and explains how the team has become a popular second team to people in Spain. Of course, none of this will interest you if you're not a Liverpool supporter, but what can I say? *No puedo o cultar que soy un Red.*

And if the game's a prole-opiate, so what? That in itself is a middle-class denigration of what has traditionally been a working-class pastime, and in recent years the game has been hijacked by the chattering classes anyway. Home Counties accents abound on the terraces. The big games are watched by a crowd largely decked out in Ironic Replica Sportswear Pour L'Homme, in the bars in university towns beneath the big screens. This can generate positives; the recent spate of financial take-overs of British teams by mega-rich foreign (chiefly American) businessmen who care more for their bulging investment portfolios than they do for the game itself, never mind the emotional mortgages of those who follow it, has prompted defiant campaigns against the turning of teams into usufruct marked by mutual support and solidarity not seen in this arena for a long, long time. As Brian Reade put it in his *Daily Mirror* article of March 8th 2008, 'the fans are REVOLTING... but this time they're fighting exploitation, not each other'. In this, he mentions how 600 Liverpool fans have formed a supporter's union called Sons of Shankly (SOS), with the aim of forcing out the club's owners, the American pair Tom Hicks and George Gillett; SOS met with Dubai Investment Capital to discuss ways of grabbing power from Hicks, who is side-kick to George W. Bush. Think about that; a group of scousers held a sit-down discussion with Sheikh Mohammed al Maktaum with the object of bringing down 'a billionaire adviser to the most powerful man on earth', as Reade put it. And why? Because ordinary fans are sick of being taken for fools; sick of berserkly-rich foreign business-men viewing their team as nothing more than another buy-in opportunity. So a fans collective called ShareLiverpool want to buy out the club, and a breakaway team called AFC Liverpool is set up (as FC United were in opposition to the takeover of Manchester United by the Glazer family). This is anger in response to contempt; anger that has resulted in creative unity. For once, people are react-ing against exploitation. It's good to see.

Football; if it needs explaining to you, then you'll never, ever get it.

It's either in you or it isn't.

DIVIDED CITY: RELIGION

The Welsh brought Methodism, the lowland Scots Calvinism, the Irish Catholicism, the northern Irish both that and Protestantism, the Russians and Greeks Orthodox, the far easterners animism, European Jews Judaism, Arabians and north Africans Islam, etc,.etc. The towers of diverse temples spike the city's skyline. In general, the faiths get along, although of course there have been exceptions, and the annual Orange Lodge parade on August 12th is allowed pretty much the freedom of the city whereas the parades of March 17th are confined to within a few square miles in the city centre (and always ending at Flanagan's Apple pub on Mathew Street). The Little Belfast area adjoining the Dingle sports St. Patrick's Church cultural centre and kerbstones painted green and white and orange and pubs called The Volunteer next to pubs called The Crown and bollards coloured blue and white and red. Such signs, codes to read the city by. Moy McRory writes about a Catholic upbringing moving between Liverpool and Belfast in her collection *Bleeding Sinners*; Bernard Fallon[7] has photographs of sectarian graffiti, of a wall outside a tenement bearing the words 'GOD BLESS OUR POPE THE VICAR OF CHRIST – DEO GRATIS PRAY FOR REBELS' and another reading 'VOTE PROTESANT', the mis-spelled alter-ation of the underlying 'VOTE PROSEANT'. Nick Danziger, in his *Danziger's Britain*, found it 'a divided city [where] your postal code could be a strong clue to your cultural and religious background... a city divided not just by colour but by class and religion'. His guide, Siobhan, calls it 'the last sectarian city in England', and he meets her outside a church in Everton where a nearby wall sports the words 'FUCK OFF TAIGS' and 'ULSTER VOLUNTEER FORCE FOR GOD AND ULSTER'. You'll remember Nik Cohn's experiences in Southport, too.

There's more; I remember a Creole/voodoo celebration in the city, which I'll tell you about in the next 'Threads' section. And in May 2004 the Dalai Lama visited the city; he was supposed to simply deliver a lecture at the Anglican Cathedral after receiving an honorary fellowship from John Moores University but a crowd had gathered outside and, on his way to his car, waylaid him. He made straight for a member of the crowd – Bill Davies – confined to a wheelchair and hugged and blessed him and patted his ruined legs. Bill said: 'My heart was pounding so fast by the experience I had to use my angina spray'[8]. Photographs of the event show the Dalai Lama's constant smile amongst a huddle of faces animated by emotion; there's one where Bill's eyes can just be glimpsed between the beak of his baseball hat and the Dalai Lama's shoulder as he leans to embrace him and it is truly wonderful. There's scripture in those eyes.

Strange phenomena; Brian Burgess's sculpture 'Cleansing of the Temple', a steel and bronze figure of Christ brandishing a whip and held in the Liverpool Academy of Art, has been shooting blue sparks from its eyes. Burgess said: 'It began when a woman who saw the statue fell to her knees and began praying. She was transfixed for more than thirty minutes and when she came out of the trance, she said she had witnessed sparks coming from the eyes of the Christ figure'[9]. Pilgrims are drawn, of course. Liverpool as Lourdes or Fatima or Knock. Brian Burgess is, apparently, a self-confessed atheist (atheists are always 'self-confessed', aren't they?), but the story of Christ seems to obsess him; an earlier piece depicted an eighteen-foot high Jesus in steel and wire and copper and bronze attacking gamblers. He attracts controversy, just as his work attracts worshippers; the manager of the Academy of Art, June Lornie, remarked that 'not since Arthur Dooley's work twenty years ago has there been such a furore in Liverpool over an artwork'[10].

Ah, Dooley (1929-94). He's one of the city's renowned sons. Liverpool born, he was a welder in Birkenhead, heavyweight boxing champ of the Irish Guards, factory worker, and cleaner at St. Martin's School of Art in London, which hosted his first show in 1962. Born Protestant, converted to Catholicism and, eyebrow-raisingly, communism in 1945. Much of his last work can be seen in churches in Britain, Latin America, and Spain; unsurprisingly, given his welding background, his favoured materials were bronze or scrap metal. In Liverpool, you can see his work in the city's Parish Church and, most impressively, hanging obliquely on a wall outside the Methodist Church on Princes Avenue. He's also responsible for the 'Four Lads Who Shook the World' piece in Mathew Street; I know, yes, yawn, The Beatles, but this sculpture utilises plastic dolls and illustrates Dooley's profound Christian sensibilities. I find much of The Beatles industry deadly dull, but I do like this sculpture. Cavanagh[11], to whose book you should go if you want more informa-tion, states 'given the nature of Dooley's approach to sculpture, it is difficult to say what is decrepit and what intentionally ragged-looking'.

Which makes it all the more interesting to look at.

Blue sparks and gold-painted dolls. Ah, it's a religious city, right enough.

GHOST/GUILT/SLAVERY, AND THE TALE OF LEAPING JACK

Leaping – or Springheeled – Jack, was first spotted in London, on Barnes Common, in 1837, springing as if from a trampoline over railings to land in front of a walker who, on seeing his pointed ears and glowing red eyes, promptly legged it. The next day, he attacked three girls, molesting one and leaving her unconscious. He molested another girl, Mary Stevens, the following day, at Lavender Hill. Stories began to circulate of a caped and cackling ghoul, able to leap over rooftops and across wide roads; able too, after another attack in Limehouse, to expel a jet of blue flame from his mouth. His eyes 'shone like balls of fire', said another victim, Jane Alsop, in Bow[12]. Another victim – this time a boy – noticed Jack's clawed hands and that he had a 'W' embroidered on his waistcoat, which led to conjecture that Jack was actually the Marquis of Waterford, a notorious prankster and something of an athlete, but Jack's appearances continued after the Marquis's death in 1859, most frequently, after London, in Liverpool, as long after the first London events as 1904, when he was seen swooping down from the roof of High Park Street reservoir, and clinging to the steeple of St. Francis Xavier's church in Salisbury Street, in Everton. A crowd gathered to watch him; he waved to them, and leapt. The crowd rushed to where he'd landed, believing him of course squashed, but scattered in panic when, as various reports have it, an 'egg-headed figure in white… ran down the street towards them, lifted his arms, and flew away'[13].

He disappeared after that, for sixteen years. Then he was seen, dressed in white, in nearby Warrington, jumping up and down between the pavements and the rooftops. Then he re-vanished, and re-surfaced in Monmouth in 1948, leaping over a river.

What was he? One theory posited an insane pyrophagic acrobat. Another, a kangaroo, dressed up. Another, a mad inventor with an anti-gravity device. Or, of course, an alien. I haven't got the first clue. But I remember many stories about him, often containing one little detail[14]; in the city centre, on Rodney Street, in the grounds of an old and decrepit church (next door to where the poet Arthur Hugh

Clough once lived; it's blue-plaqued), is an odd, pyramidal tomb. In it, supposedly, sits an embalmed corpse; an inveterate gambler in life, the man apparently wished to be interred sitting upright, at a card table, holding a royal flush. And so, it's rumoured, he was. And is. The pyramid contains a little door; I've been told, on many times and from many sources, that on the occasions of Jack's appearances, this door would be open.

I've never seen Leaping Jack. I'm kind of glad about that.

REGENERATION: CITY OF CULTURE?

Not everyone's happy; not everyone benefits. The Capital of Culture, for some, means only the Culture of Capital (and, indeed, the playwright Nicky Allt has written a novel called precisely that, in which the main character discovers, to his breakdown, that 'regeneration equals a catastrophic loss of identity'; see 'Works Consulted'). For others, it means the promotion of means of expression completely alien to their own; insular artistic endeavours from which they, and their own forms of self-expression, have always been excluded. *The Guardian*'s letters page of March 11 2006 carried these comments:

> We've been there before; the International Garden Festival now lies derelict. The Albert Dock still attracts record numbers of visitors, yet many shops lie empty due to the extortionate rents for small businesses
> .... With incomes in Liverpool below the national average, how can we sustain theatres, orchestras, and museums on these levels of poverty?
> .... We need bread and roses.

And, from the then leader of the city council, quoting the ticket collector on the Mersey ferry:

> I want a big party in 2008 [but] it doesn't stop there. It's about what
> happens afterwards – more jobs, improved prospects, a better society.

Well, let's hope. But in January 2008 the *New Statesman* carried an
interview with renowned screen-writer Jimmy McGovern[15] (*Cracker*,
The Lakes, *The Street*, etc; I'm sure you're familiar with his work), who
took the journalist Dominic Cavendish on a tour of the Liverpool he,
McGovern, knows, one that involves turning left out of Lime Street
station and away from the new architecture of the centre and water-
side and into areas where whole rows of terraces are empty and
boarded up and sprayed with the squatter-deterring words 'gas
off/leccy off'. Cavendish writes: 'the feeling of absence is palpable
and overwhelming... the living co-exist with only the memories of
their vanished community', and McGovern remarks that 'it's like the
area is being eaten away by a cancer'. This is Edge Lane (aptly, one
might think, named), being allowed to fall apart 'in the city's corri-
dors of power... as [a] prelude to regeneration'. The idea is to
transform Edge Lane, with funding of £65 million, into a major
urban boulevard, which will involve the purchase and demolition of
500 homes, but some of the residents of those homes are refusing to
move out; this is their home, their area, this is what they know and to
which they feel they belong. Such feelings go bone-deep. 'If it's about
regeneration', says McGovern, 'just look at the quality of [what] they
are knocking down. These are lovely Victorian houses and they are
going to replace them with new-build tat'.

It's a sad and angry article, Cavendish's, as well it might be; one of
McGovern's brothers, Joe, lives close to Edge Lane and has witnessed
the decimation of his neigh-
bourhood. 'They're telling me
to get out of my home while
they make a profit', he says: 'I
can't accept that'. The area
crumbles around him. His own
home crumbles around him.
Capital of Culture has
produced 'cultural vandalism'.
The plans could be scaled
down, and some of the vast
funds diverted to these people
to help them renovate their
properties; regeneration means

nothing if one of its results is catastrophic personal upheaval. In a personal email, Peter Stead, member of the Culture Award panel, wrote: 'In other highly backed cities we sometimes felt that we never got past men in suits and consultants [but] in Liverpool, uniquely, people in pubs and on the street would say 'you've got to choose us'.... We knew that in part this was the city cultivating its own mythology'. So the award was given. And now the Capital monster devours some of the people. There must be a way round this; there's money enough and brain-power enough to find a solution, surely. What's lacking is the empathic heart. 'Will Capital of Culture mean the same in Walton in the city's economically deprived north as it does in leafy, media-friendly Woolton?' asks the introduction to *Writing Liverpool*[16]. The question's rhetorical, of course. Or is proving to be. We may yet see a twenty-first century version of The Clearances.

But it's here. The Culture award and a kind of regeneration have been foisted on the city. Big losses; some gains. How big? Well. We'll see.

notes

1.   See McPherson, *The River That Changed the World*.
2.   And wrote an essay about it; see Ward, 'River of Life'.
3.   Ibid.
4.   To take it, however, you've got to really, really like the Gerry Marsden song. It's played relentlessly, on board. It drives me mad. I pity the people who still use the ferry to commute. Pity more its pilot.
5.   Some of it is held in the Museum of Modern Art in New York and the V and A museum in London.
6.   See Coles, *Both Sides of the River*.
7.   In his *Bernard Fallon's Liverpool*.
8.   See Davis, Laura, 'Works Consulted'.
9.   See Lloyd, Jessica, 'Works Consulted'.
10. Quoted ibid.
11. In his *Public Sculpture of Liverpool*.
12. See, as always in such matters, Slemen, *Haunted Liverpool 1*.
13. Ibid.
14. That seems to have evaded Tom Slemen's otherwise highly efficient radar.
15. See Cavendish, Dominic, 'Culture of Destruction', 'Works Consulted'.
16. See Murphy and Rees-Jones.

SOUTH

HALEWOOD

My maternal grandmother lived, for several years, in Halewood. It was a pretty grim area then; it's grimmer now. Her flat is still there, facing the windowless bunker of the social club; the Leather Bottle pub still stands; the precinct – most shops now covered in steel grilles, 'tinned up' – containing the butcher's from where she'd get her brawn (yick). The toyshop's no longer there, from where I once bought a small plastic cowboy and a small plastic Indian and made them fight. The Indian's legs were too small for his body. 'He's just a broad feller,' my granny said.

It's school dinner-hour when I return, hence the swarms of young teenagers, ear-hammeringly loud. Accents that could scorch through iron. *This* is rough Liverpool, yet John Lennon's Menlove Avenue lies within a five-minute walk; that affluence adjacent to this.

Another post-war peripheral estate. Began as a hunting ground for King John in the 1200s, not to be confused with nearby Hale, which we'll get to in a few pages. Ancient district, edge of the city, described at the end of the nineteenth century as 'bare and flat with wide open fields, principally cultivated, yielding crops of barley, oats, wheat and root crops such as turnips and mangel wurzels'[1]. Any historical ruins that were here have long since disappeared under the Ford car plant, a vast sprawl of industry.

I see ghosts of the younger me, here. Over that wall, spiked with spears of glass, lies a yard in which the resident's of my gran's flats would dry their clothes. My siblings and I would run through them, wet cloth forest, slap hanging knee-length bloomers into each other's faces, scream with laughter.

HUNT'S CROSS

Basically a crossroads, this, a busy one. Redbrick, a Sayers bakery (good cheese and onion pasties), a Somerfield. Not much else. Lots and lots of traffic. It's not very old, first appearing on a map of 1848, and the cross here maybe marked the boundary of the three parishes of Speke, Much Woolton and Halewood. It's typically south-end-of-the-city in that it's almost entirely given over to twentieth century housing, and, to be frank, somewhat dull. Not a lot to write about.

I hear an amusing story, though; there was a bonded warehouse here once, storing whiskey and other spirits, heavily guarded, CCTV surveillance, etc., but a lot of alcohol continued to vanish. How? Workers were frisked, exits closely watched, etc. Until a strong boozy smell was detected wafting out of a Mini Cooper in the car-park, which type of car used to have two petrol tanks. The owner was pouring whiskey into the car, driving it out and siphoning it back into bottles. Ingenious.

Not *that* diverting a story, I know. But that's Hunt's Cross.

SPEKE AND HALE

Speke, of course, is the site of the city's airport, recently re-named the John Lennon Airport and promoted with a line from his awfully mawkish, hypocritically sentimental blethering 'Imagine', emblazoned over the entrance, 'above us only sky' (which, for those with a phobia about flying, I imagine to be hardly re-assuring). The area itself was built between the 1930s and 1950s, designed as a self-contained township for workers at the industrial estate, built coterminously. Another aim was to cut the council's waiting list of over 30,000 people, 'to aid its slum clearance programme and to ease overcrowding', writes Lewis[2]. 'Speke must have seemed like the future of Liverpool', he continues; 'it had wide boulevards and bright factories, good houses with gardens, even garages for the anticipated rise in car ownership [and] crowning it all was the city's brand new Art Deco airport'. The flatness of the landscape hereabouts dictates the formality of the town planning, and the regularity (or regimentation) of its boundaries. It's not the city's prettiest district, although it boasts a unique name (there's no other 'Speke' in the UK), probably

from the Saxon 'spic', meaning 'bacon', in reference to the area's once-numerous swine fields. Getting on a bus one day in the city centre, I overheard a passenger ask the driver 'is this bus going to Speke?' The driver replied: 'No, it's an inarticulate lorry'.

Speke Hall is quite impressive. Magnificent, in fact. Grade 1 listed. Elizabethan, or earlier, inherited by Thomas Norreys in 1467, although much of it as it stands today was built by his great-grandson William, who became Lord of Speke at age twenty three[3]. The Norris line ended in 1731 with the death of Richard, and the hall began to decay, some of its wings being used as byres by Charles George Beauclerk, who sold it in 1795 to Richard Watt, 'a little merchant who made a fortune in the West Indies', says Whale[4], which means he was a slaver. The building was passed down through his family until it was leased to the National Trust. It's a pretty impressive pile, popular with school trips, and of course rumoured to have several ghosts. Fields surround it. It's another oasis in a city of many such. One field used to contain the burnt out remains of an aircraft; I remember exploring it. It's gone now. The hall's fortifications now include admission charges and car-parks but I'm pleased to see that it contains less signboards of blaring prohibition than other places like it.

And the airport? Well, the site was selected in the late 1920s by pioneer airman Sir Alan Cobham, with a farmhouse acting as the control-tower. It's much like any other regional airport, really, except for the impressive Art Deco buildings, now housing hotels and health clubs and restaurants but still boasting their original, and beautifully intricate, brick- and glass-work. This is proof of recent regeneration; in the 60s and 70s, when Speke was as run-down as run-down gets, these buildings lay derelict and the runway was used largely just for freight; worse, Manchester had a popular and gleaming terminal only forty miles or so away. Now, though, the sky screams with jet engines. Daily flights to New York. A pilot I spoke to once in a nearby pub said that he preferred landing at Speke over any other airport in the UK; the approach over the sea, the clearness of it, the aircraft-friendliness of its location, all are exemplary, he said. I've flown from there several times, and I'd agree; outstanding sense of space as you take off.

And then there's the Birdman. His name was Leo Valentin. He was French. He'd made himself a pair of balsawood wings and he'd leap out of aircraft and swoop safely back to earth and on 21 May 1956 he came to perform the trick over Liverpool[5]. This was

to be his final flight, he said. He was thirty -even, and he'd been flinging himself out of flying machines for ten years, despite claiming that, during every jump, 'I experience a moment of absolute panic, a panic of my whole being, something resembling the primordial fear of the caveman'. Brave or barmy? Both, I suppose. He suffered from recurring nightmares in which he was falling to his death. Prone to panic attacks, these would often hit him in mid-fall (unsurprisingly, you might think). Anyway, he leapt from the plane above Speke at around 9,000 feet. His wings clipped the fuselage as he jumped and he began a horrible tumbling plummet. His lines were tangled. People with binoculars observed him feverishly yanking at his ripcord. Closer he got to the ground. Spectators covered their children's eyes. There were screams. In seconds, something horrible would happen. Plunging all-shapes. Kicking as if to ward off that abysmal drop. The famed horror writer and film-maker Clive Barker, Liverpool-born, witnessed it as a child: ' "*Don't look*", my mother said, over and over', he wrote[6];

> I defied my mother's repeated edict, and looked out towards the cornfield... watching Leo Valentin plummet to his death.... The image of a man falling out of the sky, his body and his ambitions dashed against the earth, is one that trails mythologies, of course. But it would be many years before I learned the story of Icarus, or read *Paradise Lost*. All I knew at that moment was the panic, and my hunger to see what the men out there were seeing; the thing I was forbidden.

Valentin landed in a field of grain at the side of the airfield. It was

recorded that he had a peaceful smile on his face and that his eyes were closed, as if he was sleeping[7]. There were no appaling injuries, and not one trace of spilled blood. But he was dead. I hope his last thoughts were good ones.

Stay in the air for a moment, but not as high; 9 ft. 3 in., to be exact, the height of John Middleton, or the Childe of Hale. Born in 1578 and apparently of normal growth in his youth, he became something of a national celebrity at age thirty-nine, when King James I, en route to Scotland, overnighted in the area and was impressed by Sir Gilbert Ireland's huge bodyguard who he invited to London to take part in a wrestling bout, which he won. Returning to Hale, John and Sir Gilbert called in at Brasenose College in Oxford where John left an impression of his hand on a cellar doorpost, the dimensions of which are recorded: 'From the carpus to the end of his middle finger was 17 inches long, his palm 8 inches and a half broad and his whole height 9 feet, 3 inches'[8]. He was, by all accounts, a gentle fellow who, back at Hale, returned to farming. He died in 1623 and his bones were exhumed in 1768; his thigh bone measured 2 ft. 9 inches. His cottage still stands in Hale village, with its ceiling taken up flush to the roof to allow for his height. His hat-pegs stood ten feet from the floor.

It's quite an interesting place, Hale. There's a lighthouse and some twelfth century ruins and a guild of freemen who, on inauguration, are required to swear an oath on which they declare to be 'thorough' drinkers and 'fair smokers' and 'dear lovers of the fairer sex' until death. Fair enough. Reason to tarry. But let's move on.

GARSTON

An Anglo-Saxon name ('Gaerstun' = 'pasture'), yet there is little evidence for occupation earlier than the 'Roman pavement', discovered in 1855, lying seven feet under the surface of the soil and formed of boulders laid flat, without camber, and worn smooth by traffic. Old enough. For 300 years until the Reformation it was owned by the monks of Whalley and Stanlawe Abbeys. Agricultural land. Fisheries and watermills, fed by a stream that had its source in the higher ground of Allerton[9]. This watercourse was channelled into a subterranean culvert as the town grew over it and was seen for the first time in decades when work on the bypass exposed it in 1982.

An Irish area, this, settled during the potato blight of the 1840s, like much of this part of Liverpool. The earliest docks here were built in the mid 1700s, primarily to repair small boats used to carry salt from St. Helens. Dock and railway expansion in the 1850s, however, was colossal, and at its height the Garston dock complex employed 1,000 people and utilised over ninety-three miles of railtrack, but relatively recent containerisation has resulted in shrinkage, inevitably. Jack Jones, the former General Secretary of the TGWU, was born here, on York Street. Gracie Fields said that the area's Empire Theatre, now gone, figured in her 'hour of destiny'; an organisational mishap left her stranded here, but the show she gave led to her sudden stardom. And so on.

The old Bryant and May match factory is now mainly office space; LFC TV and Family Martial Arts, whatever they are. The building is visually powerful; rosettes, tiles, intricate masonry. All this space, just to make matches? There's a huge Borders bookshop and a huge HMV on the New Mersey Shopping Park and a large sign that reads 'we couldn't have done it without eu'. The library contains a One Stop Shop, which I don't think I've ever seen before. In a library, I mean. A relative on the maternal side of my family, Elsie, lived here, with her husband, Ronnie, and sons, one called Stevie. Elsie was, I think, my mother's cousin. Stevie, when still a teenager, was hit by a bus in the city centre and killed. At the moment of impact his cat, back at home in Garston, began to yowl, and did not cease doing so for twenty-four hours. A true, and sad story. I hadn't seen him for some years before his death but I liked Stevie, as a child. Liked his cat, too.

ALLERTON AND CALDERSTONES

Traditionally the city's Jewish area, Calderstones was once the home of the late, flamboyant suit-and-fedora-wearing, jazz-singing, surrealist-painting, raconteur and bon viveur George Melly. His autobiography *Scouse Mouse: or, I Never Got Over It*[10] talks about growing up in a mixed Anglo-Jewish family, with an anti-semitic Jewish uncle, and another who involved himself in Harold House, the

Jewish Boys' Club, and the Jewish Lads' Brigade of the time. Much has ben made of Liverpool's Celtic and black and Chinese ethnicity but it's long had its Jewish enclaves, too; John Belchem[11] mentions that there is a record of a synagogue on Stanley Street in 1753, and that the main Jewish occupation was in supplying goods to seafarers. 'The tolerant and entrepreneurial local spirit' attracted large numbers of Jews and the first sermon in English to be delivered in a synagogue was by Tobias Goodman in 1806, on Seel Street. The largest Hebrew community outside London grew up here, and the first Jewish mayor, Charles Mozley, was appointed in 1863, eight decades before a Catholic would take the same office. Princes Road, which heads south-east out of Toxteth towards the Calderstones/Dingle area, has on it a beautiful synagogue, designed by the Audsley brothers, a mixture of the Moorish and the Gothic and, Belchem says, 'one of the finest examples of Orientalism in British synagogue architecture'[12]. He's not wrong.

But, anyway, Calderstones. It didn't exist as a place until 1825, when Joseph Need Walker, later a Crimean War profiteer, bought up the land around Calderstone Hall and added an 's'. The hall's grounds once contained standing stones, 'Liverpool's oldest and most important archaeological relics', according to Derek Whale[13], which now stay hidden somewhere; in the mid-80s, when Whale wrote his guides, they were in the Harthill Greenhouses in Allerton Botanic Gardens, but I hear they've been secretly re-located. They're massive stones, by all accounts, several millenia old, and bearing distinctive 'cup and ring' markings and other recondite engravings which apparently relate them to the Boyne Culture of Ireland, so maybe

Liverpool's Irish links are much older than we think. A huge boulder from this area now sits outside the Wavertree Library on Picton Road. The ex-Beatle George Harrison apparently believed it to be a meteorite, but it's not. And there's an ancient oak, reputedly 1,000 years old, in Calderstones Park, on which a plaque recounts that sittings of the old Hundred Court were held under its branches a millennium ago. When it was a sapling, of course. The members of the Court must've been gnomes.

More: the old English Garden contains the grave of Jet of Iada, an alsatian dog and the first dog in Britain to be used in locating air-raid victims trapped under rubble. And at the Menlove Avenue entrance to the park are interred two ponies and a horse, pets of the owners of the original mansion. The nearby Botanic Gardens were founded in 1800 by abolitionist, poet and all-round good bloke William Roscoe, established by public subscription and share allotments. To which you've got to give the man a nod, as American writer Washington Irving (*Headless Horseman, Rip Van Winkle* etc.) did; he met Roscoe shortly before the latter's death, when he was very old, but found in him 'the fire of a poetic soul. There was something in his whole appearance that indicated a being of a different order from the bustling race around him... Wherever you go in Liverpool you perceive traces of his footsteps in all that is elegant and liberal'[14].

And Allerton? Well, there's some money in this area of the city. Large gardens and mock-Tudor fasciae abound. More megaliths, too; Robin Hood's Stone bears grooves said to be scored when the merry feller himself sharpened his arrows on it, although a likelier explanation is that local archers caused them during target practice in the park under the reign of Henry VIII. David Lewis[15] tells us that the novelist Nicholas Monsarrat, author of *The Cruel Sea*, lived in this area, off Greenhill Road. And, of course, predictably, inevitably, boringly, there's a Beatles link; Paul McCartney's family lived on Forthlin Road. House recently bought by National Trust, blah blah. Penny Lane is in Allerton too. Et cetera.

OTTERSPOOL AND AIGBURTH

Otterspool has a promenade, stroller-friendly and ambler-amenable, as proms, of course, often are. its vista is long and wide and open; you can see the Stanlow refinery far down the coast, a thin-towered city. You can watch the planes coasting in to land at Speke, see

Bromborough over the Mersey. It's misty on the day I re-visit, and peaceful, and green, and fond memories, twenty years old, of an ex-girlfriend who was living on the campus at nearby Aigburth, re-surface. We'd take hangover-banishing walks along this promenade and through its attached parks. I wonder where she is now, what she's doing. There's a whiff from the landfill close by. Can't see it but I can smell it, ripe and cheesy, when the wind changes direction.

The 'otter's pool' was the mouth of the old Osklesbrook, where it opened out into the Mersey, which attracted salmon, which attracted the eponymous mustelids. There wasn't a promenade here at all until the 1950s when the engineer John Brodie had the idea of using the spoil from the Queensway tunnel to strengthen the riverbanks. In 1984 it was the site of the first International Garden Festival, which effectively lifted the area out of decay and into something greener and enticing, although in recent years many of the donated gardens have reverted to wildness and much of the sculpture stands half-hidden in thick bracken. But there are some who like that. And I like seeing the younger me sitting on one of the benches, looking out to Wales alongside a woman once familiar now turned by time into a mystery again.

Adjacent Aigburth is intriguing (pronounce it 'Egg-buth', from 'Ackebuth', meaning 'place of the oaks'). Celtic history, Anglo-Saxon history, Roman. The Stanlaw Grange is the oldest occupied residence in the city, dating back to 1290, once part of a monastery run by Cistercian monks of Stanlawe and Whalley Abbeys. I like this area. The cricket ground, in 1883, hosted an international soccer friendly between England and Ireland, the return leg of a match which England had won 13 – 0 in Belfast. *The Guardian*'s sport archive[16]

assessed that 'the Irishmen, though novices at the dribbling game, here with characteristic vigour and energy endeavoured to master its salient features', and that Liverpool was chosen for the game because it was 'the home of large numbers of their compatriots and sympathisers'. The score, sadly, is not recorded, but I'll pretend that the Irish won by fourteen clear goals.

Yes, Aigburth is a likeable

district. It's kind of villagey and bohemian but busy with it. Green leaves and twittering birds. House prices are rising very quickly here, of course. The area contains St. Michael-in-the-Hamlet, which, if you didn't know you were in Liverpool, you'd think was somewhere else entirely; the Cotswolds, say. Sun slants through branches. Sandstone arches and a sense of organic cathedrals, the canopy overhead. This is a village purpose-built in the early nineteenth century by John Cragg, a local iron founder, who worked with the architect Thomas Rickman on building Liverpool's cast-iron churches, one of which stands here, in the middle of a hamlet made, where possible, out of iron; window-frames, doorframes, fireplaces. Surrounded by chestnut trees. The Cast Iron Shore is nearby, into which I'd throw rocks as a child to hear the splat. Big, spacious and attractive Gothic Revival houses. Conservation Area status granted in 1968. Another unexpected oasis.

Back on the Aigburth Road, I notice a group of tramps clustered around a bench, both young and old. They're sharing a bottle of cooking sherry and saluting passers-by with a cheery 'good morning'. They have caps on, and boots, and frayed string is holding up their trousers. One of them is crooning a song to himself, softly. Another gives me a nod as I pass and winks. They're like a glimpse into another age, a kinder one. Even the tramps in this part of Liverpool deserve World Heritage Status.

From here, you can see the bottom end of Lark Lane, and, at its top, Sefton Park. You're tempted by it. Sorely tempted. But we won't go there just yet.

THE DINGLE AND WATERLOO

The Dingle is the site of those famous steep-sloping streets, close-packed red terraces, huddled and secretive, leaning towards the sea, except their rush water-wards has now been blocked by the newbuild housing and hotels which clog the littoral. Poet and critic Matthew Arnold died here, in

1888, and in 1853 the American novelist Harriet Beecher Stowe visited and found it 'a beautiful little retreat.... It opened my eyes like a paradise, all wearied as I was with the tossing of the sea'[17]. It's not like that any more, although there are signs of recent prettification; flowerbeds at the heads of the streets, etc. It's a lot cleaner than I remember it being. There's still a cloistered feel to the place, however; the pubs and shops and terraces stand squeezed together, as if in clandestine conference, muttering, whispering. Concomitant with that, of course, is an enviable and admirable sense of mutually-supportive community; the weft of the place is very, very tight. Always has been. It was the setting for Carla Lane's TV series *Bread* of the 1980s and early 90s, which was heavy on the 'sit' but terribly light on the 'com'. Indeed, I thought it mawkish, speciously romantic drivel, which contributed hugely to the wider perception of Liverpool as an overly sentimental place, resulting in the epithet 'Self Pity City'. Some of Lane's earlier work – *Butterflies*, for instance – could amuse and move, but *Bread*? It made me cringe. Belchem, in his *800*, writes that the series 'received a mixed reception in the city due to the feeling that it traded on stereotypical depictions of the semi-criminal scouse scrounger', but it wasn't that aspect of the programme that I found bothersome and, indeed, risible; rather, it was all the stuff about 'ar Joey' and 'ar Mam' and taking grandad his tea every day at the same minute and how cosy it all was and how a lachrymosely-expressed sense of shrill familial love could find forgiveness for everything, including Joey's leather kex. Utter rubbish. Deryn Rees-Jones, in her brilliant poem 'Soap'[18], satirises the museum of cliché that the city became at that time and of which things like *Bread* were the curator:

> In Liverpool we have a lorra lorra laughs
> I won't be held responsible if he goes free...
>
> Why is it hard to feel so close.

The body in the garden gets up and walks.
For a year he washed his hands until they bled.

Bear in mind, here, that sentimentalised encapsulations of a place succeed in nothing but reduction. Worse; they encourage and feed the prejudices of those who have a blinkered interest in sneering and segregating. They're a kind of Uncle Tom-ism, a forelock-tugging, cowering pandering to stereotype, abjectly seeking approval. The Dingle isn't *Bread*. The Dingle produced gangsters like the Ungis and Fizgibbons, 'descended frrom Filipino sailors and... Irish immigrants [who] in the melting pot of Liverpool's slums... had formed a strategic alliance based on close familial and marital ties and driven by a desire to be the number one mob in South Liverpool'[19], very violent, very ruthless, very powerful; and the Dingle produced Eddie Braben, supplier of most of the material for Morecambe and Wise (fierce taskmasters, apparently) which 'tone was of deep Liverpool unreality', according to Paul Du Noyer[20], including a 'sketch about Ernie's fast-growing moustache seeds'. *That's* the Dingle – guns and guffaws, glassings and gallimaufry. Bollox to *Bread*. And everything else of its saccharine stripe.

Anyway; rant not so much over as temporarily in abeyance. Head off into Waterloo, named after the famous Napoleonic battle, and which, in 1815, was a popular little seaside resort for the wealthier folk of the city, until the railway was extended to Southport in 1848 (and called, at first, the 'Shrimper's Line'). Now it's... well, it's just another district, not, of course, without historical note; there was a flying school here, and indeed one of the first powered flights in the country took off from Waterloo sands, in 1910, although the War Office prohibited any flights over their gun emplacements on the same sands during World War One, when tanks were secretly tested here, too. There's a big marina here now, from which you can see over the Mersey to the Wirral. Which isn't, really, Liverpool, but quite interesting nonetheless. Let's tarry there awhile.

notes

1. See Lewis, *Illustrated History...*
2. Ibid.
3. See Whale, *Volume Two.*
4. Ibid.
5. See Slemen, *Strange Liverpool.*
6. See Mulhearn, *Volume Five: Leaving.*
7. Slemen, op.cit.
8. Whale, op.cit.
9. See Lewis, op.cit.
10. See 'Works Consulted'. Another crap title, I realise; but again, the quality of the writing within deserves a better one.
11. See the essay 'Cosmopolitan Liverpool' in 800.
12. Ibid.
13. In Part 3.
14. See Irving, *The Legend of Sleepy Hollow and Other Stories*, 'Works Consulted'.
15. Op.cit.
16. Printed in the newspaper on 6.11.07.
17. See Coles, *Both Sides of the River.*
18. See Robinson, *Seven Poets and a City.*
19. See Johnson, *Powder Wars.*
20. In his *Liverpool: Wondrous Place.*

WEST

'OVER THE WATER': LIVERPOOL?

Ah, Birkenhead. We've already established that this isn't Liverpool; it's big enough to have its own satellite towns and sense of separate civic identity, its own football team (in Tranmere Rovers), its own colleges, docks, shopping centres, etc. Plus many of its inhabitants don't take kindly to being called 'scousers', so we won't do them the disservice of doing so. When Daniel Defoe passed through it in the early 1700s, he referred to 'this narrow strip of land, rich, fertile, and full of inhabitants, though formerly, as others say, a mere waste and desolate forest, is called Wirall or by some Wirehall'; and when Tony Barnes, in his *Mean Streets*, investigated the place in the 1980s, he was told by a Professor Parker that 'the epicentre [of heroin dealing and usage] was in Birkenhead on the Wirral', and that in 1984 Merseyside Police 'set up a special squad that had some impact on the dealers who had turned Birkenhad into Britain's worst heroin blackspot'. The place continues to be associated with heavy and desperate drug use, and the concomitant crime (unfairly, of course; it's big enough, and human enough, to have many facets); Curtis 'Cocky' Warren, now imprisoned in Holland, had several properties here, bought with the colossal wealth he very quickly accrued through importing drugs; 'next to Warren, the Krays were pathetic minnows', observed *The Observer*. But we won't dwell on that, if we haven't got the time or the space to balance it out with a wider, and fairer, study. Birkenhead has a long history; fine examples of Regency architecture in Hamilton Square; an underground system; extensive docks. It can, and should, be treated as an entity separate from the larger conurbation over or under the Mersey; linked, certainly, but separate. So all we'll do here is nip into the Station Café for breakfast and a blether with Kevin Sampson, who lives nearby.

Kev's got an interesting history; author of a heap of novels and a non-fiction book (all published by Random House) and many and diverse articles, he once managed the band The Farm and edited the highly influential magazine *The*

End. When I meet him, over bacon and eggs and paving slabs of buttered toast, he's on something of a high as the filming of his first novel, *Awaydays*, has recently begun, and he's just come off the set. He's written the script himself, and has sustained a decade-long involvement with the film's development primarily because, he says, he 'cares about the book much more than my other stuff.... I have a visceral, personal relationship with it'. Set in a Birkenhead crumbling under Thatcherism, one of the film's principal actors has returned from Morocco with an orange suntan, by far the wrong skintone for 80s Merseyside, which shaded then (and still does now, except for WAGS and those ladies who work on perfume counters) towards the pale blue. As well as *Awaydays*, Kev's written a fictionalised dissection of the music industry (*Powder*); a brace of multiple-viewpoint gangster sagas (*Outlaws* and *Clubland*); a fictionalised history of the Toxteth riots (*Stars are Stars*); a kind of diary covering one football season from the personal point of view of a fanatical Liverpool fan (*Extra Time*). There've been others, too, each one furious and scabrous and funny, hilariously vile at times, swaggering, possessed of a very healthy contempt for convention. And to top it all off, he's a fine fellow to boot. He was born in Clatterbridge hospital, forty seven years ago, to a scouse mother and a Wallasey father, hence his blood, like the conurbation, is split by the Mersey, 'but the things that inspired me were all Liverpool – football, first and foremost; it became an obsession'. He grew up in Thingwall, on the Wirral; 'I wasn't an urchin from Speke or Scotland Road'. Music, too, obsessed him; 'I was very lucky to turn fifteen in 1977'. The famous Eric's club was open then, on Mathew Street in the city centre, and Kev's first gig experience was The Adverts; 'a life-changing one', he says. 'it showed me a Liverpool I didn't know existed'. The city's take on punk was a characteristically weird one, more Warholian Factory-like than anything else. Centre of the scene was the record shop Probe (since moved premises), whose staff introduced Kev to Toxteth, or Liverpool 8, 'another obsession', where he went to the Ebo

club on Princes Avenue, chiefly a black club, and threw himself into the area's counter-culture, with its dope parties and illegal shebeens. This, he says, 'was as much of an adventure as going to away games'. He was, he tells me, 'an outsider smitten with several sub-cultures and a determination to belong; the respect of people you look up to becomes the most important thing in the world, at that age'. Broke, he followed the Manchester-based band Joy Division to Paris; what meagre funds he had had been gotten from the contributions to cancer charities given by family and friends after his dad's death from that disease. He told himself that his father wouldn't've minded, which is probably true; they were, he says, very close. Kev's obsession with football came from him.

A wee digression, here; why Tranmere, though, in *Awaydays*? Why focus on their fans and not those of the two bigger clubs over the river? Well, it was easier to fictionalise, Kev tells me; those names associated with LFC at the time – Kenny Dalglish etc. – would always be 'bigger than the book'. Also, the Heysel and Hillsborough catastrophes meant that he was very sensitive to any portrayal of his club that could've been construed as negative; '*Awaydays* is a love story, but its arena, of course, is football violence'. Also, focussing on Tranmere Rovers allowed him to physically and mentally visit places like Halifax and Bury etc.; northern wastelands, devastated by Thatcherism. Cold and grey and bleak. But fertile and useful, for fiction. So then he worked in Cadbury's, in Moreton, like thousands of other people. His elder brother died, shockingly, in his sleep at age nineteen, when Kev was thirteen. As well as the profound sense of shock and loss, he left Kev a 'phenomenal' record collection. Before this, Kev liked to imagine himself as 'a normal working man', a shop steward or something, but the factory work rudely forced him to realise that 'the dreadful grind of working class life' wasn't for him. I know exactly what he's talking about. So he went to Sheffield university – English and American Literature. The interest in which came from where? Well, he'd had asthma since birth and so spent a lot of time off school, and libraries killed the boredom. He read *Sons and Lovers* at eleven and 'was hooked'. The sexy bits, obviously, had something to do with arousing his interest, and 'American writers seemed to get away with a lot more'. Inevitably, the feeling grew that, in allowing books to absorb him, he was being tugged away from his background, but he 'felt no guilt because of the strength of my conviction'. His dream job was to become a football writer for the *Liverpool Echo*. Cadbury's disabused him of the notion of any kind of working-class romance, and 'the idea of being answerable to and living my life to a time-table was a horrifying one'. Liverpool, he says, produces the ethic of 'work hard, yes, but on your own terms', and again I find myself nodding. On the terraces, Manchester United fans would sing 'get a job, you lazy bastards' and Kev would think 'why? What's the point in doing that?' In that, you can see why Thatcher expressed the wish for Liverpool to be cut away from the mainland and set adrift. It's wonderful. Work hard, but on your own terms. He left university with the ambition to write 'made even stronger... *Boys From the Blackstuff* had a huge impact'. He wrote the first draft of *Awaydays* at twenty-two, about seventy pages long, sent it to Penguin books 'and received an excoriating reply', so he 'ceremonially burnt it'. Yet the idea lingered. He began writing for the *NME* and *The Face* and other music and style magazines of the time, and his after-match routine took in certain pubs where people like Peter Hooton would drink, who was then editing *The End*, a magazine which, in Kev's words, 'dealt with unemployed life', and which, at Peter's invite, Kev began to write for, too. Peter set up The Farm, which Kev 'just drifted into managing'. On a whim, he entered a writing competition in *Cosmopolitan* magazine and won it, under the pseudonym Jenny White. He turned up to the awards, an event covered in the press, and on the strength of this was called for a meeting at Channel 4 and offered a script-reading job. He moved to Ladbroke Grove. Began to make a lot of money, 'a galvanic moment in a personal-development sense'. The Farm got back in touch, asking his advice on how to make a video. He embraced the acid house scene in London and introduced The Farm to a lot of contacts, which was 'more exciting than working in Channel 4'. Fame happened fast for the band, which 'became far more successful than it had any right to be'. Two singles reached number one, and in 1994 the band did a sixty-five-date tour of America which exhausted them and they felt it had come to a natural end; on a plane back from New York, they decided, 'nobly', as Kev says, to call it a day.

Also in 1994, Irvine Welsh's book *Trainspotting* appeared, hugely inspiring for Kev in the way it 'busted down the doors of middle-class deception... a voracious young crowd had been waiting for this'. So he re-wrote *Awaydays*. And it was quickly published. He's never stopped writing since.

We finish eating and Kev goes off to meet his partner, the novelist Helen Walsh, and their infant son, Leo. Kev and Helen and some other bloke called Griffiths make up a triumvirate of novelists who, according to Murphy and Rees-Jones, have as binding elements 'an explicit and unfictionalized version of [Liverpool's] geography [and] the use of 'scouse' as a mediator of their protagonist's experiences [which] can be seen as a linguistic marker which dramatizes what John Belchem refers to as a kind of 'self-referential otherness', which is a statement I'm happy with. Couldn't've put it better myself. What I'm also happy with is this torrent of creativity that the city is producing, has always produced, and which has always taken the stuff of Literature to be that which surrounds and is known and lived, the bricks that are bones and the mortar that is blood. It's like the city itself; if it has to be explained to you, then you'll never understand it. I'm repeating myself, I know, but it bears repeating.

Let's go to Wallasey.

WALLASEY: SAUNDERS LEWIS AND THE ISLAND OF THE WELSH

Wallasey, too, is dockland, its warehouses once more becoming desirable flats. On wasteland abutting one dock complex and behind wire mesh stands a huge and rusting submarine, the ack-ack guns still prominent on its decks. It's a somewhat shocking spectacle; the incongruity. Or if not that then the air of wrenched removal it exudes, the air of violent eviction that clings to things taken out of their elements. Like birds in cages. Fish gasping on a canal bank. O'Shea's pub, here. And, down by the Seacombe ferry terminal, the Liverpool skyline startles and stuns. Fabulous, unreal city which reminds me of

Baltimore or Brisbane, somewhere most un-British. If only the approach to the city from the airport could incorporate this view. Wallasey's main thoroughfare sports a huge and impressive town hall, but many of the shops around it are empty and boarded-up. The pubs seem to be the only establishments open, in fact. There's an air of belligerently run-down Englishness; St. George's flags being used as curtains on windows opaque with muck. This is 'the island of the Welsh', as the Anglo-Saxon has it ('Wealas sey'), and here, in 1893, on Witton Street (it's blue-plaqued now), Saunders Lewis was born, Welsh language activist, political militant (most famously as one of the three burners of the Penyberth bombing school in 1936), poet, playwright, and president of the Welsh Nationalist Party. There seems little Welsh influence abiding in Wallasey today (except the name) but it was, at one time, a strongly Cymric place. To quote Lewis from an interview given in 1960: "I am fairly certain that there was somewhere in the region of a hundred thousand Welsh-speaking Welshmen in Liverpool throughout my boyhood period. And I should say that at least half of these were monoglot Welsh-speakers who had hardly any English.... There was a monoglot Welsh-speaking community in Liverpool in my time, just as in a village somewhere in Anglesey. Thus it was not in English England that I was born at all." The Celtic-ness of Liverpool will continue to run throughout these pages, but whilst we're on the Welsh island here we might as well discuss Liverpool's Welshness, with Dr. D. Ben Rees as our guide, minister and author, lecturer, president of Cymru Lerpwl Cymdeithas Hanes (Liverpool Welsh Heritage Society). Born in Llanddewi Brefi, Dr. Ben has been living by Calderstones Park since 1968; he's recently retired from his ministerial position at Penny Lane Church on Heathfield Road, one of the five Welsh-speaking chapels left in the area. He'd encountered evacuees from Liverpool as a boy in Llanddewi Brefi during WW2 and so was impressed, at a very young age, by the depth of the city's Celtic roots. I ask him if the city still feels Welsh to him; no, he replies, but there is more awareness now of the Welsh presence in the city's history than there was in the 60s and 70s. The recent cancellation of the proposed eisteddfod in the city angered him; it was symptomatic of insularity and narrow-minded-ness. '800 years of Liverpool history?', he asks; 'that's not worth celebrating?' Similarly, people in Wales are baffled that he hasn't returned to the country following his retire-ment, but for him the borders

are porous and pellucid; he likes having 'two sides to my activities', and he feels 'rooted in both places. It's not a problem. Devolution never meant that you had to build a wall'. The Welsh-language events that Dr. Ben hosts in Liverpool often attract over 300 people, a number which impresses me, given the geographical proximity of the city to the Welsh-speaking heartland. The strongest Cymric communities are in Allerton, Mossley Hill, Waterloo, Bootle, Crosby, Litherland; 'all healthy', he says. He started writing about such communities in the mid-70s, his first being co-written with Merfyn Jones, *The Liverpool Welsh and Their Religion*, an overview of Calvinistic Methodism as practised in the city since William Llwyd opened his Pitt Street house for prayer meetings in 1782. It quotes Lord Mostyn, speaking in 1885 at the first meeting of the Liverpool Welsh National Society: 'Year after year, Liverpool became more than ever the metropolis of Wales'. The Liverpool Irish had a lot of material written about them, says Dr. Ben, but not so the Liverpool Welsh. Was this the spur, then?, I ask. Well, he says, the first Welsh chapel was built in Pall Mall (called, then, and still, at times, now, 'Little Wales') in 1784, so the bicentenary celebrations around this kickstarted him. Things snowballed after that, and the desire to chronicle Liverpool Welsh history expanded within him. His advantage was that he spoke Welsh, and a lot of material was in Cymraeg, part of a history that was being forgotten. Now, many non-Welsh groups on Merseyside are asking about the Welsh history of the place and discovering that Scotland Road wasn't just Irish. Ceredigion people and Pembrokeshire people were populating Vauxhall, too. The famous dockside Baltic Fleet pub on Wapping was opened by a Welshman. And the City of Culture award? The abysmal civic planning has been an unenviable feature, Dr. Ben says, but visitors to the city don't really seem to mind; they're anticipating its completion. Culturally, it's been successful, but the official C of C board has been 'hugely disappointing' (a lament I hear time and again). They've offered no financial support for his projects at all. Nevertheless, on the last Saturday in September 2008, Dr. Ben will present to the Maritime Museum a £3,000 model of the ship *Mimosa*, the first ship to sail for Patagonia, thereby establishing the Welsh colony there, out of Liverpool. His other books? Among them are *Wales: The Cultural Heritage* (1984), which looks at Welsh-language periodicals in Liverpool; two volumes of *The Welsh of Merseyside* (1997 and 2001), indispensable guides to a long line of Cymric Merseyside personages, including Owen Owens, builder and shop-owner, Alice Thomas Ellis, scriptwriter, and Ian

Rush, legendary LFC striker. These books look in greater depth at what I'm only, of necessity, touching on here; I recommend them highly. And Dr. Ben's most recent publication is as editor of *Alun Owen: A Liverpool Welsh Playwright*, which reprints Owen's great TV play *After the Funeral*, and is published by Allerton-based Modern Welsh Publications. He's an interesting figure, Owen; born in Menai Bridge in 1925, he moved to Liverpool aged eight, but was evacuated back to Anglesey during WW2. He travelled widely across the British Isles, became an actor, wrote plays for radio and then TV; his *No Trams to Lime Street* was broadcast in 1959. His work came to the attention of The Beatles, who commissioned him to write the script for the film *A Hard Day's Night*, which dragged him into fame. He continued to write until his death in 1994. His sense of Liverpool-ness was sharp; 'it's a Celtic town set down in Lancashire', he said, and 'its people have evolved an accent for themselves that they've borrowed from their Irish and Welsh grandfathers. The problem of identity, which is one of the greatest the twentieth century has produced, is exaggerated in Liverpool and the exaggeration makes it dramatic'. I've already mentioned how Gladys Mary Coles has credited Owen with the first representation of the scouse dialect in print, and she has this quote from Owen, from 1959, in her collection *Both Sides of the River*:

> I have fought for two years now to get plays performed in the Liverpool accent. I've had a battle to get a love scene played in the dialect. I was told the accent was ridiculous, comical, absurd and very ugly [but] people get married, live and die using the Liverpool accent, so I see no reason why they should not make love in [it].

Of vast cultural importance, this is. The Welsh contribution to the experience of the city can be traced through things other than religion or buildings. What Owen did was vital. Martin Doughty has a chapter on how the '100,000 houses constructed in Liverpool... during the nineteenth century were built mainly because of Welsh initiative and enterprise using materials imported from North Wales', and we've seen how this has become the fabric of the city in street nomenclature and architectural styles and construction materials etc., but edifices of a less palpable sort grew out of the Welsh influence, too. From Owen came Alan Bleasdale, Willy Russell, Phil Redmond, many others. So the city grows.

Tryweryn, though; we can't look at the relationship between Wales and Liverpool without looking at Tryweryn. In 1956, a proposal was put forward to flood the Tryweryn valley, outside Bala, in order to create a reservoir to provide the city of Liverpool with drinking water. This was not an empty valley; in it lay the village of Capel Celyn, a small but healthy community, described in a letter to the *Daily Post* by a Gertrude Armfield: "The way of life nurtured in these small villages which serve, with their chapel and school as focal points, a wider population – this way of life has a quality almost entirely lost in England and almost unique in the world. It is one where a love of poetry and song, the spoken and written word, still exists, and where recreation has not to be sought after and paid for, but is organised locally in home, chapel and school." Opposition to the plan was huge; thirty-five out of thirty-six Welsh MP's voted against it, there were mass demonstrations in Wales and Liverpool. Nevertheless, Liverpool MP Bessie Braddock at the time told the Commons: 'Everyone deplores the fact that in the interests of progress, some people must suffer. But that is progress', and the villages were evicted and the valley was drowned. A BBC 2 Wales programme – *The Drowning of a Village* – broadcast in March 2006 expressed what this act meant for the people; Rhodri Gwynllian Jones, a child at the time, recalled that 'the trees screamed. I can never forget the trees screaming'. He watched as his school was flattened by bulldozer; 'no care or dignity, it was ripped to shreds'. It was an act of sheer colonial thuggery, unalleviated by guilt or shame, exacerbated, indeed, by the fact that the domestic water needs of Liverpool had for a long time been met by the reservoir at Vyrnwy; Tryweryn's water, it turned out, was to be used for industry or re-sale. The arrogance and avarice is staggering. Yet the council should not be presumed to speak for its people; the demonstrations in Liverpool were large and vociferous. Liverpool City Council issued a public apology to Wales in 2005 – when, of course, crucial Capital of Culture votes were required – and then got on with its usual venal and self-serving business, as councils everywhere always do. Dr. Ben sees this apology as 're-opening the sore', the wound that, perhaps, had almost closed in the Liverpool-Welsh psyche; this was instrumental, he says, in the cancellation of the eisteddfod. It was an indefensible act, and will forever remain that way. What it did, however, was to allow in to Welsh politics a needed element of militancy; 'it was at this point that violence entered Welsh nationalist politics', wrote Gwyn A. Williams, specifically violence against property which, in my opinion, introduced a strength and a coherence into that arena which led directly to recognition. Out of

Trywreryn's waters rose the Senedd. That notwithstanding, would that Capel Celyn was still populated by people and not eels; but anger and insult can be wellsprings of advancement. Images from another programme, the 6:30 p.m. evening news following on from the aforementioned programme; Councillor Storey, in the chambers, offers his apology: 'Liverpool has a very strong Welsh community still [and] I think it's important to the links between Liverpool and Wales that this apology is given. I hope that people don't see it as just a gesture, it certainly isn't, it's about recognising the mistakes that were made in the past'. Cut to a pub interior in the business district. Neat man, white shirt, black jacket, trained hair. In an accent without the slightest trace of scouse he says: 'I think it's a total waste of time, energy, and the city council should be doing something more important than making forty-year-old apologies'. Then an older man with a lined and serious face, propping up the bar, dark serious eyes, forcefully delivers these words in a thick local brogue: 'I think it was a liberty, what they done. What rights have any council, any town, got to take the identity of another town, in another country, away from them? They have none'. This is the man I like. He understands that, when people with power and money want more power and money, they truly don't care how many lives they throw catastrophes into. Think about that; they really, really don't care. Anyway; the writers continue to appear. Nathan Jones, Wrexham-born, now lives in Liverpool. Part of the Mercy collective – a loose grouping of writers and artists and musicians – Nathan produces superb short pieces, often written in scouse/Wenglish dialect, as in his poem 'Cwm bie yer':

> Attoo watch in 'orror as it went on –
> when she went out to the pub and walked in,
>   and girls stopped their clonc and men their fightin
> to stare at my first love's round ripe breasts,
> and I had to go home to my bed with my belly
>   It was so terrible lonely in my 'ead.

And he's not Welsh, but Ramsey Campbell lives in Wallasey, one of the few truly frightening horror writers working in Britain, if not the world. Honestly, he's scary; think M.R. James with striplighting and public transport. He's been around for a while and is fairly prolific, so I won't list his books here, but Gladys Mary Coles's anthology *Both Sides of the River* contains a vicious little clout of a story called 'Calling

Card'. If you like the sensations of crawling skin and prickling scalp, then he's your man. Andy Sawyer's essay 'Ramsey Campbell's Haunted Liverpool' assesses how Campbell 'uses setting to express both a series of personal and social anxieties and a more existential response to Pascal's terrifying 'infinite immensity of spaces whereof I know nothing", and I can't disagree, even if I was sure what he meant. I wrote Campbell a letter once, when I was very young, and his reply was warm and friendly and encouraging. You don't forget these things, do you?

NEW BRIGHTON

Seaside resort. Tad run-down, still. Caught in gloriously garish eye-blasting technicolour in Martin Parr's photography collection *The Last Resort*, the purulent and penurious classes at play, an apocalypse of litter, gulls like harpies from hell. He's been attacked as a voyeur for this collection, Parr. It's a moot point. But a compelling book. As a child, I'd kneel at the edges of the rock-pools here and study the anemones; I'd drop miniscule pieces of shell into their maws and marvel as they softly but hungrily closed around the object. The Napoleonic Wars have left a legacy here; the ground beneath the fun-fair is warrened with tunnels used as storage for shells etc., and beneath Mother Redcap's pub is another network of tunnels 'in which could be hidden not only contraband goods [from the plentiful smuggling operations that occurred around here] but sailors and others keeping out of the clutches of the notorious press-gang'. And

Fort Perch – the sandstone castle out on the plinth in the Mersey – was built as a gun emplacement during the same war. It's kind of a museum now, but not open when I visit. Mainly private accommodation, really. During the American Civil War, a Union ship came to shell Liverpool, apparently, to discourage cotton trading with the Confederacy, but the Fort Perch battery saw it off – the only shot fired on British soil in the War Between the States. This is a story I've heard many times, and is widely believed, but I've been unable to corroborate it. What is provable, however, is Liverpool's contribution to the Confederacy war effort; battleships, including the *Alabama* and the *Banshee*, were illegally constructed in Liverpool dockyards.

On the promenade is a large chunk of sandstone bearing carvings that appear to blend Celtic/Scandinavian styles. An information plaque tells me that in 893 AD Irish Norsemen invaded the Wirral and left behind stones such as this and place-names like 'Thurstaston', from 'Thor's Stone'. Which is interesting enough. But New Brighton itself, as a town? Well, y'know; it's candy-floss and cones of chips and bleeping arcades and all that sort of seasidey stuff which you'd imagine was left behind in the 1950s. A lot of money has been invested to turn it again into a popular attraction, but it still remains cheaper to go to Spain. And it's not really Liverpool, anyway. So let's leave it.

ROCK FERRY

This area has always had a reputation for roughness, with some justification; I attended a day-release college here in my teens and remember the place as being home to mistrust and suspicion and the simmering violence that comes from that peculiarly English attitudinal default setting of anger. On my return, I notice long ranks of abandoned houses, all windows steel-shuttered, the squatter-deterring messages 'ELEC OFF' painted on them all; at the edge of the scrappy bombsite wasteground by the small row of shops a man berates his toddler child: 'Geroff the fucken road! NOW!' And, waiting at traffic lights, a three-legged and tail-less cat jerks across the road in front of the car. Honestly. I'm not making this stuff up.

Nathaniel Hawthorne, famously the author of *The Scarlet Letter*, lived here for a time, in his capacity as American ambassador to Great Britain, in the mid 1850s. His *English Notebooks* record his

experiences of the area, and Gladys Mary Coles, as usual, has dug up some fascinating excerpts; it appears that Rock Ferry then was, on Saturdays at least, a place of galas and festivals, attracting 'pale-looking people... from considerable distances in the interior', Hawthorne wrote; 'I believe... from Preston'. He watches the 'huge steamer' *Great Britain*, bound for Australia, take on supplies at Rock Ferry landing; he resides for a month at the Rock Ferry Hotel, 'a comfortable place [where] we have been well-victualled, and kindly treated'. From here, he witnessed the maritime business of the port over the river; split-masted vessels hobbling into dock after storms, that kind of thing. The importance of the ferries across the river was deeply impressed upon him, and the place their business had in the area's human traffic; 'I don't know any place that brings all classes into contiguity, on equal ground, so completely as the waiting-room at Rock Ferry, on these frosty days.... It is almost always crowded; and I rather suspect that many persons, who have no fireside elsewhere, creep in here and spend the most comfortable part of their day'. The poverty in Liverpool shocked and depressed him; 'I never walk through these streets without feeling as if I should catch some disease; but yet there is... a sense of being in the midst of life, and of having got hold of something real, which I do not find in the better streets'.

Malcolm Lowry, author of one of the last century's finest novels in *Under the Volcano*, liked to claim that he was born close to the place where Hawthorne stayed and 'where Herman Melville had announced to Hawthorne his desire to be annihilated'. He left Liverpool at an early age – twenty or so – and drifted, unhappy and alcoholic and self-destructive, across much of the world, settling for some years in Vancouver, before returning to Sussex where he died, aged forty-nine, in 1957. Liverpool, though, remained inside him: 'a terrible city', Bowker notes, that gave Lowry the abiding image 'of the lunatic city inside which he was to feel trapped and was to suffer, and that of the pathway to the sea and the ocean voyage, the risk-laden escape route from lunacy into uncertainty'. Murphy and Rees-Jones refer to one of Lowry's early stories, 'Goya the Obscure', in which Liverpool appears as a 'haunted city of sexual sickness and fear', yet always exerting 'a strange enchantment'. Here's Lowry's little poem 'Trinity':

> Imprisoned in a Liverpool of self
> I haunt the gutted arcades of the past.
> Where it lies on some high forgotten shelf
> I find what I was looking for at last.
> But now the shelf has turned into a mast
> And now the mast into an uptorn tree
> Where one sways crucified twixt two of me.

Sad and desperate and self-loathing and moving, like much of Lowry's work which, puzzlingly, has of late fallen into neglect, although the Wirral-based author Michael Carson (or Michael Wherly, in personal emails) has tried valiantly to arrest this with his series of Lowry-themed 'Walks and Talks', which all 'stay close to the sea. This is as it should be. There are few works by Malcolm Lowry that do not include ships and the sea, lighthouses that invite the storm, rescued seals, piers, petrified forests, ships in bottles, sailors and shorelines. He was happiest by the sea'. Michael also delivered a lecture in Liverpool in 2006 entitled 'A Merseyside Writer Responds to Malcolm Lowry', which is an intense and touching piece of work, deeply personal, examining one particular heart's reaction to the properties of both the creative urge and alcohol to simultaneously sustain and destroy. Had I more time and space, I'd look at it in depth. But I don't.

PORT SUNLIGHT: MODEL VILLAGE

This is a peculiar place. It's a 'model industrial village', founded by the soap manufacturer W.H. Lever (later Lord Leverhulme) in 1888 for the factory workers of his firm Lever Brothers. Hugely influential on the garden city movement. The factory produced soap and washing powder and detergents and the housing was quite luxurious, given the low level of the worker's wages. The village – think Ealing on Merseyside – contained a church and a theatre and an art gallery but no pub; Lever was staunchly temperance (there's one there now, however, called the Bridge Inn). The idea was to make the houses all different; uniform colours, yes, but architecturally disparate. I'm torn between finding it pretty on the one hand and scarily Orwellian on the other. There are green spaces and trees and boulevards and statuary. In the background is a constant buzz of traffic; industrial estates seethe and sprawl nearby.

Hubbard and Shippobottom's book *A Guide to Port Sunlight Village* (2003) offers a brief, but interesting, history of the place and of William Hesketh Lever himself. Born in Bolton in 1851 into a background of Liberalism, Nonconformity, and abstinence. Began to specialise in the marketing of soap in 1884, producing Sunlight Soap, which became hugely successful very quickly, necessitating new premises; the marshland site at Port Sunlight provided the location. 'Prompted by squalor seen in industrial Britain and by the social conscience which family background had engendered, Lever was determined from the first that a new factory would be accompanied by model housing for his employees', write Hubbard and Shippobottom, illustrating this text with 1890s photographs of the slum conditions extant in Port Sunlight, startling compared to the place as it is now. Architecture was a passion of Lever's, as was, to an extent, public benefaction; he was instrumental in saving the city centre Bluecoat School from demolition. 'Dictatorial and vain, but astonishingly generous....

Ruthless tycoon and autocrat, patron and philanthropist', a man with a taste for the sumptuous but 'ascetic' in his habits, driven by improving working conditions in industry but also by inflating his bank balance; these dichotomies can be seen in the physical village itself, which embodies two separate traditions in the history of town planning – the picturesque on the one hand

and the amelioration of working-class housing conditions on the other. I'd say that Lever got the balance about right, really. A tweeness does creep in, inevitably (part of the village is called 'Poet's Corner', for God's sake), but the overall feel is one of relaxation. And the centrepiece of the village – the Lady Lever Art Gallery – is magnificent; founded in 1922 to house Lever's huge private art collection (but also to  display it for the public eye; contemplation of art, he believed, could improve the soul), he named it after his late wife as a kind of memorial. It's a big, pillared and portico'd, staircased and cupola'd building with a huge collection of Victorian paintings, pre-Raphaelite works, eighteenth century furniture and, apparently, the world's most extensive collection of Wedgewood Jasperware. After walking around I pick up a copy of the latest catalogue in the shop. There are several Joshua Reynolds oils. A Gainsborough. A few George Stubbs, Turners and Constables. A brilliant Francis Derwent Wood bust called 'The Penitent Thief'. The furniture is inviting; I want to sit on it and sip port and sherry and receive guests. Some powerful tapestries too; the Mortlake stuff is superb.

But enough, here. We're not, as I've said, in Liverpool proper. So let's go back to the city. Into the city.

THREADS

WATER AND DOCKS

In Barry Unsworth's great novel *Sacred Hunger*, he tells the story of the *Liverpool Merchant*, Liverpool's first slave ship. It sailed to Africa where it took aboard 220 slaves and dropped them off in Barbados in exchange for rum and sugar and tobacco to take back to Britain (this was referred to as the 'Triangular Trade'). The ship was owned, partly, by Sir Thomas Johnson, who was responsible for the separation of the parish of Liverpool from that of Walton-on-the-Hill and became known as the founder of modern Liverpool. By the end of the eighteenth century, Liverpool controlled over 41% of European and 80% of Britain's slave commerce. Unsworth has a character expound on the geographical suitability of Liverpool to the trade in people:

> I tell you, if God picked this town up in the palm of his hand and studied where best in England to set her down for the Africa trade, he would put her back exactly where she is, exactly where she stands at present.... Why should God want to do Liverpool a kindness? .... The future of Liverpool lies with the Africa trade. It is potent and obvious to the meanest understanding.

And indeed it did. The docks were built on human suffering, sunk into the soul of the world. At the Herculaneum Dock, at the city's more southerly end, beneath what used to be the terminus for the overhead railway, the casements can still be seen, with steel rings bolted into the walls to which slaves would be secured whilst awaiting transportation. William Roscoe, in 1787, published his *The Wrongs of Africa* and spoke in favour of abolition at Parliament in 1806, shortly after which he returned to Liverpool and had to be protected by friends on horseback from seamen armed with bludgeons. Herman Melville, writing in the 1830s, reflected on how the city was brought to prosperity on the back of the slave trade, and how it led to the construction of the docks:

long China walls of masonry;

vast piers of stone.... The extent and solidity of these structures, seemed equal to that what I had read of the old Pyramids of Egypt.... In magnitude, cost, and durability, the docks of Liverpool... surpass all others in the world... for miles you may walk along [the] river- side, passing dock after dock, like a chain of immense fortresses.[1]

Shortly after this, Elizabeth Gaskell wrote about the docks in her novel *Mary Barton*, pointing out that the sense of superiority Liverpudlians felt towards other cities, notably Manchester, stemmed, in part, from the docks' presence, and the sea they serve:

Mary did look, and saw down an opening made in the forest of masts... the glorious river, along which white-sailed ships were gliding with the ensigns of all nations... telling of the distant lands, spicy or frozen, that sent to that mighty mart for their comforts or their luxuries.

Visually, the docks still retain their magnificence, in parts, although of course their trade has dwindled exponentially. Yet they remain in the city's central nervous system, and the Three Graces on the skyline abide as one of the world's most distinctive and recognised city-scapes. One of them, the Liver Building, bears the city's emblem, the cormorant-type bird with a sprig of seaweed in its beak[2], the 'guardian of shipping and sailors, commerce and counting-houses, mud and merchandise, tar and traffic, pitch and prosperity, and all other ingredients that contribute to the filling up of his pool', to quote Belchem quoting the 1847 *Liverpool Lion* in *800*. They're extraordinary sculptures, these birds, 'enormous, enigmatic, and unintentionally amusing', to quote the brilliant book *Lore of the Land*[3]:

eighteen feet high and with outstretched wings spanning twenty-four feet.... It is said... that they were meant to be eagles, the symbol of St. John, but were so badly designed that the luckless artist killed himself in shame[4].... Other[s] suggest that the statues represent two enormous [prehistoric] birds which inhabited the pool from which Liverpool takes its name, and had to be slaughtered before the city could be built – or, alternatively, became its guardians.

One fact we have about them is that they were erected in 1910, the work of German artist Carl Bernard Bartels, whose biographical details are lost, possibly erased from the city's archives during World War One.

And the docks now? Some of them are still in commercial operation, but most are given up to the tourist trade, exclusive housing, or various cultural pursuits. The Albert Dock famously houses one branch of the Tate Gallery, which hosted the Turner Prize ceremony of 2007 and contains work by Bridget Riley, Edgar Degas and Francis Bacon; Rodin's 'The Kiss' takes your breath away in the foyer. Ron Jones's glossy little book *The Albert Dock Liverpool* gives an extensively-researched history of the dock, from its founding in the mid 1800s by Pontefract-born Jesse Hartley to its boom-period to its abandonment and decay to its resurrection, which has 'been credited with being the catalyst for much of the new development that has taken place'. Hartley was sixty-one years old when he started work on Albert Dock, which is kind of astonishing. It was modelled on St. Katherine's Dock in London, designed so that goods could be unloaded straight from ship to bonded warehouse, no waiting around on the quayside because 'the Liverpool system', as Jones says, 'or... lack of system [meant] that fraud, evasion, pilferage and, let's not mince words, downright plunder, was being undertaken on a massive scale'[5]. Hartley went on to design the Stanley and Wapping Docks, 'heroically scaled', according to Giles and Hawkins[6], who offer a fascinating illustrated history of

Liverpool's dock storage systems; I never thought the design and construction of warehouses, and the differences between the private and bonded varieties, could be so interesting. I'm serious; I was gripped. Well, fairly tightly clasped, at least.

I re-visit the Albert Dock on Derby Day – Liverpool v. Everton at Goodison Park. I should be at the game or at least in a pub watching it, but the Pumphouse on the quay here isn't showing it. Not cogent to the tourist trade, y'see. So informative texts come at regular intervals to my mobile and I'm told about Dirk Kuyt's equaliser for Liverpool whilst I'm in the Warhol Room. I let out an involuntary and happy yelp. And do so again later when Kuyt gets the winner with a last-minute penalty. Joy and uproar. I can taste the beer already. And be avoiding any blue shirts for a week or two.

The Albert Dock of late 2007 is all cafés that sell speciality coffees and paninis. Souvenir shops with window displays of clichéd tat. The Blue Bar and Baby Cream, WAG hangouts both, bottled tan and bling. Today, the quayside access to the Museum of Liverpool Life is closed and I can't find the signposted alternative entrance; the arrow points nowhere. Ridiculous. So I amble along the dockside between the river and the million-pound flats that look out over it. I imagine footballers and soap stars and pop stars behind those windows, watching me shamble past. The new pavilion building being built here, which from the air resembles a giant butterfly cake, swells up suddenly from the wharf in an abrupt bulge of glass and criss-crossed steel girdering and a racket of power tools and pong of paint. No way, I think, will this be ready for 2008 (but, remarkably, it is). The Chavasse Park development nearby, over the Goree, is more of the same but bigger and with a lot more cranes. This activity, this constructive buzzing, maybe there's an echo in it of the way these docks once were – the ceaseless activity, the endless noise of throat and engine and hammer and saw. The million different voices. And there's a group of workers, yellow vests and hard hats, sitting on the dockside, drinking mugs of tea and smoking, their faces a mixture of black and white and Chinese. Things progress.

I go for a cappuccino and a toffee florentine at Costa Coffee. Sit outside so I can smoke. 'Yellow Submarine' starts up from somewhere and my heart sinks and I realise with sudden horror that I've chosen a table next to the entrance to the Beatles Story. Of all the cafés in all the docklands and I choose this one. Time I wasn't here. I leave and follow the quay around to the north, walk miles, and find a sign: 'EXIT CLOSED. USE ALTERNATIVE EXIT ADJAS-CENT (sic) TO THE BEATLES STORY'. Oh bloody hell. It's raining now as well. I retrace my steps. 'Paperback Writer' now, God help me. But at least I see a couple of cormorants on the quayside, their wings spread like vampire's cloaks to dry in the barely-there sun. Little black Liver Birds mirroring their bigger steel cousins up there in the falling sea-mist. I find a way out of the dock, go up Hanover Street towards the Prohibition Bar and the old Post Office buildings at the foot of Bold Street. Hanover Street is one long building site. Smell of raw cement.

DIVIDED CITY: FOOTBALL

Everton Football Club; founded 1878, ground Goodison Park (capacity 40,200), nicknamed 'The Toffees' because the original Everton mints were first made in Mother Noblett's Toffee Shop, based in Everton, and were striped like Everton FC's original kit (they play in blue and white now, of course). The liverpoolcity/sports/everton website says that 'the club's roots lie in an English Methodist congregation called New Connexion', and goes on to talk about St. Domingo's and the rent dispute and all that, which we've already discussed. Apparently, according to the site, 'Goodison is the only ground in the world that features a church in its grounds – St. Luke the Evangelist at the corner of the Main Stand and the Gwladys Street End', but then it also states that the Liverpool/Everton rivalry is 'one that is generally perceived as being more respectful than many other "derbies" in English football', so I don't know whether to believe it.

EFC calls itself 'The People's Club', which is what a team calls itself when it's not doing as well as its same-city rivals. Ho ho. To be fair, Evertonians I meet stress the approachability of their team's players; the club hosts lunches, for example, at which players and fans sit side-by-side. The historical idol is Dixie Dean, whose record of sixty goals in a thirty-two-game season remains unsurpassed, and is incredible. Their modern folk hero is the Scot Duncan Ferguson, although he's retired now. Wayne Rooney *was* shaping up for hero status, when he scored and pulled up his jersey to reveal on his vest the words 'ONCE A BLUE ALWAYS A BLUE', which held true for a few months until the red of Manchester offered him more money. The barracking from his ex-fans that he received on his return to Goodison led him to whinge to the press (you'd imagine that his wages of eighty grand a week or thereabouts would go some way towards palliating the hurt he felt at this terrible expression of betrayal), which led of course to more barracking, which led to him running to the stand in which his family were sitting and ostentatiously kissing the Manchester United badge on his jersey. This, to me, encapsulates everything that is wrong with modern football. No humility, no dignity, and absolutely no class.

DIVIDED CITY: RELIGION

Flashback to a summer about fifteen years ago

Something's going on in the city centre. Black people with dread-locks and wearing animal-print capes and odd high hats. Talking in southern American accents. Drumming, insistent and fervid and incantatory, in side streets, often accompanied by dancing which seems touched by ecstasy and delirium. This is odd. I see a sign saying 'Po' Boys' above a barrel of bubbling oil and I ask for one. The guy grins at me as he splits French bread.

That awk-cent, cher. I love this place.

He fishes some hissing things out of the boiling oil – oysters, deep-fried – and stuffs them into the bread with sliced tomatoes and shredded lettuce, squirts mayonnaise and shakes hot pepper sauce into it, wraps it in paper and gives it to me. It is one of the most delicious things I have ever eaten.

Some hours later I am in the Casablanca basement bar, taking advantage of the offer on Cockspur rum. I see those people again; the animal-print cloaks and the interesting accessories which appear to utilise bones. They are surrounded by locals and are animated, laugh-ing, dispensing potions, dancing. I ask an older man at the bar what's going on. He waves his glass at a large, fat man, wearing a necklace of what looks like teeth, holding court to a rapt crowd at the edge of the dancefloor, in the flashing lights. *See him?*, the older guy says. *He's some kind of voodoo priest. Was flying over to London for some kind of convention from New Orleans like and he comes into British airspace and starts going on about how he can feel something pulling at his feet. Looks out the window; sees a coastal city. It's pulling him down, calling to him. Stewardess tells him he's flying over Liverpool. So soon as he's done in London he gets on the first train to Lime Street with his crew. Says the city called to him. Said he had to listen to it.*

★

There's an eerie, almost foreboding spirituality to the

city. The many dark spires of the old and blackened churches piercing the creeping haar. The two cathedrals, staring each other down. Unpious and unsanctimonious, hearts here follow a yearning parabola in the only ways they know how, with unmeek voices and burdened backs. There's little that settle for the middling, here. There's little fast contentment in the palms that bleed and the sides that slide open or the mud-clogged and sodden murmurings of the river-spirits. Which only some ears can hear.

GHOSTS/GUILT/SLAVERY

In the 1990s, the author Caryl Phillips, as research for his book on the slave trade *The Atlantic Sound*, visited Liverpool. The city, and its denizens, had already presented him with ugly, problematic experiences; he'd been called 'a nigger' by visiting football fans and noted the refusal of Everton to sign black players (changed now, of course). 'There was something disturbing about Liverpool', he writes. Then, ten years after the Toxteth riots, he watched a Liverpool/Everton game on the TV and noticed that 'not only were there countless non-white faces on display, but the captain of Liverpool was a black man.... I did not recognise this suspiciously multi-racial Liverpool'. So he decides to tour the city with a guide called Stephen, a man passionately engaged with 'Liverpool's hidden history [and] its relationship to the slave trade'. Shortly before this, there had been a well-meaning but misguided campaign to change the name of the Goree, a dockland street, as it referred to an island off the coast of Senegal where a slave

fort/prison once stood. Stephen objected; by 'renaming the street in this manner the city would be endorsing the historical amnesia which already prevailed'. He tells Caryl that the city 'doesn't want to acknowledge' its history, that it has a 'guilt problem'. Caryl becomes unsure about the suitability of Stephen as a guide when he, Stephen, launches into an anti-Semitic rant.

So Phillips wanders the city

alone. Stands in the square behind the town hall (the building's stonework still bearing the pockmarks of Luftwaffe strafing) known as Exchange Flags, where maritime trade was conducted in the eighteenth century, 'the stock exchange of its day'. He regards the statue there, 'a powerful sculpture of four semi-clad and chained men'; it's meant to commemorate four of Nelson's victories, but the 'shackled prisoners in poses of anguish and resignation... recall Pietro Tacca's bronze slaves', to quote Terry Cavanagh[7]. The symbolism is obvious. Phillips enters the town hall where he rapidly 'feels glutted with the visual evidence of excess' and gives in to a 'strange feeling of disgust'. He crosses town to St. George's Hall, passing on the way young homeless people holding cardboard signs that read: 'Hungry. Need food'. 'Why does everybody seem clinically depressed?', he asks.

There's not much in Phillips's chapter on Liverpool that lifts it above the glum and grim. He visits the slavery museum, but is underwhelmed, and he concludes that it

> is disquieting to be in a place where history is so physically present, yet so glaringly absent from people's consciousness. But where is it any different? Maybe this is the modern condition, and Liverpool is merely acting out this reality with an honest vigour. If so, this dissonance between the two states seems to have engendered both a cynical wit and a clinical depression in the souls of Liverpool's citizens.

It's changed, though, in recent years, and the Capital of Culture award shares only some of the credit; the rising cohesion in a collective black consciousness can be celebrated, as can the increased awareness of the ongoing narrative of human history. The International Slavery Museum Research Institute and Education Centre will, in 2010, move into the Dock Traffic Office in the Albert Dock, a grand and imposing building; 'it will become, over time', the promotional leaflet tells me, 'one of the world's leading research insti-

tutes in the field of human rights'. Its director is Richard Benjamin, a descendant of Guyanese slaves. In his *Observer* review of the exhibition, journalist Stephen Bayley[8] called it 'exemplary.... Such harrowing material cannot be called beautiful, but it is fascinating   and thought-provoking... [It can't] redress sinful injustices of the past, but [now] hard-pressed Liverpudlians can salvage some moral dignity from this dark history', for the museum also contains references to Roscoe, 'a brave, pioneering abolitionist, [so] if Liverpudlians were mired by the start of the slave trade, they also distinguished themselves by ending it'. Another journalist, Tristram Hunt, continues the theme: 'Liverpool confronts [its] past', he writes[9], with a 'progressive, vigorous approach to the past [that] has led the debate away from the dead end of apologies and guilt'.

The problems remain, of course; there are none more aware of this than Antony Walker's bereaved and heartbroken family. But these acts of commemorative remembrance are not being foisted on the public; there seems to be a genuine desire to be informed. So hope does a little bit of springing, doesn't it?

REGENERATION/CITY OF CULTURE?

A new building is going up on the seafront, which is a designated UNESCO World Heritage site. It'll be a museum, it'll cost £65m, and its purpose will be to 'celebrate the rich heritage of Liverpool, from prehistory to its days as a hub of the British empire, to the Beatles and Alan Bleasdale'[10]. Denise Fergus, mother of James Bulger, was understandably, and naturally, furious when she found out that the exhibits would make mention of her son; David Fleming, director of National Museums Merseyside, has denied that this will ever happen. 'We are launching a project which will change Liverpool for ever', he goes on to say; it will be 'the biggest purpose-built English national museum for almost a century'[11].

So regeneration goes on, in concrete and controversy. Michael Wherly, who we met earlier, sums it up in a personal email: the Capital of Culture board

> goes on about 'chaos' being at the centre of Liverpool culture. That seems to me to be making a virtue out of necessity. The very word 'culture' is messy, chaotic and covers quite wretched areas of the waterfront. To laud the messiness could be interpreted as lauding the beauties of the rubbish dump. My hope for the year is that people will see the river in all its moods.... The culture is there. What will be produced, what drops off the back of the culture lorry from elsewhere, what PC quangos manage to compile... it will be but a garnish to what exists already in the substance of the place.

I'll hear this over and over again; calls to resist the importation of some committee's idea of what 'culture' is into the city. It can't be defined, of course, and it's in the play of sunlight on water as much as in what people achieve in terms of expression. Kenn Taylor, of the *Mercy* collective[12], emails me (punctuation sic throughout) that a certain pub 'in the city now displays a sign saying: 'People Wearing Tracksuits WILL NOT Be Admitted'. Kenn goes on: 'This is Liverpool: home of the tracksuit! For the people who have enjoyed their rites of passage within [that pub's] walls, lost their virginity in the alleyway up the side, it is a slap in the face: the natives of this city and their precious moments in time; frozen and forgotten.... Where was the interest, the recognition then, when this cultural city extraordinaire and its people really needed support? It seems this history is being painted over with tapas'.

Hard to disagree. Even if I wanted to.

notes

1. See *Redburn*.
2. As some say. Others insist that the bird is a phoenix or a roc – that is, entirely mythical.
3. See Westwood and Simpson, 'Works Consulted'.
4. Remember this detail when, later, we get to St. George's Hall. There's an interesting coincidence.
5. Indeed, crime, both petty and organised, was one commodity exported from the Liverpool entrepôt. Owney Madden, friends with Stan Laurel, lover of Mae West (who said of him, 'hmmm. So sweet yet so vicious'), owner of New York's famous Cotton Club in the 20s and 30s, was 'a product of the Liverpool docks and Hell's Kitchen – two of the world's toughest neighbourhoods' (see Repetto, 'Works Consulted'). He was actually born in Leeds in 1891 but moved to Liverpool with his family at a young age, a city which, 'like New York,

was a melting pot. People were friendly, shouldering poverty with a cocky resilience', to quote Nown (see 'Works Consulted'). Nown's book isn't good – it's a poorly-written hagiography – but it'll do, in the absence of any alternative, as a guide to the immigrant who became one of the biggest gangsters in Prohibition-era America. In Coppola's film *The Cotton Club*, Madden was played by Bob Hoskins. With a daft accent.

6. See *Storehouses of Empire*.
7. In his *Public Sculpture of Liverpool*.
8. See his 'Barbarity begins at home', 'Works Consulted'.
9. In his 'A bold step away from the dead end of guilt and apology', 'Works Consulted'.
10. See Ward, 'From the Beatles to James Bulger', 'Works Consulted'.
11. Quoted ibid.
12. Which he describes in an email as 'a guerrilla art collective [that] carries out conceptual anarchy and cultural mischief in warehouses, bus stops, and galleries'.

CITY
CENTRAL

TOXTETH: WAR TOUR

Bohemia. Somali Town. No-go area. Toxteth's been synonymous with rioting and civic deprivation and disturbance since 1981 when, on the night of 5th July, the place exploded. Crippling unemployment married to institutionalised racism and a catastrophic breakdown in police community relations. Not only disaffected black people, 'as involvement in the disruption also spread to local whites, as the dispossessed of the inner city rose into a poor people's revolt against authority'[1]. CS gas was used in the two weeks of rioting; a disabled young man, David Moore, was killed; hundreds of police and civilians were injured and £11m worth of damage done to public buildings, homes, and shops. Thatcher's government appointed a special Minister for Merseyside in Michael Heseltine supported by the Merseyside Task Force; to be fair, Belchem records that this did create 'over 1,000 jobs through the re-development of 35 hectares of previously derelict railway sidings into the Wavertree Technology Park [and] dramatically changed [the city's] features by encouraging the adoption of a regeneration strategy based more on tourism, leisure, housing and tertiary employment'[2]. Which is something. But did I hear the words 'too little, too late'? Or the word 'sop'?

Anyway, the place *has* changed, now. Or rather, grown. Little of the rioting's scarification remains, but it still retains that alluring aura of secretive pleasures and veiled danger which makes it unique, and exciting. John Cornelius, in his book *Liverpool 8*[3], sums up its singular identity:

> I always maintained that Liverpool 8 was not so much a place as a state of mind; an unpunctuated state of mind that wrapped up the pubs the shops the art college the cathedral the early mornings the late nights the dawn chorus the clubs the police vans the architecture the poets the musicians the prostitutes the students the down and out the luxurious tasteful homes... the seedy bedsits of the failures the has-beens and the never-will-bes... the alcoholics the shallow poseurs the stunning geniuses who never got a chance... into one cerebral parcel.

Liverpool 8, as a postcode, includes not just Toxteth but Princes Park and the Holy Land[4] and the Cast-Iron Shore and Chinatown and Edge Hill as well. Faulkner Square is within it, a popular filming spot due to its cobbles and Regency housing, standing in recently for London and Prague and Moscow and Dublin and featuring in numerous whiskery Dickens adaptations. Levi Tafari lives here, poet and performer; his latest book is *From the Page to the Stage*. And I still return to a peculiar anthology published in 1990 called *Undercurrents: An Illustrated Anthology from the Inner City*[5], with its striking portfolio of graffiti photographs: RESCUE ME, says one, MAGICK FOR ALL another, BLOW YOUR BASTARD BRAINS OUT OK and I HATE THE POLICE AND THE SOIL WE TRED ON VINNY C. Raging haikus, snippets of delirium.

There's Little Wales, here. Egerton Street, whose pubs the Baltic Fleet and The Grapes were rebuilt by John Meakin, the original owner of the Jacaranda Club, who would ride a horse through the streets, and wearing a top hat. Huskisson Street, where we've already been. Wonderful, wonderful pubs; Kavanagh's, Ye Cracke, The Pilgrim. Kavanagh's, under threat of closure since the smoking ban has driven people outside where their laughter and singing and chatting disturbs the pubs' newly-upmarket neighbours. Scour and scrape it all clean and featureless and disinfected. This pub's closure would be an utter catastrophe. Kevin Sampson set his latest novel *Stars are Stars* in this area, the story of Danny May's coming-of-age, culminating in a night of rioting; the child heroine of Grace Jolliffe's novel *Piggymonk Square*, Sparra, wanders these streets in the 1970s, playing on the bombsites and avoiding bogey-men. Creativity, of a million different sorts, boils in the place; gangsters and poets and playwrights and junkies and seadogs huddle together at a distance and the talk is all pidgin and patois, polyglot and motley. And it's ancient; Domesday gives it the name 'Stochestede', or 'stockade', and in 1207 King John established a royal hunting park here when he bought it from the Molyneuxs. The crown kept a close eye on it, employing forty-nine men to police it, with ten horses, two packs of dogs, and fifty-two spaniels[6]. In the seventeenth century, Puritan families were enticed into the area to populate it, which gave rise to the 'Holy Land' area (and Arthur Askey; see note 4). Richard Mather appeared here at the age of fifteen, and became increasingly radicalised, enough to attract the attention of the Established Church authorities, persecution by whom drove him to America in 1635, where he sired Increase Mather, president of Harvard, and of course Cotton Mather, founder of Yale university. The Victorians pushed the place up, up, with Italianate elegance. Princes Park was laid out in the 1840s. Poverty, as it always does, appeared alongside the opulence; between the boulevards spread 'mean, narrow streets, filled with those gloomy courts into which as many dwellings as possible were packed, irrespective of light and air'[7]. Filth, squalor, disease, malnutrition.

Toxteth has 'an edge', writes Lewis[8], 'a creativity, a cosmopolitanism, that marks it out from the rest of the city'. Black settlers here have brought blues, jazz, soul, funk. It's stolidly, still, working-class. Much of my second novel, *Sheepshagger*, was written in a flat here, on Bedford Street South. My memories of the place are mixed; boredom, danger, a thrill, a soaring, a path through life made ponderous by penury. Waiting for people who never turned up. Avoiding people who did. And remembered moments that still make my skin prickle and heart fly which I wouldn't change for anything I could ever imagine.

SEFTON PARK/LARK LANE

Today, Sefton Park's trees are wearing autumn's colours. The Palm House – recently renovated, of course – is too dark to photograph. Netherland's circus is here, so the place is mushroomed by marquees. There's a wedding going on, too. A statue of Christopher Columbus used to stand before the Palm House; Cameron and Crooke's book *Liverpool – Capital of the Slave Trade* uses a photograph of it as a frontispiece. The place is central to Liverpool cultural life, particularly that of an alternative stripe; fungi are picked and consumed here, music played and listened and danced to, trips taken on the lakes, in the head (or out of it). 'Larks in the Park', a free festival, at one of which I saw American know-it-all Henry Rollins come out onto the stage they'd erected on the island in the largest lake and say something like (and I paraphrase, but retain the spirit): 'There's 3,000 of you here, all drink-

ing and getting stoned and enjoying yourselves, having a good time. But statistics show that before the year is out, twelve of you will have committed suicide, two of you will have been murdered, four raped', etc. Disbelieving looks were made, disgruntlement rumbled; doesn't he think that we *know* this? And that that's precisely the reason why we're sitting here drinking and getting stoned and having a good time?

That we're taking an opportunity to escape temporarily the perils of our existence? Meatheaded nincompoop.

Nick Danziger[9] visited here in the 1990s and found it 'a sad, vandalised relic, the statues' stone inscriptions removed and replaced by obscene graffiti: The striking Victorian palm house had virtually all of its several thousand panes of glass smashed. A scheme had been initiated to Sponsor-a-Pane towards the reglazing and refurbishing of the building'. Well, it's refurbished now. Close to magnificent again, even, as is the park itself; big, spacious, green, quiet. I like it here. There used to be a Pet's Corner, when I was a child; rabbits and birds. A masturbating monkey. Adjoining the park is Lark Lane, more of a self-contained village than a city thoroughfare; there are delis and bars and tattooists, the Amorous Cat bookshop, a junk shop called 'Remains to be Seen'. Faded, but surviving, bohemia. Close enough to the city's more troublesome spots for the windows to necessitate steel grilles and bars, but nevertheless there's an air to it of leafy respite. The Albert, a good pub. Keith's wine bar – many an afternoon whiled away in there over vino and cheesy nachos. This is a place I like.

WAVERTREE

Wavertree is another one of those districts with the appellative 'village', or, to give it its full name, 'Wavertree Village and Garden Suburb'. It's about three miles from the city centre, and predates it; Domesday lists it as being worth '64 pence'. It has a nice name; picture the branches gesturing in a hello or a farewell.

Mike Chitty's book *Discovering Historic Wavertree* is an extensive guide to the area. He talks about the famous landmark Picton Clock, presented to the people of the area in 1884 by Sir James Picton and designed by him as a memorial to his wife, who died after half-a-century of marriage. Sweet. Close by the school stands one of

Liverpool's last surviving tenements, designed by the interestingly-monickered Lancelot Keay in 1935, City architect between 1939 and 1948. On High Street lived a William Quiggin, shipbuilder, whose firm supplied blockade runners to the Confederacy in the American Civil War (the more I dig, the more these connections surface). George Harrison was born here on Arnold Grove, just round the corner from where Felicia Dorothea Hemans lived, at No. 17 High Street, between 1828 and 1831, a once famous poetess ('The boy stood on the burning deck', remember that one?); her house was, at one time, and still, to a lesser extent, is, 'a place of pilgrimage for American tourists', according to Chitty. Hemans was born on Duke Street, in the very centre, but moved to Dublin.

There's more, of course; this is a rich district. Bronze Age burial urns and arrowheads discovered here. The Monk's Well, attached to legends of secret passages, supposedly leading to Childwall Priory. The Liverpool Progressive Synagogue on Church Road North, testament to the area's old Jewish connections. Blue Coat School, established originally in 1708 by a Mr. Byron Blundell and Rev. Robert Styth as a 'school for teaching poor children to read, write, and cast accounts' (says Chitty), but it's been associated for as long as I can remember with the posh kids. Blundell, again, a profiteer from slavery. As always. Anterior to the library on Picton Road, a boulder stands in the gardens, just behind the gates. A meteorite, everyone says; George Harrison wrote a song about it, once. But it's from the Lake District, not outer space. Glaciation brought it here. It's just a stone.

KENSINGTON

Or, as the locals have it with their propensity for nomenclative abridgement, 'Kenny', as in the great Shack song, 'Streets of Kenny', off their legendary *HMS Fable* LP, a brilliant piece of work about, amongst other things, heroin addiction (as, indeed, are many songs that came out of Liverpool in the 80s and 90s, however cryptic; 'There She Goes' by The La's, remember that one? Same subject, apparently). I spent quite a lot of time in Kensington, in younger years; a good friend used to live there. In the early to mid 90s, this was. Certain local pubs would offer 'Giro Specials'; each Wednesday, the day when the local unemployed would receive their giro cheques, a mere one pound door charge would buy you a pint, a pie, and a gawp at an 'exotic dancer'. And there was the health-food shop which, along with the mung beans and tofu, had an extensive selection of powerful and highly illicit drugs. That burnt, or *was* burnt, down, years ago.

The place was named Kensington in 1804, before which it was called Prescot Lane; whether this indicated an urge to emulate London or not, I don't know. The mayor, in 1903, William Fanwood, recalled growing up in the area in the 1840s; 'a very charming and attractive suburb', he said[10], with 'houses large and handsome'. Hmmm. One of the residents of one of these houses was, for a time, Dr. Salomon, who developed the 'Balm of Gilead', a supposed panacea which made him an extremely wealthy man. He died in 1819, leaving behind Balm Street and Gilead Street. Christ Church is impressive and imposing, as is the adjacent library. Deane Road is the site of one of the city's lost Jewish cemeteries, now closed and tree-choked.

It's now one of the city's poorest areas. Many shops are boarded- or bricked-up. So many lifeless eyes. Rumours of the demolition of large tracts of the area persist. The terraced streets are tight and winding and I lose myself in them, start to feel cloistered and panicky, relieved when I manage to escape. Slum Liverpool, this, still, and captured beautifully, powerfully, and movingly by director Terence Davies in his film *Distant Voices, Still Lives*; he grew up in this area during World War Two, and left it shortly afterwards. His film, according to Liverpool-born novelist Beryl Bainbridge[11], is about 'the mosaic of memory.... I am still mesmerised by its originality of structure, its use of music, its attention to detail. A coral filter was used to subdue all primary colours, except the red of lipstick, and further bleached to intensify the stark reality of the past'. Sounds beautiful, no? Or let Paul Farley persuade you[12]: '[The film] manages to synthesise memory to an extraordinary degree: looking back is both joyous and painful at once. It is nostalgia in an etymologically accurate sense – to return home and to suffer pain in some way.... It deals with a break, an old wound, using stories and memories; it feels as necessary and creaturely as storytelling around a fire'. It's about growing up gay and poor and Catholic in one of the most repressed and repressive areas of a repressed and repressive city at a repressed and repressive time. It has a ferocious power. Davies's films also include *The Long Day Closes*, the *Trilogy*, *The Neon Bible*, and *The House of Mirth*. A novel, too, called *Hallelujah Now*, although the only copies I could track down online were prohibitively expensive. He hasn't lived in Liverpool for ages, but he's one of the jewels that the place has always generated. Yes, they exist.

Alison Cornmell, in *Nerve* issue 11[13], has written about the Murals Project[14], which posited the idea of covering all the gable ends of Kensington terraces with huge paintings. The subject matter was to be, yawn, the Beatles, but it's motives were laudable; inspired by a visit to Belfast, the plan was to employ two muralists from that city, one a Loyalist (Mark Ervine) and the other a Republican (Danny Devenny). The Northern Irish press loved the idea, as did the locals on this side of the Irish Sea, but the Culture Company rejected the idea in 2006 for not being 'edgy enough'. For God's sake; where's the edge in Ringo Starr singing sentimental drivel on the roof of St. George's Hall? Phil Redmond, however, is allowing all the rejected proposals another chance to present their case, so something might yet come of it. I hope so. The area needs colour.

A touch of the rainbow is being offered by Mark Diston, whose work will hopefully be included in the forthcoming *Liverpool Magazine*, edited by Kenn Taylor. He emailed me a brilliant short semi-autobiographical piece called 'The Only Tourist in Sheil Road Writes Home', a desperately funny missive from 'The House of Incompetent Men' in 'the random asylum that is Kenny' to which the writer has been confined for 'chronic financial naivete and crimes against the work ethic'. A comical Kafka in Kenny. A voice, undoubtedly, to watch.

EDGE HILL AND THE MOLE: THE WILLIAMSON TUNNELS

Edge Hill is the last rail stop before Lime Street, the city proper. In a predominantly Catholic city in which coitus interruptus was seen as the only viably sin-less method of contraception, 'getting off at Edge Hill' came to mean... well, I'm sure you can guess the rest.

Famously, the earth beneath Edge Hill is Swiss-cheesed with tunnels, the work of Joseph Williamson, the 'Mole of Edge Hill'. He was a tobacco merchant in the nineteenth century, and used his wealth to build, in the words of James Picton in the 1870s, 'some of the most extraordinary operations that can be conceived'[15]. Williamson filled Mason Street with – to quote Picton again – buildings 'of the strangest and most uncouth character... projections and recesses in irregular disorder, storeys of all heights, some rooms without windows, others apparently all window', etc. None of these survive today, alas, but his tunnels do; miles of subterranean cavities, supposedly built by Napoleonic War veterans with nothing to do, and engineered and bankrolled by Williamson. Edge Hill is a honeycomb, 'excavated and pervaded by caves, vaults and yawning chasms utterly without meaning, plan, or object' (again, Picton, more vexed and exasperated and baffled). This mad enterprise almost bankrupted Williamson and he died in 1841, and was buried in St. Thomas's churchyard; when the cemetery was cleared in 1905, his remains alone were allowed to continue lying there.

The Friends of Williamson Tunnels are dedicated to preserving the area, even opening some of the tunnels as tourist attractions. Les Coe categorises their importance to the city as being part of 'the heritage and the sensation of the unknown'[16]. Apparently, they cost £100,000 to build; £22m in today's prices, according to Les. They're extraordinary examples of visionary engineering, in truth, built of sandstone and brick, comprising tunnels of varying sizes, dead-ends, vaults, huge cathedral-like caverns. Various theories have been expounded as to their purpose; one, that they, in part, were secret means of ingress to the bedrooms of Williamson's many mistresses across the city. But maybe they're just a mark; the impression that Williamson wanted to make on the earth. The stamp of one man's presence and passing. Something which, when the souls queueing up in stellar relays are given corporeality, will communicate to them the existence of one unique personality, on and on and on. Intrepid and purpose-giving, testaments to the incomprehensible mysteries of the human soul. I'm glad they're there. If you want to know more, log on to www.williamsontunnels.com; read John Stonechaser's words, regard the creepy sketches. It's good stuff. As the poet Kit Wright said:

> For who can explain
> The excavation of nothing whatever for neither
> Light nor gain?

notes

1. See Belchem, *800*.
2. Ibid.
3. Written in 1981, revised in 2001. See 'Works Consulted'.
4. An area so-called because of its Biblically-named streets. Arthur Askey was born on Moses Street, 6th June, 1900, and went on to music hall 'comedy' fame and that bloody song 'Busy Busy Bee'. Not that I'm boasting-by-association or anything.
5. See under 'Various Editors', 'Works Consulted'.
6. All this info from Lewis, *Illustrated History. . .*
7. Lewis, op.cit.
8. Ibid.
9. See *Danziger's Britain*.
10. See Lewis, op.cit.
11. See her 'Bittersweet Symphony', 'Works Consulted'.
12. In his BFI book named after the film. See 'Works Consulted'.
13. *Nerve* is a superb and free magazine 'promoting grassroots arts and culture on Merseyside'. It's produced by Catalyst Media; see www.catalystmedia.org.uk.
14. And also see http://theliverpoolmuralsproject.blogspot.com.
15. Quoted in Lewis, op.cit.
16. See Jones, Catherine, 'Our Tunnel Vision', 'Works Consulted'.
17. From 'The Losing of Liverpool', excerpted in Coles, *Both Sides of the River*.

CITY
EYE

VAUXHALL: LOVE LANE AND PALL MALL

Once fenland, Vauxhall quickly grew into a heavily industrialised area, with a reputation for terrible squalor and overcrowding, in the 1850s, when it was rapidly settled by Irish immigrants escaping the Great Hunger. The great Catholic communities of Scotland Road had their origins here. Clarence Dock has a plaque which commemorates its history as the main place of entry into the city for colossal numbers of displaced Irish – up to 1.3 million, apparently, in five years. Vauxhall offered work on the docks and the canal. Political allegiances were also imported, and Fenianism flourished in this area, caches of weapons often being discovered in the packed houses. The Luftwaffe shattered the docks here in World War Two and industry, in Lewis's words, 'drifted away'[1]. Many of the slums were demolished and the inhabitants re-housed although many chose to remain in the district; those who lived on Eldon Street formed the 'Eldonians', and worked with housing associations and architects to create the Eldonian Village, neat semi-detached houses with large gardens abutting the canal. This has brought some stability to the area, and Vauxhall is ticking along; there has been some small-business investment, some new housing, that kind of thing. It's an intensely populated part of the city, especially in the 'Little Ireland' of Eldon Street, the enterprise of which, according to John Murden[2], 'demonstrated the viability of bottom-up regeneration and provided a template for further development' in the wider city.

So something of a success story, then. Remember the Alan Bleasdale-scripted series in the 80s, *Boys From the Blackstuff*? Yozzer Hughes, 'gizza job' and all that?[3] Well, its closing scenes were of Love Lane being demolished, and the area is still fighting for rebirth. Ron Noon, a writer and history teacher at John Moores University with a special interest in researching the sugar industry in TU/Labour history, is setting up the Love Lane Lives website (google it), 'to promote public history', he tells me in the Punch and Judy pub just off Lime Street. He calls it 'a community with a hole in the middle of it', although it's a hole he's trying to fill; his short film, also called *Love Lane Lives*, was screened in 2007 at the Tate. Ron's Scotland Road Liverpool-Irish, a politically inspired and committed feller who's 'never felt comfortable with academia... public history's my thing'. He tells me about the 'asset stripping' inflicted on Liverpool's public buildings, how even the churches were emptied, including the sixteenth-century marble altar from St. Mary of the Angels. He puts his bag up onto the pub table and he takes out an architectural blueprint of Tate and Lyle's Love Lane sugar site. The older fellers around us, all ex-workers at the factory, are absolutely rapt. 'I know more about fucking sugar than fucking anybody!' Ron says (the Guinness has been flowing freely), and he's not just exaggerating. His interest in sugar began because he was asked by the Love Lane veterans to research it. 'Sugar's a metaphor for capitalism', he says. A left-wing historian, he got absorbed in the decade-long struggle to keep the plant open (it closed in 1981), and was asked by the laid-off workers to write their story up sympathetically. 'It's a legal drug', he says, and it's obvious that sugar, and the usage and manufacturing of it, has swallowed him as a subject; it's a 'hunger-crop, it's intimately bound up with slavery. In a grain of sugar, you can see capitalism'. The cultivation of sugar exacted a vast amount of slave labour; 'it's the quintessential slave-crop, much more so than tobacco'.

Ron's tremendous. He's fired up with righteous ire and political will. I'm kind of unsure what he's on about, though, because of the Guinness and all that, but some days later he sends me a xerox of his essay 'Liverpool Love Lane Refinery Lives' from the publication *North West Labour History*, issue 32, which is a fascinating piece of work, examining, as he said, the inescapable ties between sugar production and the slave trade, and consequently the centrality of sugar to the public history of Liverpool. Added to this is the 'abandonment' of Liverpool by Tate and Lyle (or, as Ron says, 'Take and Lie') in favour of more profitable enterprises elsewhere; 'day-to-day struggle', he writes, 'makes it very difficult to see the chicaneries and strategies that multinationals can play out at the worker's expense'. 2,000 jobs were lost, which almost obliterated a community. Ron quotes Bob Parry, House of Commons speaker, on the announcement of closure: 'The Tate and Lyle company, which made the announcement this morning about sacking these people and throwing them on the scrap heap, also announced that its profits had increased.... This is the naked and vicious face of capitalism'.

What saves this from being simply another story of rapacity and callousness is the fact of the Eldonian Community Housing Project, which in 2006 held its twenty-fifth anniversary, with the result that, in Ron's words, 'this Liverpool story is never dead'. With that, and with Ron's impassioned analysis and research and exposure, it also becomes a story of defiance and empathic warmth. In another of his articles[4], Ron quotes Auguste Cochin: 'The story of a lump of sugar is a whole lesson in political economy, in politics and also in morality'.

I think of the old boys in the Punch and Judy, surrounding Ron and his blueprints, fascinated, animated, nostalgic and angry and proud.

That's Love Lane.

MOORFIELDS AND BUSINESS DISTRICT

Grand architecture in this part of town, great stone bulks of build-ings, sooty statuary, alleyways and ginnels and shadowy cobbled narrow capillaries that link the larger traffic-crammed thoroughfares of Tithebarn Street and Water Street and Dale Street. Superb subter-ranean pubs such as JP Molloy's and those dark but warm little bolt-holes in places like Hackins Hey. You could live here for years and still be discovering these hidden, hunched hostelries. There's the Ship and Mitre by the tunnel entrance on Dale Street with its hundreds of draught and bottled beers[5]. And it sells Tayto crisps; best accompaniment to chilled lager ever. Made in Armagh, they are. Difficult to get on this side of the Sea. There's the Brunswick. There's Ned Kelly's on Cheapside. The main arteries in this area are wide and open but the dark buildings loom roundabout and there's a feeling of Dickensian antiquity, despite the cars and buses and sirens and underfoot rumbling from the underground trains. It's a part of the city I like very, very much. Equal promises of skullduggery and fun.

The area – especially as centred around Mathew Street – can lay claim to being the epicentre of Liverpool's abidingly thriving music scene. The Cavern Club stood there, of course, opened by Alan Sytner in 1957 and demolished in 1973 to make room for a car-park

and then re-built when the Heritage Industry realised their stupid mistake. Eric's was there, too, a nightclub predom-inantly recalled as being punk-flavoured, the Liverpool equivalent of New York's CBGB's, although there are some who remember it differ-ently: 'My memory of sitting in Eric's', says Kevin Sampson[6], 'trying to make a pint last for ever, was of the most played record on the jukebox being

'Suzanne' by Leonard Cohen.... I remember seeing Matumbi there, Prince Far-I or Rockin' Dopsie and his Cajun Twisters'. One of the club's founders, Pete Fulwell, says[7]: 'There was a strong affinity with new York.... It was an attitude rather han a dress code. It was a brief period when people were open to things'. The club's lifespan covered three years only, and it closed in 1980, not particularly

a victim of the thuggish club wars of the time, more of civic politics and jurisprudential zeal. But it was a volcano, throwing out bands like Big in Japan and Echo and the Bunnymen and The Teardrop Explodes, and a magnet, attracting people like Courtney Love (but let's draw a shame-sparing veil over her involvement) and Bill Drummond, who would go on to form the KLF Foundation and have a number one novelty hit and perform the preposterous 'artistic' stunt of burning £1m on a remote Scottish island and selling the ashes. He has written that what attracted him to Liverpool was the fact that 'it had neither respect for its heritage nor any realisation that this heritage could be exploited'[8], and Mathew Street, with its space where the Cavern used to be, encapsulated this. Around the corner, on Dale Street, Probe Records used to operate (it's moved premises, now, to Wood Street), a brilliant shop where, if the owner didn't approve of what you asked for, he'd give you an insult with your change (I remember buying Don McLean's 'Vincent' as a present – honest – and being called 'a great big fucken puff'). Then there was Cream, on Wolstenholme Square, arguably the country's first 'superclub', opened by James Barton, who is now, according to DuNoyer[9], 'a Liverpool entrepreneur in the tradition of its top-hatted Victorian merchants'. With Cream, clubbing became cool, and was taken away from the gangster/retired footballer/blotchy legs/lads on lager/meatmarket kind of thing it'd for a long time been. Zoo Records had their offices here, on Whitechapel. Elvis Costello, when he was Declan McManus, had connections. Still has. Bill Drummond saw the area as being one point on a leyline that ran from Iceland to Papua New Guinea and centred on a Mathew Street manhole cover. I could go

on, but there'd be no point, really, as I can only scratch the surface here; but if you want to know more about the music scene in Liverpool, go to Paul DuNoyer's book or to Pete Wylie's virtual tour on the Liverpool08.com website. No better guide than him, 'a man who's been there, done that, and got the hit record', says Chris Salmon[10]; 'your cool Scouse uncle, spinning entertaining yarns about everything from the site of Brian Epstein's office... right up to its current standing in UK clubbing'.

It was inevitable, really, that such a sizable port would produce a typhoon of musical creativity. It still does. Paul DuNoyer again:

> Liverpool's past has been preserved in the genes of its people.... Every colour and creed was represented in a city which, like New York, had so little indigenous heritage that it became the creation of its immigrants.... Nearly all the imported music in Liverpool was available to anyone in Britain, though Liverpool might have had a few weeks' lead time. The real difference was that Liverpool wanted this music more badly; its craving was stronger; and once it had learned the words it took the songs to its heart and howled them back to the world.... Liverpool only exists because it is a seaport. Its virtues and vices, its accent and attitude, its insularity and its open-mindedness, are all derived from that primary fact[11].

So there you go; music was unloaded with the bananas and cotton and tea. Perfect. Of course.

This area can be an exhilarating, mad, intensely alive place. Smoking a cigarette on the steps of Flanagan's Apple pub one Saturday night I smell curry and onions and spices and meat and coconut and perfume and hair grease; I hear fiddle music, techno, a bodhran, an electric guitar, someone somewhere singing 'Liverpool Lou'; a hundred different languages bounce off the jostling heads and sweating walls; scruffy dogs scarper past with styrofoam cups strung to their necks to collect money for their busking owners; a legless man in a wheelchair scoots past with another fully-limbed man sitting on his lap, four arms and two legs dancing. Cities that this one was once umbilically connected to, and still in a way is, echo; Cairo Singapore Boston Bombay Dublin Zanzibar, more. Above me, Johnathan Drabkin's plaster-and-bronze bust of Jung looks approvingly out over it all. 'Pool of Life', he said. He's not kidding.

LIME STREET

Lime Street station is a vast arch, ribcage of a leviathan, curving girders way up there somewhere, echoing, flying, huge. Seems to belong to another age, one more given to bombast and grandeur. The railway cuttings here have been made through deep sandstone, and the view of them from the slowing train windows rising redly up, hung with dripping green ferns, comprises one of the iconic images of the city for anyone who knows it and has visited or left it by rail. The temperature drops, here, in this chugging canyon, and I welcome it today, after several sweaty hours spent on an overheated cattle car or hanging around stations for trains that didn't come or were interminably delayed on the rare chance they weren't unexpectedly cancelled. Being told by tannoy only what you're NOT allowed to do, scurrying over stairways and bridges to find some travel information or asking a uniformed someone who appears to have been lobotomised (especially on the platforms at Wolverhampton). God but I *hate* travelling by train in this country. Eight, nearly nine hours to travel just over a hundred miles. Pathetic.

But, anyway, I've arrived. I'm breathing easy, again. The station's elevated position gives you a view over the city, an impressive vista. On the train, I'd read Koeck's and Robert's essay 'The Archive City: Reading Liverpool's Urban Landscape Through Film'[12], which says of this view:

> A virtual panorama of Liverpool's famous waterfront rises from a busy stretch of pavement leading to and from the railway station. For the

urban *flaneur*, the iconography of this symbolic cityscape... is momentarily woven into the otherwise prosaic fabric of everyday urban space. The panorama's transitory location inhibits any lingering or reflection.

Oh, does it? As I regard the view a *Big Issue* seller approaches me. *Crackin view, lad, eh? Yer first time?* No, I'm returning. *Ah, well, welcome home. Love this pitch, me. Get to look at that all day.* He sweeps his arm across the seething city. I buy a magazine.

Lime Street is traditionally seen as the city's red-light area, as described in the famous folk song 'Maggie May', although that's associated more with Hope Street and its environs these days; prostitution is a peripatetic business as much as anything else. Adrian Henri's great painting 'The Entry of Christ into Liverpool' (1964) depicts a processionally packed Lime Street bedecked with flags and protest symbols. The view from the front entrance of the station is inevitably dominated by the great white bulk of St. George's Hall[13], which, in the mid-80s, Alan Bennett visited:

> The massive municipal temple on the Plateau at the heart of Liverpool. Ranged round the vast hall are statues of worthies from the great days of the city, and on the floor a rich and elaborate mosaic, set with biblical homilies [and] badges stuck there at a recent People's Festival. 'He hath given me skill that He might be honoured', says the floor. 'Save the pits', say the stickers. It is a palimpsest of our industrial history[14].

One of the few things in Liverpool that impressed Bennett, then. The hall was built in the 1830s along with the nearby museum and library and Walker Art Gallery, during a spurt of civic pride when the architectural city, as we know it today, was taking shape in what C.H. Reilly called 'neo-Grec architecture, combining Greek refinement and scale with Roman strength and magnificence... this new spirit of civic pride reached a high point with the construction of St. George's Hall, 'that noble building, one of the noblest in the modern world"[15]. All is grand and great and gargantuan in this area. Columns, iron lions, wide stone staircases, cobbled aprons the size of football pitches. I can't go in the Hall so I sit on its steps as the sun starts to set over the frantic traffic before and below me. I've sat on these steps

many times. The 2008 City of Culture opening ceremony was held here, on these steps, and on the forecourt, and on the roof of the building. Central to the life and history of the city. I don't know; when something's so big as to fill the landscape, referring to anything other than its magnitude becomes impossible, doesn't it? Stand looking up at the Great Pyramid of Giza and all you can think is: PYRAMID.

I cross through the Gardens to William Brown Street. There's some sick on the steps of the museum. Inside, the place has undergone extensive renovation, but there are still some exhibits which hurtle me back to childhood; the Irish elk skeleton, the mounted spider-crab, the display-case of the amblotherium, a tiny, shrew-like mammal (one of the first) drinking water out of a puddle made by the footprint of a three-toed dinosaur. All as I remember them. And the aquarium; that's always been one of my favourite places in the city. The nipping shrimps. The colours in the coral reef tank. Hurtled back to childhood. Feel both happy and sad. My reflection in the glass of these low-lit tanks flitted over by pretty fish. I see that reflection as of an excited child, and then as a wasted adult. Kind of want to leave.

The Walker Art Gallery is colossal and it swallows you. It's named after A.B. Walker, a brewer, who funded it, of a long-lasting dynasty with roots in the fourteenth century. Its scale and design is monumental. If you visit, be sure to take a guide, or a sleeping bag and some sandwiches to tide you over until the search party finds you. The first floor contains fifteen rooms, chronologically arranged; there's Poussin, Rembrandt, Rubens, Stubbs, Gainsborough, Millais, Constable, Rossetti, Monet, Degas, Cezanne, Matisse, Spenser, Freud, Lowry.

More contemporary work in changing exhibitions and special displays. Ground floor contains ceramics and sculpture in several rooms. I tire myself out walking round it. Stand for a rest and gawp at David Jacques's magnificent 'Irish Emigrants Entering Liverpool'. The place spins my head so I leave and sit, again, on another huge stone staircase. Look out over the Gardens which, today, for some reason, teem with teenage goths and emo types running crazed in playful panic and drinking bottles of cheap cider. Hence the sick, probably. It was on these steps that George Garrett, Liverpool-Irish writer and political activist, held his protest on 12th September 1921, when he and several hundred other members of the NUWM were 'batoned down by troops during a non-violent protest... and many more arrested, tried and accused of receiving funds from Communist Russia', raising the issue, which troubled Garrett deeply, of whether non-violent protest 'has any value in a world where the struggle for working-class rights seems to be ruthlessly crushed time and time again by uncaring authority'[16]. What incensed Garrett was the callous indifference in Liverpool towards those in need – especially veterans of World War One – from those with plenty and in a strong position to ameliorate. As he wrote in his brilliantly enraged essay 'Liverpool 1921 – 1922'[17]:

In Britain in the post-war years 1920-21, with the 'Homes for Heroes' illusion already exploded; two million brooding unemployed; second-hand shops glutted with furniture surrendered cheaply for rent and bread; and the pawn- shop windows piled with medals, now so much worthless junk; Sir Alfred Mond, Minister of Health, posed the fatuous question: 'Is anyone starving?.... In Liverpool, with its sixty thousand out-of-works, mass disillusionment, degradation and raggedness were pronounced. But resentment only seethed in small groups around the Labour Exchanges, or was muttered on back-street corners, or screamed inside slum hovels. It had yet to be joined.

Garrett unified, mobilised, built up cohesion and strength. Of *course* it was worthwhile; such protest always is. It can stay a greedy and ignorant hand. Good man, Garrett. He's fondly remembered. And remains an inspiration.

And it's not strictly located in the Lime Street area, but see that tall structure piercing the sky, like a giant spindly mushroom? That's St. John's Beacon. Bennett again:

> [it's] a restaurant, set on a concrete pole (may the architect rot); now empty, it boasts a tattered notice 300 feet up advertising to passing seagulls that it is TO LET. [Beneath it] is graffiti on a bus-stop: 'HOPE IS FUCKING HOPELESS'[18].

I'm sure you've gathered by now that Bennett disliked Liverpool intensely. Leaving aside his prissy misgivings, it must've seemed apocalyptic to him at that time, unsalvageably wrecked. But look again at St. John's Beacon; now, lasers fork from it at night-time and slash the stars and their background velvet red and blue and green. Creative human activity goes on in it, now, because it's the offices of Radio City, and on their staff is an old friend of mine from school, David Brown, who shows me round. I meet him at an inconspicuous doorway in St. John's market and an elevator slurps us up into the sky.

The tower was built as the flue for the shopping precinct at its foot; it's basically a glorified chimney. It became a restaurant in the 1960s and used to revolve, but the turning gears stay still now. The top floor of the mushroom head, where I stand, used to be an open-air observation deck. Radio City took the place over in 2000. They were based in Stanley Street and were going to re-locate to the Albert Dock but listed building status there disallowed much of what a radio station needs, like signage, and Tom Hunter, the managing director at the time (not from Liverpool, so able to see the city with unaccustomed eyes), had the vision of occupying the tower, which was fast becoming a civic and political embarrassment. The Council breathed a sigh of relief at his proposal. All equipment had to go up in the lift as

cranes couldn't get that high (so how, I wonder, was it built in the first place?). Moving in took two years. A massive undertaking.

450 feet high, the tower wobbles in the wind. Can cause motion sickness amongst the workers. The view is absolutely astonishing; the breath is punched from my lungs. You can see Anglesey in one direction, the Lake District in another. This new perspective on the city... I feel like a bird. I can see down into back yards, onto church roofs. The city's secrets revealed. The Mersey looks narrow from up here, due to the foreshortening effect of the dockside buildings' sheer size. It's amazing. I can't look away. I don't want to come down.

But I do. And take a quick detour past the Adelphi, the lounge of which figured in a recent film of *Brideshead Revisited* as the interior of a transatlantic liner. Its entrance was, for a time, junkie-haunted, but today, as I pass, a chauffeur-driven limo is dropping off an Arabian-looking feller. It's no longer on hard times, indeed it's reclaiming some of its opulence. It retains a wildness, however; I recently had a wonderful all-night drinking spree in its bars with my girlfriend and a Greenlandic Inuit called Niels. The foyer was full of drunkenly-slumbering Irish people. And it doesn't, but it should, have a banner above its plush main door reading: 'Just cuke, will yeh!' (If you know what I'm referring to here, you'll no doubt snort or chortle. If you don't, I'm not going to explain it. Let the mystery remain).

HOPE STREET: CATHEDRAL CITY

Where to start, with Hope Street? In cultural/historical terms, it's immense, like Mathew Street, or Lime Street. Leaves me floundering. The two cathedrals, the Everyman Playhouse and Bistro, Ye Cracke pub... it's a cultural jungle to get lost in.

We'll start at its northern end, by Brownlow Hill, with the Catholic cathedral, Paddy's Wigwam, or, to give it its proper title, the

Metropolitan Cathedral of Christ the King. You'll know it to look at, I'm sure; like a giant upturned metal dustbin with spikes. Initially, it was to be built to a design by Edward Lutyens, commissioned by the charismatic Archbishop Richard Downey in 1930; it would've been 510 ft tall (60 ft higher than St.Peter's in London), second cathedral in height only to St. Peter's in Rome[19], but, by the end of World War Two, the projected costs had soared from £3m to the truly impossible figure of £29m. So Frederick Gibberd took the project over, and built up from Lutyens's crypt, after it had been consecrated in 1967; the finished thing, Glancy writes[20], 'is crowned by a daring lantern adorned with superb stained glass designed by John Piper and made by Patrick Reyntiens... a fine, fascinating building, [but] an architectural minnow, a church mouse, compared with Lutyens's greatest design'. Ah well. We have what we have. And what we have is monumentally spectacular, awe-inspiring, of a fierce beauty, sublime and sacred and eternal. Inside, the air seems coloured blue, from the refractive qualities of the glass; I imagine myself drifting in amniotic fluid. I pick up more historical info; the Catholic Diocese of Liverpool was established in 1850, and the commission to design a cathedral was entrusted to Edward Welsby Pugin, but only the Lady Chapel of the edifice was completed, in Everton, before funding ran out. The idea of the cathedral bubbled on the backburner until 1922 when, as we know, Downey and Lutyens got involved. Foundation stone laid on Whit Monday, 5th June, 1933. Pope Pius XI suggested the name 'Christ the King'. After World War Two, Archbishop Heenan posited the idea of a cathedral that would express the new spirit of the Liturgy then being formulated by the second Vatican council.

Gibberd's design was chosen. Building began on Whit Sunday, 14th May, 1967. Year after I was born. It's a young cathedral. It's designed primarily for liturgical celebration; the huge central circular space seats 2,300 people. At each chapel around the perimeter, there are artworks from contemporary artists, most impressively the Stations of the Cross, in manganese bronze, by Sean Rice, made between 1993

and 1995, with accompanying meditations by Fr. Gerald O'Mahony. It's extremely powerful stuff. The First Station – Jesus is Entombed – is so effective as to almost defy description; the faces, the contortion, the endurance, the impossible grace in pain. Utterly enthralling. Space restricts further discussion of the artwork here, and indeed much more of the cathedral, but I'd like to mention the Lantern Tower, the Chapel of St. Columba, the Chapel of Unity, the Chapel of the Holy Oils, more. You'll have to go and see it for yourself. Gaze agog. It has a light and celebratory quality to it which I find incredibly uplifting; here is a God who understands the value of laughter, and of rejoicing in the body. My maternal grandfather's name is in the Book of Remembrance. He died on New Year's Day, 1964, two years before I was born, ten days before my brother was born. I read his name.

The pilgrims and praying and the poets, too, come. Roger McGough was commissioned to write a piece celebrating the buildings' completion. It contained the lines:

> Let it not be a showroom
> for would be good Catholics
> or worse...
> But let it be a place
> Where lovers meet after work
> for kind words and kisses
> Where dockers go of a Saturday night
> to get away from the missus
> Tramps let kip there through till morning
> kids let rip there every evening...
> And let the cathedral laugh
> Even show its teeth
> And if it must wear the cassock of dignity
> then let's glimpse the jeans beneath[21]

And Nathan Jones, who I've already mentioned, a Squelch writer ('Scouse' + 'Welsh'), emails me one of his poems from the showmercy.co.uk website. Called 'Trick or Treat', it references the cathedral as a simple landmark in the quotidian life of the city, and thereby fulfils, a bit, McGough's prayer:

> The Cathedral has its picture taken
> from some of the cars. Dull, pointless pictures of the mist
> punctuated by dough-kneed school-girls shying from the flash,

smiling moving closer pandering to it just once
as they forget their teeth, their skin, and smoothing down their
glittered
hair

glow a moment.

Next Hope Street stop must be the Everyman Playhouse and, of course, the bistro beneath it, brightly-lit subterranean world with fine food and exotic beer. It was a popular haunt when I was younger and lived in the city and, to judge by the huddled and chatting heads in it today, still is, or is again. It's central to the history of the 'Mersey Sound' scene, the loose poetry 'movement' that began in the 60s and did a great deal to popularise the discipline as practised by its three principal figures – Adrian Henri, Roger McGough, and Brian Patten, whose shared *Mersey Sound* anthology received a needed update in the late 80s with the *New Volume* (Penguin). This was a huge commercial success, and came from the fact that 'poetry in Liverpool is more uninhibitedly colourful, more deliberately "public", than at any other place in the British Isles', to quote Edward Lucie-Smith[22]. Undoubtedly true; Henri, now dead, was also a highly popular painter, and McGough was a member of the group Scaffold – remember 'Lily the Pink?[23]. He's recently published an autobiography, *Said and Done*, the most recent in a line of over fifty books that have gleaned him a CBE and freedom of the city of Liverpool. He mentions that the Everyman Bistro, as it's now known, was once called Hope Hall, in which himself and a feller called John Gorman,

'to keep the idea of an arts festival in the public conscience... organised weekly events [which] consisted of satirical sketches and surreal dialogues, interspersed with a poet and perhaps a folksinger or guitarist'[24]. These evenings became hugely successful, and from them sprung great things. What great things? Well, read the book. Roger's ostensibly breezy, punning style isn't to everyone's taste, but this book

addresses the balancing seriousness at the heart of the verse. There's something life-affirming about it. And the whole 'Mersey Sound' thing was part of a wider artistic phenomenon which, in retrospect, conforms more to the perceived idea of the 'avant-garde', which is a story 'of locals and visitors, and of the established and experimental', to quote Sam Gathercole[25]. Making poetry popular at that time, taking it out of academia, was, of course, avant-garde, and its legacy can be seen, now, in the waves of little-press magazines that are flooding out of the city, and also in the activities of groups like the Dead Good Poets Society[26], which is a group based in the Bistro 'where it provides 'open floor' sessions in the Everyman's famous 'third room' on the first Wednesday of the month'[27]. So it continues. Thank God it does.

To digress from Hope Street just a tad, there are some real jewels to be found in Liverpool's current small magazine scene. Hybrids of fanzine and music paper and poetry press, and personal exultations or execrations, they keep appearing, of inevitably varying quality but never less than intriguing. *Mercy* has already been mentioned, as has *Nerve*; there's *TVS*; and Ade Jackson's *Back to the Machine Gun*, begun in 2004 'by a group of like-minded misfits aiming to lift the dull skies an inch or two higher, cut some diamonds in the rough and generally do something elegant, pointless, and true'[28]. Ade's got a collection out, too, called *latenight sistersongs*, with Gladys Mary Coles's Headland Press. A snippet:

> Flattened, moon-drenched clouds hang over the old
> school at the top of Mount Street[29].
> Chinatown whispers behind the hushed
> hours between the pub rush and the club rush and an ill wind
> off the Mersey runs grubby mittens through the trees,
> twisting the city's guts, digging beneath her corruption of
> yellow light.

And the Everyman Theatre, of course, continues to push and promote innovative and powerful drama. Recent highlights, for me, include Tony Green's *The Kindness of Strangers*, an often extremely funny and moving piece of work about the city's immigrants and prostitutes, and *Unprotected*, by Green and several others, a harrowing play based around the murders of three young women (who happened to be working as streetgirls), with the dialogue taken verbatim from interviews with those involved in the city's sex trade, including clients, outreach workers, policemen and women, the working girls themselves. At the play's close, a tape recording of the voice of one of the murdered women is played; it's an unbearably poignant moment. Murphy and Rees-Jones, in *Writing Liverpool*, call these productions 'a balance between a particular Liverpool sensibility and sentimentality [and] an unashamed attempt at producing the kind of ideas-driven, state-of-the-nation drama too long absent from the Everyman stage.... [The] indication is that the Everyman's commitment to fostering new writing talent may initiate a new golden age in the history of the theatre'.

The Hope Street area is the setting for Helen Walsh's fine and successful first novel, *Brass*. The story of Millie and her adventures with drugs and local prostitutes, it aroused wildly mixed reviews when it first appeared; equal parts love and loathing, 'a tornado of booze, beak and lustily described bodily fluids', as Katy Guest has it[30]. I loved it, personally, and declared so on its back cover. If you haven't already done so, then I urge you to read it.

So many treasures on Hope Street. A rich place. Into the Philharmonic Pub, once designated by the Egon Ronay organisation as the Most Ornate Pub in England. Ronay himself said, 'if a pub could be a work of art, the Philharmonic is that pub'. Grade A listed. Gin palace interior, marble toilets, snugs and unexpected little rooms. Quite splendid, Victorian flamboyance that truly dazzles. I meet Deb Mulhearn in here, editor of the brilliant *Mersey Minis* series. Over Guinness she tells me that the Culture Company is overlooking

Liverpool's literature; *Mersey Minis* are an attempt to counter that, the model for which was a series of short books published in Cork in 2005, when that city received the Capital of Culture award. The original idea was for one large book, but Gladys Mary Coles's *Both Sides of the River* already laid claim to that, and besides, Deb wanted to focus exclusively on prose, the sheer diversity of which based in and around Liverpool drove her interest; 'all the visitors over the centuries', she says, 'why were they here?' The wide and hugely impressive research was done herself, and 'amazing connections were discovered', such as the Croft siblings, escaped slaves who fled to the city in the 1860s and wrote: 'It was not until we stepped upon the shore at Liverpool that we were free from every slavish fear'[31].

It's been fortuitous for Liverpool poets that the city's two cathedrals stand at opposite ends of Hope Street; a nice symbol in that. I could choose numerous examples, but I'll settle for one, from Henry Graham's fine collection *Kafka in Liverpool*:

> At each end of a street named Hope two different
> gods stand glowering at each other through
> the festering air.

See? So here's the Anglican Cathedral, colossal edifice, positioned on St. James's Mount, designed by Sir Giles Gilbert Scott (1880-1960), only twenty-two when he won the commission. Foundation stone laid 1904, building completed in 1978; over seven decades in the making. Men did their very first and last days of work on the same job. Largest Anglican cathedral, and fourth largest cathedral of any denomination, on the planet. It's very, very big. Joe Queenan, visiting American humourist, wrote about it in his *Queenan Country*: 'The gloomy, fortresslike Protestant cathedral [is] physically the most massive structure in Anglican Britain. It pays homage to a dour, cheerless god the English people stopped believing in back in the eighteenth century when they started worshipping Mammon'. Well, yes, maybe: but I find something celebratory and uplifting just in the building's sheer scale. The ingenuity of will and application of muscle is an affirmation of the human, I feel. It dominates the city; John Cornelius in his *Liverpool 8* has a funny section about the building sentiently, and creepily, regarding him as he walks past it stoned at night-time. Undoubtedly, it can have the effect of stunning you into silence.

Facing the cathedral is LIPA, the Liverpool Institute of Performing Arts, established largely thanks to Paul McCartney, who invested £3m in it. Each of its undergraduate places attracts twenty applicants. And behind that is Cubitt House, opposite the London Carriage Works restaurant, supposedly very good, although I haven't, yet, been. I lived in Cubitt House, some years ago, but now it's coming down. Through the top-floor window that I used to sit and gaze out of, I can see sky. There's no roof left.

BOLD STREET

Central shopping thoroughfare, pedestrianised. Usual chainstores, vertical-drinking bars, Mr. Chips, clothes boutiques both retro and designer. A large Waterstone's. Matta's, a world-foods supermarket, its shelves and fridges a wonder to explore. Christian's fruit and veg stall; go there at day's end to pick up bargains. Microzine, a male-orientated emporium that sells gadgets, bikes, books, beer, sportswear. Contains also the Microzine gallery, where people like Jimmy Cauty of the KLF and punk iconographer Jamie Reid have exhibited their work. Resurrection is a great vintage clothing store. Hairy Records, a trove of used vinyl. And one of the street's highlights is News from Nowhere, so-called 'radical bookshop', and without doubt something of a weirdly wordy wonderland; it's run by a five-woman cooperative, and is a place you could spend some happy hours and a lot of cash, which I do. Then I wander down to Waterstone's, outside which is a long, long queue of eager people all itching to get their books signed by Michael Palin, of whose affable-hamster face I catch a quick glimpse between the mountainous shoulders of his minders. And then the store's own security guard appears, clutching the puny bicep of one of Liverpool's more wretched-looking denizens, at the sales counter. *Whatjer want me to do with this one?*, he asks. I don't hear the answer. I look for the 'Local Interest' section and tut when I realise that it's directly behind Mr. Palin. No chance of getting past those huge fellers in shades to browse the shelves. They're very menacing. The city's not *that* bad.

I walk up towards St. Luke's church. There've been stories of time-slips here, on Bold Street; of fifty-year old coins dropping out of the air, of the world becoming suddenly unfamiliar with vans appearing bearing logos of long-gone shops, the street all of a sudden filled with people wearing 50s fashions. Brief time-slips. Just for a matter of seconds, then all is once again normal. The men working on convert-ing the old post office at the street's foot would often talk about such phenomena, how disconcerting they were; some refused to return to work. Odd tales.

It's a busy street, this, even at 3 p.m. on a weekday afternoon (it'll be much busier twelve hours later when the pubs and bars kick out). Walking up it, I hear very little spoken English, and the faces are multi-coloured. Used to be called the 'Bond Street of the North'. High hopes were held for the regeneration of it and its adjoining Ropewalks area, and whilst these visions of happy and harmonious city-centre living haven't quite materialised here, the night-time economy of clubland keeps it buoyant and relatively prosperous. Plus there's Arena Studios, and FACT (Foundation for Art and Creative

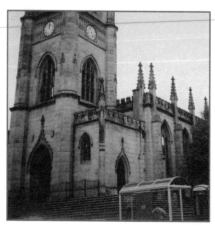

Technology), which offers space for artists working primarily with moving image and new pixel media, so the area scores highly on any arty/bohemian checklist. I like it. It's a lively, decent place.

From anywhere on Bold Street you can see the ruins at its head; this is St. Luke's church, set ablaze by the Luftwaffe and left to stand in ruins as a commemorative reminder. Eerie tales are attached to this, too, of ghostly choirs heard among its blackened fallen beams and strange light seen through its glassless windows. One night, I saw two bright white objects zoom across the sky above it; about spire-height, the size maybe of small cars, an odd sense of solidity to them. Peculiar. The church's grounds were once junkie-stalked and not, really, a place you'd want to spend any time, but now they are fragrant

and flowery and colourful and safe, a welcome oasis in this traffic-strangled part of the city. And there's a sculpture in these gardens, a monolith bearing a shallow indentation, today containing an inch or so of rainwater, nothing else. This is the Empty Bowl, or, in Erse:

AN POBHLA FOLAMH

The Bowl tells me that, between 1849 and 1852, 1,241,410 Irish people arrived in Liverpool, fleeing the Great Hunger. 7,000 died of malnutrition in one year. There is also a memorial at the gates of Clarence Dock, where the refugees disembarked, hollow-faced and hungry and, perhaps, hopeful.

The Irish and Liverpool... again, where do you start? Michael Kelly, in his *Liverpool's Irish Connection*, starts in 1378, when records show Irish burgesses settling in the city, a dank little village then, of course. A larger influx followed the 1798 rebellion, and then the Hunger, and by 1841 twenty per cent of all Irish people in Britain were to be found in Liverpool, often living in appaling conditions. Kevin MacManus, in his *Ceilis, Jigs, and Ballads*, offers more statistics; 12,000 Irish people in Liverpool by 1821, and 83,813 thirty years later. In 1847, Liverpool had four Catholic churches; by 1880, there were nearly fifty. Irish nationalism, music, food, attire, and language thrived in the Irish communities, along with disease, in the Wards of Exchange and Vauxhall and Scotland. Mortality rates were high. Squalid conditions prompted bigotry in those whose own conditions were better. Orangeism grew, and so did sectarian bitterness. Clashes, riots. In

1929 a general meeting of the Irish communities was held in Scotland Road with the aim of dissolving the Council of Irish National Societies, which, at that time, were made up of the Gaelic League, Sinn Fein, the Irish Self Determination League, the Irish Musical Society of Liverpool, and the Irish Foresters. The end of World War Two saw another huge wave of Irish immigration in the cause of reconstructive labour. More ceili clubs appeared. This new wave regarded the older Liverpool-Irish askance, with their funny old language and strange dancing. In 1948, the Irish Association of Merseyside was formed, another attempt to yoke all the groups together, but this failed; the older members couldn't understand why the younger ones weren't conversing in Erse and dancing sixteen-hand reels, when some of these newer arrivals were seeing the dancing and hearing the spoken language for the first time in their lives.

The Irish Centre opened on Mount Pleasant in 1964, with 1,635 members. An extension was required in 1973. It was subtle in the ways it promoted Irish culture; nothing was painted green, yet the Claddagh symbol was present, St. Brigid's Cross, etc. Auld ones sipping Guinness and reading the *Irish Times*. Nothing of the bejaysis or begorrah.

The Comhaltas Ceóltoirí Eireann (Association of Irish Musicians) was set up in the city in 1957. Shannon Star Band, the Brian Boru Ceili Band. The Liverpool Ceili Band won the All Ireland competition twice. Cream of the Barley made the boat trip to Dublin even more raucous, kicking off with 'The Leaving of Liverpool' as the boat left dock. Session pubs: Ye Cracke, Flanagan's Apple, Guinan's. Hundreds more. The culture, especially as encapsulated in the music, became an exportable commodity, and the Irishness of the city runs marrow-deep: 'So deeply engrained in the history of the place that it will never disappear', McManus says[32]. St. Patrick's Day remains a happily riotous affair. For all that, the first officially organised Irish festival in the city was not set up until 2003, because sectarian division had always militated against it. Why did this subside in 2003?

C of C award. Of course. Here's another possible attraction; another string to the city's bow on which to play a tune. The 2007 festival was sponsored by Cains brewery, itself founded by an Irishman. Dubliners, Ron Kavana, Cora Dillon, Ardal O'Hanlon. Aptly-named butcher John Bones created the Liverpool-Irish sausage.

That's the potted history, basically. Ireland runs through Liverpool like a seam of coal, in the accent, the musicality, the lexical wordplay, the swagger, the lack of self-censure when it comes to displaying emotion. In Ireland, I've heard Liverpool called 'East Ireland'; in Liverpool, I've heard Ireland called 'West Liverpool'. The country lies there, reachably over the waves, close, at hand. The regular boat trips between the two places are an umbilicus. During research on this topic, I found myself nearly downed in a sea of reference books and poetry and plays and prose exploring and promoting the Liverpool-Irish identity, too many to list, although Belchem has a few interesting essays in *Merseypride* and *800*. Michael Kelly's aforementioned book is a collection of short biographies of the Liverpool-Irish great and good (not always so good, admittedly); he mentions Alderman Richard Shiel, a wealthy merchant and town councillor, born Tipperary 1791, came to Liverpool in 1828 to represent the Scotland Ward, an unusual combination, for the time, of socialist and Catholic. He has a park and road named after him. And Thomas Power O'Connor, known as 'Tay Pay', born 1847 in Athlone, moved to London to work on the *Telegraph*, edged his way into politics, saw Liverpool as an outlet for his ambitions as the Liverpool Scotland Division needed an Irish Nationalist for their parliamentary seat in the 1885 general election. Tay Pay's oratorical skills drew celebrity status upon him and he became Film Censor in 1916. His politicking was a big influence on Jim Larkin, probably the leading light in Liverpool-Irish political mavericks; there's a painting of him in the Newz Bar on Water Street, by David Jacques, and on 24th June 1996 the James Larkin Republican Flute Band was formed. Fondly remembered in the city, he was born on Cambermere Street in 1874, became member of

Independent Labour Party at seventeen, and stowed away on a ship to Montevideo in 1893. On his return to Liverpool he became foreman dock porter in 1903 for the firm T.J. Harrison, soon acquiring a reputation as a non-drinker (rare amongst dockers), and a fair and honest man whom the degradation of the labouring classes profoundly shocked and appalled. Joined the National Union of Dock Labourers in 1901, fomented the strike of 1905 which failed, but was his making and after it he became a charismatic and compelling spokesman for exploited peoples: 'his... oratory, his infectious enthusiasm, his determination, his fearlessness, and his devotion to the men on strike transformed him from the model foreman to the militant leader of men', writes Eric Taplin[33]. His vision was of uniting all workers against capitalist exploitation. The NUDL appointed him national organiser, after which he left Liverpool for Derry and Dublin, probably the first time he'd ever visited the country of his parents. After his death, the playwright Sean O'Casey said: 'he combined within himself the imagination of the artist, with the fire and determination of a leader of a down-trodden class'[34].

In terms of creative artistry, the Liverpool-Irish community has produced writers like a dandelion produces spores. George Garrett you've met, and J.G. Farrell, so now meet James Hanley, a much neglected writer, bafflingly so, born 1901 in Dublin, moved to Liverpool when still a child, ran away to sea at thirteen, jumped ship at New Brunswick and fought and was gassed in World War One with the Canadian Expeditionary Force. Back in Liverpool, he wrote frantically and feverishly, as if it was too late. From 1930 until his death in 1985, he published forty-eight books. Left Liverpool for north Wales and became friends with John Cowper Powys and R.S. Thomas. Buried in Llanfechain churchyard. Many of his books are out of print, but the web is wondrous, and I've managed to track several down. The majestic *The Furys* fictionalises Liverpool as Gelton, and is full of shame and rage and anger; *No Directions*, set in a London tenement block one night during the Blitz, was described by Henry Miller as 'one long roar of oceanic trash drowned in a green jungle of cracked ice, dementia, hysteria, vomit, flames and hallucinations'[35]; *The Ocean* is set completely on a life-raft fleeing a torpedoed ship and host to a sailor, a priest, and three civilians; and *Boy* is probably his most well-known work, but still, by any definition, neglected. It concerns a young boy, Fearon, who escapes a tyrannical father by stowing away on a ship bound for Alexandria. Ill-treated and bullied by the crew, he experiences a sexual initiation in an

Egyptian brothel, contracts syphilis, and is put down by the alcoholic ship's captain and thrown over the side. He's fifteen. It's a spectacularly upsetting book. On publication, the brouhaha was huge; Sir Hugh Walpole publicly tore a copy up in a London bookshop. Oh for such publicity today, but Hanley suffered; his devoutly Catholic mother and sister were devastated by the scandal of the burning of one hundred copies of *Boy*, and Anthony Burgess, in his introduction to the re-issued Penguin edition, wrote that 'the attachment of obscenity to Hanley's reputation, very far from justified, haunted him for the rest of his life... *Boy* is a typical expression of his view of the novelist's art. It seems to deny art in being pungent with the horrors of the real world [but] it is considerable art all the same'.

He's not wrong. Scour the second-hand bookshops, trawl the web, hunt for Hanley's work. I've pocketed a couple from the shelves of pubs. Resurrect his reputation. He deserves it.

Growing up in Liverpool, Ireland and everything that happened over there felt very close. This was, in turn, exhilarating and, during the 70 and 80s, frightening, but never less than colourful. It remains that way.

LEECE STREET/HARDMAN STREET/MYRTLE STREET

More shops, more traffic, more renovated (and thus spoiled) pubs. Great Arabic caff on Myrtle Parade, with a superb hangover-lightening breakfast; falafels, fried eggs, pitta bread, black olives, tomatoes, and coriander. Brilliant Greek restaurant behind it, too. Myrtle Gardens, tenement-style corporation housing, 50s fashion and well preserved, which is more, sadly, than can be said for the People's Centre at the top of Hardman Street, a Grade 2 listed building which has been forced into moving by gradual and attritional reductions in council funding. The Picket was based here, a bar and music venue, for over twenty years, 'the only venue in the city not run on a purely commercial basis'[36], and as such 'able to take more creative risks, acting as a breeding ground for young musical talent'[37]. Last time I was there, the 'For Sale' sign had been taken down; I don't know who's bought it, or for what purpose, but it's a big loss.

Magnet, over the road, one of my favourite bars in the city, and aptly named; the crowds that fill Hardman Street of a weekend night all seem to be drawn towards it. The *Liverpool Guide* for 2007 spoke about 'pre-meditated mayhem in the labyrinthine basement'. The music is never less than spot-on. Slug on the Loaf, a few yards further down, also good. Fried chicken joints etc. The street heaves, at night-time. Just off it is Abercromby Square, heart of uni-land, surrounded by trees and lawns which reflect something of a siege mentality; they were designed to be used as quasi-moats to protect the houses of the rich merchants[38] who once lived here. It's named after Sir Hugh Abercromby, who defeated the French at Alexandria in 1801. Barbara Hepworth's sculpture is here, 'Square with Two Circles', on a raised plinth; Hepworth in 1965 explained that she was 'interested in the proportion of the sculpture in relation to the human figure and [thus] the apertures are placed in relation to human vision and help to give the sensation of depth'[39]. And so they do.

These sloping streets form a running hill that seems to aim you at the very heart of the city centre. From the top of them, at the cross-roads where Myrtle Street becomes Hardman Street, the city is laid out before and below you; tall glass and girders catch the sun and cranes lattice the sky. There is much noise. There is a feeling of promise and enticement.

PARK LANE/WAPPING

This is dockland without the interesting bits. Or no, not entirely; there's the Gustav Adolfs Kyrka, the Swedish seaman's church, opened in 1884, offering both spiritual and practical guidance to Scandinavian sailors in port. Park Lane's the old Sailortown that Melville wrote

about. One of a myriad local spaces in a world city; a section localised and familiarised by yearning transients. As in every port, there are many such areas in Liverpool.

Wapping Dock's massive wall still bears a few of the iron columns that supported the Overhead Railway. The district is the original home of the 'Superlambanana', a bizarre and brilliant and bright yellow lamb/banana hybrid sculpture commissioned in 1998 for the Art Transpennine exhibition from Japanese artist Taro Chiezo. Theories about it abound; that it reflects Liverpool's heritage of exporting lamb and importing bananas; that it addresses the issue of genetic engineering with irreverent humour. It's eighteen feet tall, made of concrete and steel and weighs eight tonnes, and was built at a cost of £35,000 at Garston's old Bryant and May matches factory. It travels around the city now[40], attracting graffiti, frequently repainted and seemingly spawning; six-foot replicas have appeared in the foyers of the Capital and Plaza hotels, both on Old Hall Street. The Malmaison Hotel has one too, called 'Superstarrylambanana', painted black and pinpricked with holes and lit from within. There were recent rumours that the original was to be taken out of the city but it hasn't been, yet, and I hope it never is. It's a wonderful thing. I have a small, rabbit-sized replica on my windowsill at home.

CHINATOWN

Chinatown is Nelson Street, and the thin capillaries off it. It's supposedly the oldest overseas Chinese community on the planet, although of course the original settlers would be in many ways unrecognisable to today's inhabitants; as Belchem says in *800*, 'despite the reinvention and refurbishment of Chinatown with lacquered street furniture and a colossal arch... the old hybrid culture based round sailors from Shanghai and elsewhere has gone, replaced by a new 'all-Chinese' community, drawn mainly from immigrants from post-1949 Hong Kong replete with grandparents and grandchildren'. Which, of course, doesn't make it any less of a Chinatown than it's ever been. The giant arch, which forms a gateway to Nelson Street, has attracted criticism but I find it magnificent; forty-four feet high, designed by a Mr. Zhang, constructed in Shanghai by the South Linyi Garden Building Company, shipped in pieces to Liverpool and re-assembled

there. It amazes me; the detail, the intricacy, the constant busy engagement of the eye. It evokes a kind of awe; and, as you face it, you're always aware of the immensity of the Anglican cathedral at your back. Interesting part of the city, this. Here, you can feel insignificant and mighty at the same time.

To your left is the Blackie, or, to give it its proper name, the Great George's Community Cultural Project[41], founded on the 'privileging of communality'[42]. It was established in 1968 by Bill and Wendy Harp, and immediately 'integrated community involvement and avant-garde art with an organically evolving institution.... A site of communal creativity and play'. Still is. Down from it is Chinatown proper, all ideograms and duck's feet hanging from skewers behind windows. Tremendous food, here. The Chinese New Year celebrations are something to be experienced, too. And some great pubs, the Nook being one of my favourites in the entire city, frequented by locals who can trace their pedigree back to the early eighteenth century when the Blue Funnel Line, sailing out of Liverpool, established the first direct steamship link between Britain and China. In terms of depth of roots, these people are more scouse than those descendants of Celts who blinkeredly lay claim to 'true scouseness', whatever the hell that might be. They'll look Chinese, they might even speak a Chinese dialect, but their English is pure catarrhal vernacular. From the outside, the Nook looks like a bunker in a warzone (and indeed, whenever I've directed people to it, they've thought it was shut down), with its rusty shutters and chicken wire, but step inside and you're in snug and dusty joy. Oriental gewgaws everywhere. Big gantry behind the bar, and a poster of Liverpool's

1978 European Cup Winner's team. Huge map on the wall of maritime trade routes, so old that some of the places on it don't exist any more. No food here, apart from what can be bought in bags, but why would you need it when Ma Bo's or Mr. Chow's are ten mere yards away? And, for an entirely different ethnic experience – actually, no, not *that* different, except in style of music and skin tone – take a walk down one of the little ginnels off Nelson Street to White Street, where you'll find the pub Pogue Mahone, which is Irish Gaelic for 'kiss my arse'. Main drinking den of Liverpool's Russian community[43]. Another dingy cosy niche in which to sit and sip and listen to the city go about its busy life far, far away behind the frosted glass.

It's a settled, rooted Liverpool community, the Chinese one. Maria Lin Wong, in her book *Chinese Liverpudlians*[44], writes that 'during the 1940s Liverpool, as wartime headquarters of the Western Approaches, was the home of the Chinese Merchant Seamen's Pool which led to a massive expansion in the number of seamen based there [,] said to have been between eight and twenty thousand men registered'. The community hasn't had a problem-free history, of course; in 1906, thirty-two Chinese arrived in the city without the 'guarantees of employment' required by the recently introduced Aliens Act of 1905, and the reaction to this was hysterical; the day's tabloids shrieked about 'Chinese Vice in England'. Docker leader James Sexton – friend of Jim Larkin, remember, and an immigrant himself – 'deployed', according to Belchem[45], 'explicitly racist discourse, condemning the 'beastly' morals of the Chinamen: 'He comes here like an international octopus, spreading its tentacles everywhere, and he undermines and corrupts the morals, and pulls down the wages of the English people". There was talk, inevitably, of opium dens, brothel-keeping, gangland violence. Does any of this surprise you? The council appointed a commission to investigate Chinese settlements in Liverpool; all allegations of criminal behaviour were repudiated; all laundries, supposedly a cover for all manner of deviance, were declared morally and hygienically clean. The Tongs did exist, of course, whose secrecy tended to facilitate gang warfare and illicit activities, but even their overriding function was found to be 'collective mutuality and welfare'[46]. The Chinese were declared to be 'a highly functional migrant community'.

So there you go. Liverpool's Chinatown, like similar communities across the world, I find to be colourful and lively and exciting and happily free of danger or menace. No doubt there's a dark side to it;

sweat shops in the cellars, snakeheads, the problems that beset all other ethnic communities in the city. But these I don't know about, and I did dig – but by their very nature, they're hidden. And I'm not, here, wearing my investigative journalist hat. What more can I say?

HAN(G)OVER STREET: LONGEST BAR IN THE WORLD

Fairly unremarkable back lane, Hanover Street, except that it seems somehow to shrink the city; it makes the docks seem closer to the centre than they actually are. Aim yourself dockwards via Bold Street and Church Street and the Pier Head from, say, Central Station and by the time you get there you'll be knackered; but head there via Hanover Street and you'll be there in a blink. Of course it's to do with civic topography and pedestrianised routes and all that but it still feels somewhat Tardis-y. Today, though, there's so much construction work going on at the foot of Hanover Street at Chavasse Park for the Paradise/Liverpool 1 Project, which will be a colossal temple to consumerism when it's finished, that the air is thick with brick dust and cement; I'm coughing and in need of a shower by the time I'm half-way down. A drink, too, so I go into the Hanover Arms. Handsome boozer; exterior of whitewashed walls and darkened glass. Huge inside, again Tardisly so, with several rooms and snugs off the main bar area which is cavernous in itself. Walls sport drawings of ships and liners, as most pubs in this part of the city do. Stuffed birds and fish. A sign says 'The Longest Bar in the World', and it might well

be that; stand at one end and use binoculars to see the other, way off there in the distance.

Hanover Street is named after the Royal House of Hanover. In the early 1700s it marked the edge of the town; beyond it were green fields. It's the edge of both the Ropewalks area and the Bluecoat Triangle which, if you take School Lane opposite the pub, you'll be smack in the middle of. The Bluecoat Chambers is down there, begun as a charitable foundation, now a busy arts centre. A wee bit lower are the cranes and clattering of the Paradise Project. Quiggin's used to stand here; a grand and beautiful old building housing various clothing stalls and record stalls and general peculiarities. It was compulsorily purchased for demolition as part of the Grosvenor-Henderson Paradise Project and this act throws into question the whole notion of the City of Culture award. Quiggin's was unique – an essential ingredient of the city's distinctive identity, an institution indispensable to its singular expression elbowed aside to make room for identikit citification. 10,000 names were on the petition to save it. Change hurts, yes, but how have we reached the stage where homogenisation is equated with change? How can antithesis equal its opposite? The Paradise Project will contain new shops, leisure facilities, residential apartments, offices, a meeting hall, gallery, two hotels, a new bus station, 3,000 parking spaces and a new public park. What it won't contain is anything as special or as interesting or as peerless as Quiggin's was. The stalls still exist – they occupy new premises off Ranelagh Street – but the building itself is gone, flattened, built on. Progress? Of what sort?

This part of the city, it's not how I remember it. Which is fine, but I'm not sure I like what this district is becoming. Or what new shapes it's being forced into.

RANELAGH STREET/RENSHAW STREET

Heart. Ugly 1980s shopping mall of Central Station. Rushing hub, movements of urgent purpose. Take-aways, strip-clubs, pole-dancing, casinos. The plastic and glass bunion of Clayton Square shopping centre. Pedestrianised Church Street – Schuh, Marks and Spencers, HMV. Everycity. Renshaw Street, known as 'Rapid Hardware Street' as one side of it is almost entirely occupied by that DIY store (also to be relocated, I'm told, this time to a retail park on the outskirts). Perpetually busy, this. The Central Hall building is impressive; redbrick Art Nouveau style, built by Welsh Methodists. Drinking establishment, now.

Ranelagh Place means one thing – the Adelphi Hotel. Where you've briefly visited. Opposite it, at the foot of Ranelagh Street, is Lewis's department store, bearing above its entrance the famous 'exceedingly bare' statue, built by Jacob Epstein; the building itself was entirely rebuilt after the bombing raid of 3rd May 1941, and the statue – 'Liverpool Resurgent' – represents rebirth. Eighteen foot high bronze naked man on the prow of a ship, one arm outstretched with fist clenched, other raised above his head. 'Apt', some might say, for these times of fervid regeneration. Others might say 'ironic'. Still others, 'cruelly inappropriate'. Or something like that.

Who were Renshaw and Ranelagh, to warrant streetnames? Dig as I might, I can't find out. I know that there's a district of Dublin called Ranelagh, but that provides no clues, and not even Google can help. I'm flummoxed. Not a place to linger anyway, really, fume-filled and feverish as it is. Escape it by scooting into the Dispensary, a 'modern pub in an old pub's shell', as Lewis[47] observes; the pub used to be called The Grapes, but at some point morphed into the pub it is now, renovated with respect for Victorian architecture, all creaking wood and leather and engraved glass through which mote-floated sunbeams fall at a slant. 'A better metaphor for the city's regeneration could not be found', says Lewis[48]. Hm. Discuss. At long and increasingly vociferous length.

JAMES STREET/PIER HEAD

James Street; first stop in Liverpool on the underground system, or last, of course, if you're leaving the city for the Wirral. Liverpool begins and ends at the river. Old James Street; added to the city in 1677, along with Lancelot's Hey and Hackins Hey, part of what Belchem, in *800*, calls the 'haphazard... physical expansion [which] created problems of overcrowding and squalor'. Later, the foot of the street was turned into a landing-stage for cross-Mersey and more distant passenger traffic; this open space also led into Water Street and Brunswick Street. At the corner of James Street and the Strand stood the Mersey Mission to Seamen, one of many charities in the city that offered pastoral care to sailors of all nationalities. This, in 1984, was relocated to Crosby. One of the country's first curry houses, the Anglo-Indian restaurant, stood at number 116, until it was burnt down by white gangs on a night of rioting on 31st July 1948. The reason? Competition for jobs in the aftermath of World Wwa Two. Racial tensions heightened. Violence, arson, destruction. Most victims, and arrestees, were non-white. Look at the White Star Building, with its pink and cream bricks. It looks lickable. As if it would taste of rhubarb and custard. I thought it a giant sweetie as a boy and still do.

You can find Derby Square down James Street. Can't miss it, in fact; it stands anterior to the Law Courts and contains a huge monument to Queen Victoria. The city's castle once stood here, a long time ago; built somewhere between 1232 and 1247, it was allowed to crumble for centuries. Finally demolished in 1726 to make way for St. George's Church, itself pulled down in 1898. So the site rings with historical

significance. Victoria died on 22nd January 1901; on the 13th May of that year it was decided to commemorate her reign, here, with statuary, funded by citizen subscription; the Mayor, Arthur Crosthwaite, petitioned 6,000 of them, but didn't raise anywhere near the required amount, provoking criticism of the purported motives behind the raising of the monument as representing the wishes of the majority of Liverpudlians. Media at the time questioned the morality of such fund-raising in a city crippled, in large parts, by penury. But the money was, eventually, raised; rich businessmen chipped in, as did banks and other industries. Hooper and Co. of New York auctioned a bale of cotton. Designs for the monument were invited, and on 6th March 1902 the commission was given to the team of C.J. Allen and Simpson, Willink and Thicknesse. More financial shenanigans ensued, too dull to go into here[49]. But the thing went up, and was unveiled by Princess Louise, Duchess of Argyll, on September 27th 1906, and has remained unchanged since. It's pretty impressive. The sculptor, Charles John Allen, did a grand job. It's more of an edifice than a monument, really; four broad staircases ascend from a low, circular plinth to a central podium. Each staircase is flanked by tall pedestals topped with lead urns. Balustrades and bays. A 'domed baldacchino', writes Cavanagh[50], 'supported by four clusters of four unfluted Ionic columns positioned on the diagonal axes'. Allegorical figures representing Fame, Justice, Industry, Education, and Commerce. And so on. Surrounding it are some ugly square featureless post-war boxes of buildings, so it stands out further. Last gasp of bombast? One final melodramatic howl to bid farewell to the Victorian age? Undoubtedly. But physically striking it is.

After James Street, the Pier Head and docks. Salthouse Dock, the

oldest complete dock on the waterfront, opened in 1753. Near the carpark is a garden for the 'Blind and disabled', as Lewis writes in *Walks Through History*, 'with water trickling over a granite bollard and plants chosen for their strong texture or smell'. Nice. There's Duke Dock, the only private dock in the system, built for the cotton boats of the Duke of Bridgewater in 1773. Tony Cragg's iron and stone sculpture 'Raleigh' stands, or rather lies, nearby. Then the Pier Head, a twentieth century creation, site of the city's famous skyline. The Three Graces; Port of Liverpool Building (1907), the Cunard Building (1916), and the Liver Building (1911). The waterfront, and indeed the entire city when viewed from this angle, are dominated by these colossi. The riparine space before them is open and pedestrianised, with grassed areas and cobbled walkways. Many monuments and memorials to those lost at sea. Canada Boulevard, named in honour of the Canadian dead of World War Two, and an avenue of maple trees. Peaceful here, usually, but today I can hear the fuss from the opening-day ceremony of the Liverpool 1 Project, lots of loud music. I walk up there. Much as I expected. But I do buy some nice shirts from Debenhams. Just accept it. It's here.

James Street dangles its toes in the river with which the city begins and ends. But I've already said that, haven't I?

notes

1. See his *Illustrated History*. . .
2. In Belchem, *800*.
3. You're probably familiar with some of Bleasdale's TV work, but as a fictionalised examination of religious divides in Liverpool, check out the film he scripted in 1986, *No Surrender*. If you can't find the film, get hold of the script (bibliographical details in 'Works Consulted'). Brilliant times ten.
4. 'Goodbye, Mr. Cube'. See 'Works Consulted'.
5. It has a website, too: www.shipandmitre.co.uk.
6. See DuNoyer, *Liverpool: Wondrous Place*.
7. Ibid.
8. In his book *45*.

9. Op.cit.
10. See his article 'A trip down Penny Lane', 'Works Consulted'.
11. Op.cit.
12. Collected in Grunenberg and Knifton, *Centre of the Creative Universe*.
13. Apparently, according to popular but uncorroborated rumour, built back-to-front; when he saw the finished thing, the architect hung himself. Supposedly.
14. From *Writing Home*.
15. In Belchem, *800*, and incorporating a quote from Muir.
16. From Murphy and Rees-Jones, *Writing Liverpool*.
17. See *The Collected George Garrett*, 'Works Consulted'.
18. Op.cit.
19. See Glancy, 'A mirage on the Mersey', 'Works Consulted'.
20. Ibid.
21. Collected in Coles, *Both Sides of the River*.
22. From his introduction to *The Liverpool Scene*, as extensive an anthology of that place at that time as you're ever likely to get.
23. Many evidently do; drinking with Roger recently in a small Welsh town, I was amazed at how unbroken the accompanying refrain of 'oooohhhh we'll *drink*-a-drink-a-drink' from fellow tipplers was. It was everywhere. The moment Roger came through the door, it started up. It was inescapable.
24. From *Said and Done*.
25. In Grunenberg and Knifton, *Centre of the Creative Universe*.
26. Check out deadgoodpoetssociety.co.uk.
27. From Murphy and Rees-Jones, *Writing Liverpool*.
28. So says Ade himself, in a personal email.
29. Which runs off Hope Street down towards Chinatown. Amanda Ralph's 'Suitcase Sculpture' marks the corner.
30. In her article 'Young, gifted, bold as brass'. See 'Works Consulted'.
31. See *Mersey Minis Five: Leaving*.
32. In *Ceilis, Jigs, and Ballads*.
33. Collected in Nevin, *James Larkin: Lion of the Fold*.
34. Ibid.
35. For all bibliographical info on Hanley's books, see 'Works Consulted'.
36. Belchem, *800*.
37. Ibid.
38. See Lewis, *Walks Through History*.
39. Quoted in Cavanagh, *Public Sculpture of Liverpool*.
40. And, indeed, further afield; to celebrate Liverpool's Welsh links in 2008, a replica will appear on top of Moel Famau, a mountain in north Wales. There's been protest, of course, humourless and blinkered protest, but personally I'm glad it's going up there. It's not permanent, anyway. It'll be gone soon.
41. The building itself began as the Great George Street Congregational Church. The Rev. Thomas Raffles (1788-1863) was minister there for forty-nine years.
42. See Grunenberg and Knifton, op.cit.
43. That's a joke.
44. Quoted in Coles, op.cit.
45. Op.cit.
46. Ibid.
47. In *Walks Through History*.
48. Op.cit.
49. See Cavanagh, *Public Sculpture in Liverpool*, if you want to know more.
50. Ibid.

APPENDIX ONE

A GLOBAL REACH

Or a global brand? There are towns and cities called 'Livrepool' in New South Wales, New York State, Illinois, Nova Scotia, Pennsylvania, Texas, Ohio (two), Costa Rica, and a chain of department stores in Mexico (because the Frenchman who founded them imported much of his goods through the city in England). A man called Phil Bimpson has visited them all; 'my criteria', he said, 'is there needs to be an established community with a graveyard, a governing body and a police or fire station... I know there is a Liverpool in the Amazon in Brazil, but it's basically a tree. It has a population of about 30 people spread over 40 kilometres'[1]. The Liverpool in New South Wales, within driving distance of Sydney, has a population of 165,000 and was the first white settlement officially established in Australia. It was founded in 1810 by Governor Macquarrie as an agricultural centre and named after the Earl of Liverpool who was the then Secretary of State for the colonies. It has two of Australia's oldest surviving bridges; the Lansdowne and the Lapstone, both built by Scottish stonemason David Lennox, who was taught by Thomas Telford. The town sits at the head of the Georges River.

And it's not a pretty place. I visited there, in the summer of 2007, in endless grey rain. It looked like Halewood or some other run-down district of its British counterpart; red-brick low-rise flats with the washing out, rusty railings, there was even a stoat-faced guy in a Burberry cap and shellsuit. The resemblance was uncanny. I saw an overturned supermarket trolley on a patch of scrubby and dogshitten grass. Gridded streets between a few square housing blocks. One

main street with shops on. Torrential rain. Graffiti.

I went into the museum, where the attendants, pleasant as they were, appeared to feign interest in the fact that I was born in the British Liverpool. It was a well-kept and fascinating little museum, albeit depressing, recounting as it did in the exhibits the frequent massacres inflicted on the aborigines in this area by white settlers. I read a quote by a J.D. Lang:

'this is a dull, stagnant, lifeless sort of place'. In a caff over tea I leafed through the local paper, the *Liverpool City Champion*; read how buses used to transport disabled people had been vandalised out of service; of arson attacks; of how the 'drugs fight is failing'. I'm being selective, of course, but I did experience a strong sense of dislocation when reading paragraphs such as this one:

> When it comes to the streets of Liverpool, alcohol, tobacco, and prescription medications are the most common legal substances being abused while cannabis, opiates and amphetamines feature among illegal substances.... Drug users [in the area] typically have mental health problems ranging from anxiety to schizophrenia, have been exposed to trauma, and are involved in crime[2].

I shook my head and looked out of the window. Am I still in Australia? Outside looked much the same as Halewood. I picked up a copy of the *Liverpool Visitor's Guide* ('creating the future together'), and flicked through that. 'One of Australia's fastest growing regions', it said. 40,000 years ago, the place was known as Gunyungalung, in the Darug language, spoken by the Cabrogal people. It has a church called St. Luke's, not attacked by the Luftwaffe, built in 1818. Became a municipality in 1872. 'By 2021, 255,000 people are expected to call Liverpool home.... Pertaining to its heritage, Liverpool still consists of semi-rural areas but also has an expanding and lively city centre where major commercial and retail opportunities exist'. There's not a Collingwood Dock but there is a Collingwood Hotel. There's a Liverpool Catholic Club. A New Brighton Golf Club. A Mount Vernon. A George's Hall. I drink tea and a planet shrinks.

So I didn't linger long in Liverpool, NSW, as I perhaps didn't in Liverpool, GB; maybe I'll visit Liverpool, NY, so as to be able to leave there quickly too. But the city – the British one, that is – has always been marked by diaspora, not just among those who passed through its docks on their way elsewhere but among those born there, too. The critic Helen Carr makes the case for a specifically 'Liverpool diaspora': 'After all', she says, 'there's increasing discussion of Scottish writing in terms of postcolonialism, so why not Liverpool?'[3]. Michael Murphy and Deryn Rees-Jones, in their introduction to *Writing Liverpool*, point out that

> it is a central element in the essays and interviews that follow just how many writers from Merseyside have felt an urgent compulsion to leave. The reasons for this have been many: George Garrett was

appalled by both Liverpool's sectarian divisions and the brutality with which the city council and central government... connived to treat striking Liverpool transport workers in 1911; Malcolm Lowry hit not only the bottle but the high seas; Terence Davies left to escape the kind of spiritual and sexual slow death so harrowingly depicted in his film *Madonna and Child;...* and of the Liverpool poets... only Adrian Henri, born in Birkenhead, was to stay.

We return, of course; Terence Davies's new film, *Of Time and the City*, mixes autobiography with an examination of the city's regeneration (or so I've read; I haven't seen it yet). In an interview with the director, Frank Cottrell Boyce[4] writes:

> We talk about the business of leaving. For me, being moved out into suburbia made Liverpool a magical place – of childhood and forgotten ways. I couldn't wait to move back in. But you don't recapture the magic by moving back. You lose it. The magical 'old house' turns out to be just another house. The terrifying bully turns out to be smaller than you thought with problems of his own.

The many 'Liverpools' scattered across the globe suggest the parent city's uncontainability; it can never be enclosed, caged, or, indeed, escaped – it follows you. I've met Liverpudlians on mountaintops or in deserts or on icesheets or in bars or on ships on most of the continents; on the Great Pyramid of Giza; in caves. I've eaten fried eggs in a cafe in Nuuk beneath a girder bearing the words 'MADE IN LIVERPOOL' (it was, I was told, salvaged from a wreck in Disko Bay); there is a street-market in Lima dismantled and shipped over from Liverpool, so that its aisles and stalls are signposted with 'Scotland Road' and 'Lime Street' etc. When a man first explores Mars, he'll discover a crater in which 'LFC' is written in the red sand. Next to 'EFC'. And between them the marks of a scuffle.

I've barely scratched the city, in the preceding pages, and its breakneck pace of change renders much discussion very quickly obsolete; the fierce debates about regeneration, for instance, will no doubt continue for decades, as will those concerning what the City of Culture added or subtracted from the city. What should've happened and what shouldn't. What did and what didn't. All of this will only augment the astonishingly rich and fertile personality attached to that ugly, stupid, bright, sharp, ruined and sparkling, maverick, and utterly individual city at the wet and windy western edge of Europe, happy in its oddness, at ease with being Other.

So, I'll repeat my question: what's your opinion of Liverpool? You'll have one. Everybody does.

notes

1. See Jones, Catherine, (B), 'Cities in One World', 'Works Consulted'.
2. See Marchetta, 'A druggie's other ills', 'Works Consulted'.
3. See Murphy and Rees-Jones, *Writing Liverpool*.
4. See his article 'A walk through the city of ghosts', 'Works Consulted'.

APPENDIX TWO

Doggerel Written on a Beer-mat in a Dock Road Pub, Sometime in the Early 90s

The same fluid moves in me
as reflects the Liverpool lights;
maybe that's why I, too,
can sometimes smell of shite.

THE PHOTOGRAPHS

WORKS CONSULTED

Allt, Nicky, *The Culture of Capital*, Liverpool University Press, 2007
Anderson, Michael, *Liverpool Alehouses*, Sigma Press, 1995
Anon., *Domesday Book: A Complete Translation*, Penguin, 2003
Anon., *Sir Gawain and the Green Knight*, James Winny ed. and trans., Broadview Press, 1992
Babel, Isaac, *Red Cavalry and Other Stories*, Penguin, 2005
Bagshaw, Chris, et.al., eds., *Bloody Britain*, AA Publishing, 2002
Bainbridge, Beryl, 'Bittersweet Symphony', *Guardian*, 21.4.07
Balaque, Guillem, *A Season on the Brink*, Weidenfield and Nicholson, 2006
Barnes, Tony, et.al., eds., *Cocky*, Milo Books, 2000
Barnes, Tony, *Mean Streets*, Milo Books, 2000
Bayley, Stephen, 'Barbarity begins at home', *Observer*, 2.9.07
Behan, Brendan, *Borstal Boy*, Black Swan, 1983
Belchem, John, ed., *Liverpool 800: Culture, Character, and History*, LUP, 2006
Belchem, John, ed., *Merseypride: Essays in Liverpool Exceptionalism*, LUP, 2006
Benedictus, Leo, 'The World in One Country: A Unique Atlas of Multi-Cultural Britain', *Guardian*, 23.1.06
Bennett, Alan, *Writing Home*, Faber, 1994
Black, Arthur, 'The Save Our City Campaign', *Mercy*, issue 30, Oct/Nov, 2007
Bleasdale, Alan, *No Surrender: A Deadpan Farce*, Faber, 1986
Bowker, Gordon, *Pursued by Furies: A Life of Malcolm Lowry*, Flamingo, 1994
Boyce, Frank Cottrell, 'A walk through the city of ghosts', *Guardian*, 15.5.08
Cameron, Gail, & Crooke, Stan, *Liverpool – Capital of the Slave Trade*, Picton Press, 1992
Capper, Andy, 'Music', *Guardian*, 15.12.07
Cavanagh, Terry, *Public Sculpture of Liverpool*, LUP, 1997
Cavendish, Dominic, 'Culture of Destruction', *New Statesman*, 17.1.08
Chitty, Mike, *Discovering Historic Wavertree*, Wavertree publications, 1999
Cohn, Nik, *Yes We Have No: Adventures in Other England*, Secker & Warburg, 1999
Coles, Gladys Mary, ed., *Both Sides of the River. Headland*, 1993
Cornelius, John, *Liverpool 8*, LUP, 1981, revised 2001
Cornmell, Alison, 'The Liverpool Murals Project', *Nerve* issue 11, no date
Cottrell, David, ed., *Liverpool: The Guide 2005/06*, Trinity Mirror Merseyside publishing, 2006
Cox, Alex, 'Scousers are the culture', *Guardian*, 14.1.08
Danziger, Nick, *Danziger's Britain: A Journey to the Edge*, Flamingo, 1997
Davis, Laura, 'Dalai Lama makes day 'magical' with a hug', *Daily Post*, 28.5.04
Defoe, Daniel, *A Tour Through the Whole Island of Great Britain*, Penguin, 1978
Doughty, Martin, *Building the Industrial City*, Leicester UP, 1986
Drummond, Bill, *45*, Abacus, 2001
Du Noyer, Paul, *Liverpool: Wondrous Place*, Virgin Books, 2004

Elsa, Peter, 'Liverpool's 'greatest' artist', *Daily Post*, 26.12.05

Evans, Gwynfor, *Fighting for Wales*, Y Lolfa, 1997

Fallon, Bernard, *Bernard Fallon's Liverpool: Photographs 1967-1974*, Bluecoat Press, 2007

Farley, Paul, *The Boy From the Chemist is Here to See You*, Picador, 1998

Farley, Paul, *Distant Voices, Still Lives*, British Film Institute publishing, 2006

Farley, Paul, *Tramp in Flames*, Picador, 2006

Farmer, Hugh David, *Oxford Dictionary of Saints*, Clarendon Press, 1978

Farrell, J.G., *Troubles*, Phoenix, 1995

Ferguson, Euan, 'The Grief of Liverpool', *Observer*, 26.8.07

Ferguson, Euan, 'Suffer the Children', *Guardian*, 31.10.99

Fortean Times article, 'It ain't necessarily so', anon., issue 206, 2006

Fryer, Peter, *Staying Power: The History of Black People in Britain*, Pluto Press, 1992

Gaskell, Elizabeth, *Mary Barton*, Oxford, 2006

Giles, Colm, & Hawkins, Bob, *Storehouses of Empire*, English Heritage publishing, 2004

Grant, Ken, *The Close Season*, Dewi Lewis/Open Eye publishing, 2002

Green, Tony, *The Kindness of Strangers*, Oberon, 2004

Green, Tony, et.al., *Unprotected*, Joseph Weinburger, 2005

Grunenberg, Christoph, & Knifton, Robert, eds., *Centre of the Creative Universe: Liverpool and the Avant-Garde*, LUP and Tate Liverpool, 2007

Guest, Katy, 'Young, gifted, bold as brass', *Independent*, 13.3.08

Hanley, James, *Boy*, Penguin, 1990

Hanley, James, *The Furys*, Penguin, 1983

Hanley, James, *The Ocean*, Mayflower-Dell, 1965

Hanley, James, *No Directions*, Andre Deutsch, 1990

Henri, Adrian, McGough, Roger, & Patten, Brian, *New Volume*, Penguin, 1987

Hetherington, Peter, 'Clash of the Titans', *Guardian*, 1.3.2006

Hubbard, E., & Shippobottom, M., *A Guide to Port Sunlight Village*, LUP, 2003

Hunt, Tristram, 'A bold step away from the dead end of guilt and apology', *Guardian*, 23.8.07

Irving, Washington, *Legend of Sleepy Hollow and Other Stories*, Penguin, 1988

Jackson, Ade, *latenight sistersongs*, Headland, 2007

Jenkins, Russell, 'ASBO bars gangster from city centre', *Times*, 10.4.2006

Johnson, Graham, *Powder Wars*, Mainstream publishing, 2005

Jolliffe, Grace, *Piggymonk Square*, Tindall Street Press, 2005

Jones, Catherine, (A), 'Aboriginal remains are to be sent home', *Liverpool Echo*, 16.10.07

Jones, Catherine, (B), 'Cities in One World', *Echo*, 28.8.06

Jones, Catherine, (C), 'Our Tunnel Vision', *Echo*, 6.1.06

Jones, Ron, *The Albert Dock Liverpool*, RSA Ltd., 2004

Jung, Carl Gustav, *Memories, Dreams, Reflections*, Harper, 2005

Kelly, Michael, *Liverpool's Irish Connections*, AJH publishing, 2006

Kiely, Aaron, *Exhibition Catalogue*, Gemini Print, 2007

Lady Lever Art Gallery, *catalogue of exhibits*, anon., Bluecoat Press, 2004

Lear, Edward, *The Lear Omnibus*, ed. R.L. Mégroz, Thomas Nelson, 1938

Lewis, David, *The Illustrated History of Liverpool's Suburbs*, Breedon Books, 2003

Lewis, David, *Walks Through Liverpool*, Breedon Books, 2004

Lewis, Saunders, *Presenting Saunders Lewis*, University of Wales Press, 1991

Lloyd, Jessica, 'Hundreds flock to see sculpture', *Wirral News*, 21.2.2007

Lowry, Malcolm, *Hear Us O Lord From Heaven Thy Dwelling Place*, Penguin, 1969

Lowry, Malcolm, *Selected Poems*, City Lights, 1962

Lowry, Malcolm, *The Voyage that Never Ends*, NYRB, 2007

Lowry, Malcolm, *Under the Volcano*, Penguin, 1977

Lucie-Smith, Edward, *The Liverpool Scene*, Donald Carroll publishing, 1967

Macilwee, Michael, *The Gangs of Liverpool*, Milo, 2007

Marchetta, Ilona, 'A druggies other ills', *Liverpool City Champion* (NSW), 13.5.07

Maritime Mercantile City: Liverpool: Nomination for Inscription on the World Heritage List, aon., LUP, 2005

McGough, Roger, *Said and Done*, Arrow, 2005

MacManus, Kevin, *Ceilis, Jigs, Ballads: Irish Music in Liverpool*, Institute of Popular Music, 1994

McPherson, Colin, *The River That Changed the World*, Bluecoat Press, 2007

McRory, Moy, *Bleeding Sinners*, Minerva, 1989

Melville, Herman, *Redburn*, Penguin,1986

Melly, George, *Scouse Mouse*, Futura, 1985

Miller, Anthony, *Poverty Deserved?*, Liver Press, 1988

Morrison, Blake, (A), *As If*, Granta, 1997

Morrison, Blake, (B), 'Life after James', *Guardian*, 6.2.03

Mulhearn, Deborah, ed., *Mersey Minis One: Landing*, Capsica, 2007

Mulhearn, Deborah, ed., *Mersey Minis Two: Living*, Capsica, 2007

Mulhearn, Deborah, ed., *Mersey Minis Three: Longing*, Capsica, 2007

Mulhearn, Deborah, ed., *Mersey Minis Four: Loving*, Capsica, 2007

Mulhearn, Deborah, ed., *Mersey Minis Five: Leaving*, Capsica, 2007

Murphy, Michael, & Rees-Jones, Deryn, *Writing Liverpool*, LUP, 2007

Nevin, David, *James Larkin: Lion of the Fold*, Gill & Macmillan, 2006

Noon, Ron, 'Liverpool Love Lane Refinery Lives', *North West Labour History*, issue 32, 2007-08

Noon, Ron, 'Goodbye Mr.Cube', *History Today*, October 2001

Nown, Graham, *The English Godfather*, Ward Lock Ltd., 1987

O'Keeffe, Greg, 'You've got Knowsley all wrong, Kirstie', *Echo*, 16.10.07

Owen, Alun, *A Liverpool Welsh Playwright*, edited with introduction by Dr.D.Ben Rees, Modern Welsh publishing, 2008

Parr, Martin, *The Last Resort*, Dewi Lewis publishing, 1998

Parrott, Kay, *Pictorial Liverpool: The Art of W.G. And William Hardman*, Bluecoat Press, 2005

Phillips, Caryl, *The Atlantic Sound*, Vintage, 2001

Preston, Peter, 'Let the Bulger killers build useful lives in peace', *Guardian*, 17.2.03

Priestley, J.B., *English Journey*, Folio Society, 1998

Queenan, Joe, *Queenan Country*, Picador, 2004

Reade, Brian, 'The fans are REVOLTING...', *Daily Mirror*, 8.3.08

Rees, Dr. D. Ben, and Jones, Merfyn, *Liverpool Welsh and Their Religion*, Modern Welsh pub., 1984

Rees, Dr. D. Ben, *Wales: The Cultural Heritage*, Hesketh, 1981

Rees, Dr. D. Ben, *Welsh of Merseyside Volume One*, Modern Welsh pub., 1997

Rees, Dr. D. Ben, *Welsh of Merseyside Volume Two*, Modern Welsh pub., 2001

Repetto, Thomas, *American Mafia*, Owl Books, 2004

Riddell, Mary, 'The mob must not rule', *Observer*, February, 2003

Riddell, Mary, 'Don't seek revenge on violent gangs: Take responsibility', *Observer*, 26.8.07

Robinson, Peter, ed., *Liverpool Accents: Seven Poets and a City*, LUP, 1996

Salmon, Chris, 'A trip down Penny Lane', *Guardian*, October 2007

Sampson, Kevin, *Awaydays*, Johnathan Cape, 1998

Sampson, Kevin, *Clubland*, Cape, 2002

Sampson, Kevin, *Extra Time*, Yellow Jersey, 1998

Sampson, Kevin, *Outlaws*, Cape, 2001

Sampson, Kevin, *Powder*, Cape, 1999

Sampson, Kevin, *Stars are Stars*, Cape, 2006

Sereny, Gitta, *The Case of Mary Bell*, Pimlico, 1995

Slemen, Tom, *Haunted Liverpool 1*, Bluecoat Press, 1998

Slemen, Tom, *Strange Liverpool*, Bluecoat Press, 2004

Smith, David James, *The Sleep of Reason*, Century, 1994

Spiegl, Fritz, *Scouse International*, Scouse Press, 2000

Sprackland, Jean, et.al., *Ellipsis 1*, Comma, 2005

Sprackland, Jean, *Hard Water*, Cape, 2003

Sprackland, Jean, *Tilt*, Cape, 2007

Stacey, Miranda, *The Black Presence: The Representation of Black People in the Paintings of National Museums and Galleries of Merseyside*, NMGM pub., 1999

Tafari, Levi, *From the Page to the Stage*, Headland, 2006

Torpey, Paul, 'Bards, Barbs, and Biscuits: HMHB and Birkenhead', *TVS magazine*, 2006 (?)

Thomas, Hugh, *The Slave Trade*, Phoenix, 1997

Topping, Alexandra, 'Party cross the Mersey', *Guardian*, 9.1.08

Townsend, Mark, 'Racism? It's endemic here', *Observer*, 12.12.05

Unsworth, Barry, *Sacred Hunger*, Penguin, 1992

Various artists, *Undercurrents*, Strange pub., 1990

Wailey, Tony, *The Irish Sea*, Soft Net Books, 2002

Wailey, Tony, & Higginson, Steve, *Edgy Cities, Northern Lights*, 2006

Walsh, Helen, *Brass*, Canongate, 2004

Walsh, Helen, *Once Upon a Time in England*, Canongate, 2008

Ward, David, 'Miracle on Merseyside', *Guardian*, 15.12.07

Ward, David, 'The Beatles to James Bulger', *Guardian*, 17.11.07

Ward, David, 'Liverpool moves out of the shadows with a little help from its friends', *Guardian*, 1.1.08

Ward, David, 'From bad to verse', *Guardian*, 21.12.05

Ward, David, 'River of Life', *Guardian*, 19.9.07

Ward, David, 'Liverpool says sorry for flooding Welsh valley', *Guardian*, 13.10.05

Westgaph, Laurence, *Read the Signs*, English Heritage pub., 2008

Whale, Derek, *Lost Villages of Liverpool Volume I*, T. Stephenson & Son, 1985

Whale, Derek, *Lost Villages of Liverpool Volume II*, T. Stephenson & Son, 1985

Whale, Derek, *Lost Villages of Liverpool Volume III*, T. Stephenson & Son, 1985

Williams, Gwyn A., *When Was Wales?*, Pelican, 1985

Williams, Peter, 'Origins of scouse', Letters, *Guardian*, 29.9.07

Westwood, J., & Simson, J., *The Lore of the Land*, Penguin, 2005

WEBSITES

anotherlatenight.biz

artinliverpool.com

deadgoodpoetsociety.co.uk

edgycities.com

encyclopedia.thefreedictionary.com/Saint+Domingo

idler.co.uk/crap

liverpoolblackhistory.com

liverpoolcityportal.co.uk

LiverpoolConfidenial.com

liverpoolfc.tv

liverpoolmuralsproject.blogspot.com

liverpoolsubculture.com

liverpool08.com

loveliverpoolbooks.co.uk

mysouthport.co.uk

old-liverpool.co.uk

showmercy.co.uk

rossbullock.co.uk/runcornhistory.html

runcornhistsoc.org.uk

sthelenschat.co.ukanotherlatenight.biz

visionsofbritain.org

visitsouthport.com

williamsontunnels.com
writingonthewall.co.uk
yoliverpool.com
visionsofbritain.org
visitsouthport.com
williamsontunnels.com
writingonthewall.co.uk
yoliverpool.com

JOURNALS/PERIODICALS

Back to the Machine Gun
Daily Mirror
Daily Post
Guardian
History Today
Independent
The Kop
Liverpool City Champion (NSW)
Liverpool Echo
Liverpool Visitor's Guide (NSW)
Nerve
New Statesman
North West Labour History
Observer
Times
TVS
Wirral News

INDEX

THE AUTHOR

Niall Griffiths was born in Liverpool in 1966, studied English, and now lives and works in Aberystwyth.

His novels include *Grits* (2000), *Sheepshagger* (2001), *Kelly & Victor* (2002), *Stump* (2003) and *Runt* (2006). *Stump* won the Welsh Book of the Year. *Grits* was made into a film for television, and *Kelly & Victor* and *Stump* are also being made into films.

Niall Griffiths has also written travel pieces, restaurant and book reviews, and radio plays. His last book was *Real Aberystwyth* (2008), also in this series.